Educating Professionals for Network-Centric Organisations

IFIP - The International Federation for Information Processing

IFIP was founded in 1960 under the auspices of UNESCO, following the First World Computer Congress held in Paris the previous year. An umbrella organization for societies working in information processing, IFIP's aim is two-fold: to support information processing within its member countries and to encourage technology transfer to developing nations. As its mission statement clearly states,

IFIP's mission is to be the leading, truly international, apolitical organization which encourages and assists in the development, exploitation and application of information technology for the benefit of all people.

IFIP is a non-profitmaking organization, run almost solely by 2500 volunteers. It operates through a number of technical committees, which organize events and publications. IFIP's events range from an international congress to local seminars, but the most important are:

- The IFIP World Computer Congress, held every second year;
- open conferences;
- working conferences.

The flagship event is the IFIP World Computer Congress, at which both invited and contributed papers are presented. Contributed papers are rigorously refereed and the rejection rate is high.

As with the Congress, participation in the open conferences is open to all and papers may be invited or submitted. Again, submitted papers are stringently refereed.

The working conferences are structured differently. They are usually run by a working group and attendance is small and by invitation only. Their purpose is to create an atmosphere conducive to innovation and development. Refereeing is less rigorous and papers are subjected to extensive group discussion.

Publications arising from IFIP events vary. The papers presented at the IFIP World Computer Congress and at open conferences are published as conference proceedings, while the results of the working conferences are often published as collections of selected and edited papers.

Any national society whose primary activity is in information may apply to become a full member of IFIP, although full membership is restricted to one society per country. Full members are entitled to vote at the annual General Assembly, National societies preferring a less committed involvement may apply for associate or corresponding membership. Associate members enjoy the same benefits as full members, but without voting rights. Corresponding members are not represented in IFIP bodies. Affiliated membership is open to non-national societies, and individual and honorary membership schemes are also offered.

Educating Professionals for Network-Centric Organisations

IFIP TC3 WG3.4 International Working Conference on Educating Professionals for Network-Centric Organisations August 23-28, 1998, Saitama, Japan

Edited by

Peter Juliff
Deakin University
Australia

Tsurayuki Kado
Hitachi Ltd.
Japan

Ben-Zion Barta
Bar-Code Computers Ltd.
Israel

KLUWER ACADEMIC PUBLISHERS
BOSTON / DORDRECHT / LONDON

Distributors for North, Central and South America:
Kluwer Academic Publishers
101 Philip Drive
Assinippi Park
Norwell, Massachusetts 02061 USA
Telephone (781) 871-6600
Fax (781) 871-6528
E-Mail <kluwer@wkap.com>

Distributors for all other countries:
Kluwer Academic Publishers Group
Distribution Centre
Post Office Box 322
3300 AH Dordrecht, THE NETHERLANDS
Telephone 31 78 6392 392
Fax 31 78 6546 474
E-Mail <services@wkap.nl>

Electronic Services <http://www.wkap.nl>

Library of Congress Cataloging-in-Publication Data

IFIP TC3 WG3.4 International Working Conference on Educating Professionals for Network-Centric Organisations (1998 : Saitama, Japan)
Educating professionals for network-centric organisations : IFIP TC3 WG3.4 International Working Conference on Educating Professionals for Network-Centric Organisations. August 23-28, Saitama, Japan / edited by Peter Juliff, Tsurayuki Kado, Ben-Zion Barta.
p. cm. — (International Federation for Information Processing ; 17)
Includes bibliographical references and index.
ISBN 0-412-84690-X
1. Information technology—Study and teaching Congresses. 2. Multimedia systems Congresses. I. Juliff, Peter Laurence, 1938- . II. Kado, Tsurayuki. III. Barta, B.Z. IV. Title. V. Series: International Federation for Information Processing (Series) ; 17.
T58.5.I32 1998
658.4'038'011—dc21 99-30335
CIP

Printed on acid-free paper.

Printed in the United States of America.

Table of Contents

Preface

The short history of the International Working Conference on Educating Professionals for Network Centric Organizations is a good illustration of the tremendous rate of development of global networking, its impact and of its deep penetration into management of business, industry and administration.

In 1996, when the theme and name of the conference had been set, there was yet no heavy use of networks in the fields just mentioned. However, it has been already established well enough to enable those with a visionary sense to feel that it will be an important subject and it could be an interesting theme for a conference to be held within two years. It seemed a risky decision at the time but it turned out to be very successful when conducted in 1998.

It has been stated that "it took until 1997 for the business world to discover the Internet". In less than two years, the Internet and the Intranets are a vital component for running major parts of the business world.

This fast pace puts some pressure on writing papers and holding a conference – effort has to be made to have meaningful contents despite the changes. A time span of 9 months between writing a paper and having it published, seemed once to be very short, but it is not so any more when referring to a dynamic issue like global networking.

About half of the papers in these proceedings refer to the world of Business and Management. Most of the others address the issues of Education and Training, with no strict boundaries between the two.

Concerning Business and Management, the main issues covered are applications of Internet and Intranets in Business, implications for small businesses, networked business simulations, implications on management of work, distributed, remote, networked work organizations. Social changes and ethics issues also belong to this group.

Networked Education and Training Systems, public and corporate, are covered by many of the papers. Starting form general issues like requirements, enablers and negative aspects of networked educational multimedia or knowledge-navigation in Hyperspace; evaluation and effectiveness of networked corporate training systems; descriptions of several working systems for creation and delivery of training, uses of networking for management of training and teaching support; some aspects of networking for monitoring students' projects and for the assessment of academic activities.

In addition to the usual papers and related discussions, several dedicated discussion groups dealt with two main subjects: Educating Professionals for Network Centric Organizations – an analysis of the range of professionals using networks for their daily activities and of their respective educational needs; Tele-education in Network Centric Organizations – dealing with new roles and processes in educational and training activities, learning styles, student to student and student to teacher communications, group activities and the use of various media.

An additional discussion group dealt with methodology and tools for assessing the activity of academic institutions.

Short summaries of these discussions are an important, even if rather short part of these proceedings. The outcomes of these discussions may well provide issues for further research and perhaps future publications.

A large group of institutions and persons contributed to the organization and success of this working conference: First of all, its two main co-sponsors, namely, Hitachi Group of Japan and Working Group 3.4, of the International Federation for Information Processing (IFIP), acting under its Technical Committee on Education (TC3), which volunteered to undertake the organizational burden of the conference, to be active with the programme committee and to contribute some of the material means needed to run it. Then, the Information Processing Society of Japan and the Japan Society for Information and Systems in Education cooperated with the Ministry of International Trade and Industry, the Ministry of Education, the Japan Society of Educational Technology and the Center for Educational Computing contributed by the Support Center for Advanced Telecommunications Technology Research, the Japan Information-Technology Engineers Examination Center, Fujitsu Ltd., NEC Co., NTT Information and Communication Systems Laboratories and Toshiba Ltd. In addition there was the personal contribution of the staff members of these institutions, of the members of the Programme Committee and of the Organizational Committee and the secretariat of the conference. Finally, the authors of the papers presented and the participating audience; without them and their active participation the conference would not have been possible.

The developers of web based training systems that provided the exhibition day have to be specially mentioned for their efforts to install the systems and have them operational and for providing the demonstrations during the nominated day.

Special thanks to the director and the staff of the conference venue, the National Women's Education Centre of Japan, who hosted the conference and provided hospitality on the beautiful site which they are managing.

To all these and to those whom we may have omitted to mention, our deep appreciation and thanks for their remarkable and fruitful contribution.

The Editors

Educating Professionals for Network-Centric Organisations
P. Juliff, T. Kado, B.Z. Barta (Eds.)

EDUCATION IN CHANGING ERA -- A VIEW FROM JAPAN

N.Tokura
Department of Informatics and Mathematical Science
Graduate school of Engineering Science, Osaka University

1. Short introduction to Japanese history [1]

It would be suitable to talk about current Japan's situation. The present situation is not independent of the past history.

When Japan was first known to the western world, Japan was a country of Gold.

In the Edo period (1600-1868), the national seclusion policy and powerful administration of Tokugawa shogunate achieved more than two centuries of peace. The Tokugawa system was oppressive in many respects, however, Japanese created its own rich culture. The heritages of the culture in the Edo era have much profound influences on our behaviors and our disposition.

This peaceful life was threatened in the 19th century as Russian, British and American vessels begun to push their claim for trade with China and Japan. This leads to Meiji restoration of 1868. The slogan of new leadership of Japan was Fukoku Kyohei (enrich the Country, Strengthen the Military). The modernization of Japan was quickly attained. The reason could be that many of feudal clans in the Edo era were very earnest about their children's education and ready for new era. In their small schools, one important subject was the Chinese classics of Confucianism.

After the Meiji period, the Taisho period (1912-1926) and the Showa period (1026-1988) followed. Japan got acceptance as a major power in the world. In the early Showa period, ultra nationalism and political oppression at home eventually led to the World War II with the United States and the Allied powers in Asia and the Pacific.

The defeat of Japan in 1945 under the mushroom clouds brought the Allied Occupation and drastic changes in society: e.g. demilitarization, dissolving of the old financial and industrial combines, renunciation of divinity of the emperor, a new constitution, democratization, and a new educational system (the 6-3-3-4 system). After a painful period of postwar reconstruction, the Japanese economy begun to show a high growth rate in the 1960s and 1970s. The Japan's continued prosperity has been based on the United State-Japan security treaties, a consistent stress on economic growth and business-oriented policy making, an emphasis on education, and the saving, energy, and sustained efforts of the Japanese people. The unusual expansion of economy in 1970s, 1980s ended in 1990; that is, the bubble economy collapsed. After that many severe problems revealed themselves. There is a word "system fatigue." We are now experiencing another pain of restructuring or reform of our traditional systems. The former Hashimoto Cabinet promised six reforms (1996) but the action is too slow. The items of the six reforms are listed below:

1. Administrative reform
2. Fiscal structural reform:
3. Structural reform of social security:
4. Economic structural reform:
5. Financial system reform:
6. Educational reform:

2. Japanese companies and vocational education

2.1 *Japanese companies*

Japan has over 2 million corporations, of which slightly more than 99 percent were medium and small enterprises with less than 300 employees. There were over 1,700 corporations (i.e. "big business") listed on the Tokyo Stock exchange. Also, 99.0% of manufacturing companies are small-to-medium-sized companies with 71.9% of all manufacturing industry employees and with a 51.3% share of the total manufacturing shipments (1995 statistics).

The characteristic structure of Japanese manufactures is the pattern of strong connection of a core enterprise and its subsidiaries and subcontracting firms. The word 'keiretu' is used in English articles. These smaller firms pay lower wages and provide a smaller package of benefits compared to the parent enterprise. Hence, it is a considerable economic advantage to use smaller firms as suppliers of those components or subassemblies that require less-skilled labor. The high quality products are supported by these smaller firms' efforts partly.

2.2 *Japanese company's characteristics:*

A. Lifetime employment

Most Japanese companies adopt the system of career long employment with an expectation that employees stay with the company until their retirement. The forced retirement age are around 55 to 65. (For example, it is 60 in Tokyo University, 63 in most major universities, 65 to 70 in private universities.) In this lifetime employment system, an employee's rank, salary, and qualifications within a company are based on the length of her or his service in it. This system is beneficial to employees by the stability of employment and to employers by the strong worker loyalty and the resultant ease with which they can formulate personnel plans. This system is now changing gradually to a new system in which workers move to another company to get more good position. The fixed idea based on Confucianism that anyone should be loyal to his organisation (worker should stay in the same company life-long) is not accepted by younger person.

B. Seniority system

Educational background, age, sex, and type of job determine starting wages, while wage increases are primarily governed by age and length of service; retirement allowance also depends on length of service, position, and wage level at the time of retirement. Seniority is also an important factor in promotions.

The seniority system are not traditional one; its origin can be traced to a period of serious labor shortages during World War I when Yokosuka Naval Shipyard adopted it in order to secure enough technical and skilled workers.

This system is now forced to change because of rapid increase of labor costs. So companies must place more emphasis on employee ability and less on seniority.

In Appendix, two statistical data are shown: (1) the starting wages of new graduates, (2) Retirement pay.

C. Labor union

In contrast to European nations, Japan has enterprise Unionism after World War II. Paternalistic management and enterprise unionism have both supported lifetime employment and promoted labor-management harmony.

2.3 Reinforcement of corporate culture

Confucian thought, which contains the conception of the social order, the acceptance of hierarchy, and emphasis on social identity, was rather familiar to Japanese and conveniently adapted as an ideology for modern Organisations. Japanese tend to defer to or obey the group, particularly its leaders. Due to the general absence of strong personal religious beliefs and concomitant ideological commitment, Japanese have little trouble accepting that companies will try to mold their members to fit a particular ethos and style. The worker's character, attitudes, and values are properly subjects of company concern. Therefore, new employees usually undergo intensive corporate education and training programs.

Most employees are willing to participate in informal company-sponsored activities. Relations within small work groups are expected to be personal, warm, and actively developed outside working hours. The ideal boss is one who will aid subordinates in personal problems, give advice, and maintain a close association.

2.4 Vocational education in companies

The companies are also very eager in vocational training and education. Let us see a common image of educational activities in big companies of Japan.

The company have the education division which formulates a plan of educational programs and recruits teaching staffs from inside and outside the company, make's schedule of the program, execute it and evaluate the program. It may have special facilities for educational and training programs; usually in the firms and in resorts and the remote facilities are connected by communication satellite channel and leased circuits. So the lecture taught in the classroom of the training center can be relayed to the remote classes. This gives good chances for many workers to refresh their knowledge and skills for experienced workers and to introduce to new jobs for fresh workers. The programs are of very broad range targeted to all ranks.

The effects of training or education are rather difficult to see. The managers usually prefer immediate outputs to the future possible contributions of workers. It is the time of recession and restructuring. So the education and training programs are in very severe situation.

There are many distinguished persons in this area and some of them come to this conference. So the details of educational programs in companies will be reported. We can exchange ideas and/or reports of trials in several conferences, for example, Japanese Society for Engineering Education(Nihon kougaku kyouiku kyoukai) and others. The members are from companies, universities, colleges of technology, special training colleges and others. There are other efforts to promote the vocational education.

3. Educational System in Japan

Here the general educational system in Japan is reviewed briefly (See Fig.1).

What schools are doing the vocational training and education? There are high school for technology, commerce, forestry and agriculture, fishery and maritime education. Colleges of Technology are also in charge of educating good engineers. How about engineering schools of universities? There is some gap in the evaluation of Engineering education between university professors and company persons. This problem will be touched later in my talk.

I add one more topics. We have the University of the Air in Japan. It is a regular university that uses TV channel and FM radio channel and some schooling. It has a faculty of liberal arts. Almost 300 subjects for 6 courses are taught. One of 6 courses is the industries and technology course. I am in charge of 2 TV subjects.

		Schools	Teachers	Students
1	Kindergarten	14,790	103,518	1,798,051
2	Elementary school	24,482	425,714	8,105,629
3	Junior high school	11,269	270,972	4,527,400
4	Senior high school	5,496	278,879	4,547,497
5,11	College of Technology	62	4,345	56,396
6,12	Special training college	3,512	36,830	799,551
8,9	University	576	139,608	2,596,667
10	Junior college	598	20,294	473,279
14,15	Graduate school	NA	NA	NA
7,13	Miscellaneous school	NA	NA	NA
-	Schools of the blind, deaf, physically Handicapped and mentally retarded	975	52,723	86,293

Fig.1 Education system (Based on the report of Ministry of Education as of 1996.11.)

One is "Introduction to computer science" and the other is "Fundamentals of programming." Students must submit mid-term reports on which they can write any comments in addition to the answers to the exercises. I found one problem reading their comments; that is, many students whose title is SE (system engineer) are taking my lecture. Typical comments are as such: "I am en experienced SE with 10 years service to the job, but I am graduated from school of economics with little experience of computer usage. I do manage to do my job with only the knowledge of COBOL taught in the training period of a new employee. But I can not follow the trend of Information Technology without any computer science background. So I am taking your lecture for some support.

In the high economic growth period, shortage of SE is severe so many companies employ students with any background. They were proud of good training course, which trains any graduates with any backgrounds into SE in very short period. After collapse of the bubble, the demands are decreasing and the technology itself changed radically. Engineers with knowledge and skills in new technology are demanding but engineers with limited knowledge and skills are surplus. In recession age, such improvised engineers are targets of restructuring. Indeed, some students say that I am dismissed and I must try to build up from the basics. These are tragic stories and it should be a problem.

4. Other activities

4.1 Government projects

Several projects supported by the government for promoting IT education are carried out.

A. 100-school Networking Project

Project Objectives
In the twenty-first century elementary and middle school education is expected to be more advanced and aggressive. It will embrace computer and network technologies, bring about dramatic results, and help students foster their creativity, express their own ideas effectively and think freely through improved access to domestic and international communication and information sources.
Project Overview
This project was initiated under the combined auspices of Ministry of International Trade and Industry (MITI) and Ministry of Education. Project operations are managed by Information Center for Educational Computing.

This project encompasses four on-going sub-projects:

- ☐ "National Germination Map"-- a group -learning project for elementary school students observing the growth of pumpkin seeds planted at various locations throughout Japan on 2 May 1995.
- ☐ "Acid Rain Survey"-- on the realities of local and national environmental problems utilizing data provided by participating schools.
- ☐ Mailing Lists for Project teachers and project management staff to exchange information as a touchstone toward future information exchange programs.
- ☐ Trial news groups for elementary, junior high and high school students to exchange information. (from URL. http://www.edu.ipa.go.jp/kyouiku /100/100_e.html)

B. Space Collaboration System (SCS) project

The SCS is an inter-university satellite network designed especially for the exchange of images among universities, colleges, and national institutes. It was financed in 1995 by the Ministry of Education based on the result of research in the National Institute of Multimedia Education. Its operation was initially started with 51 sites in 37 institutions in October 1996, with the number of stations in the network scheduled to increase year by year. In 1997, stations at 89 sites in 73 institutions will be connected, with participation of private universities also planned. The SCS is becoming one of the important education and research infrastructures among universities, colleges, etc. (from URL. http://nime.ac.jp/)

4.2 Information Processing Society of Japan

The Information Processing Society of Japan (IPSJ) was established in 1960. At the time of its establishment, IPSJ joined the International Federation for Information Processing (IFIP) as a Full Member. The member of this society, which reached almost 30,000, consists of those students majoring in the information processing science and technology, scholars, professionals, research workers, engineers and practitioners. There are 26 SIGs at present, and each SIG holds four or more study meetings annually. Symposia, seminars and tutorials are held frequently by SIGs. Another major activity is publication. IPSJ publishes monthly journal, "Joho Shori"(Information Processing) in Japanese, and monthly research papers, "Transactions of Information Processing Society of Japan" mostly written in Japanese (each with English abstract) and some English papers. "Information Processing Handbook and several other publications are also issued by IPSJ. It also drafted and established the Code of Ethics of the IPSJ. (Effective from 20 May, 1996).

IPSJ has many committees and commissions. Two of them will be introduced.

A. Information Processing Education Commission

The commission has made many activities so far.

1. Designs of standard curricula:

- □ CS curriculum (J90) Core curriculum for Computer Science programs are formalized.
- □ Information System curriculum:
- □ Curriculum for the general education level
- □ Curriculum for the junior colleges
- □ Curriculum for the non-CS programs in Faculty of Engineering
- □ CS curriculum (J97):

This curriculum covers the broad range of subjects considering the results in computer science area and new trend for information age. It contains subjects for communication and networking, HCI, and others.

2. Symposia

B. Accreditation committee

Recently, some system of accreditation of engineering programs is sought. Prof. N.Takahashi proposed to organize the accreditation committee in IPSJ. This is the first committee in academic institutes of Japan. Both the committee and the Information Processing Education Commission consist of various members from academic field (Universities, Colleges of Technology and others), private companies, the governmental institutions and the government. Hot discussion is one of characteristics of these committees. This committee starts this fiscal year and we hold the committee almost bimonthly. A terminal report will be published at the end of this fiscal year. This committee will hold several symposia or panel discussions in IPSJ conferences. This is to inform our process and results of discussion to the member of IPSJ.

5. Final remarks

There are two or three problems in this context. The traditional way of companies is now collapsing; seniority system and lifetime employment is not easy to maintain. This will have many effects on workers spirit and behavior. Young employees are loosing loyalty for the company and they will move to other company if the wage or conditions are better for them. To what direction should the training and education programs in companies direct?

Is it good to focus on very limited target to gain an immediate profit? How do you consider the SEs who were fired because of their narrow knowledge and inflexibility to new technology.

The recruiters of many companies changed their attitude and demand that the graduates of universities should be persons who can work in the firms quickly without long training period. Their previous attitude was that they would train and educate graduates from universities (more effectively than universities) if the graduates are healthy and active. This attitude gives bad effects on students who consider that the companies can teach well and we need not study so hard in universities.

The half of 18-aged young persons can enter the university and the level of students is going down. But, the demands of the companies are now very severe. To bridge this gap, universities should consider how to do. The ministry of Education and its councils propose many reform plans. Universities must deal with these moves. So far, university members have focused on research but education is becoming stressed. It is requested to include new subjects such as Engineering ethics, problems of intellectual properties, social issues for new information era.

Japanese have spent much money in consumable goods and real estate but they learned much from the collapse of the bubble economy. Knowledgeable persons claim that Japanese should invest their money in themselves. In other words, self-learning and/or refresh studies should become popular. There are business chances in education area especially in network-centered education/learning.

Many say we are in opaque age and we can not find how to proceed. My last claim is that if we can go back to the origin or deep points of ourselves and consider seriously about our problems, we could find out some better way even if it is not the best possible way.

References

[1] The Kodansya Bilingual Encyclopedia of Japan, Kodansya, 1998.
[2] Japan Almanac, 1998, Asahi Shinbun 1997.

Appendix Some statistical data [2]

Starting wages of new graduates (1996) unit Yen

Junior High school(15 yr. old)	male	146600
	female	130800
Senior High school(18yrs old)	male	154500
	female	146100
University (22yrs old)	male	193200
	female	183600

Retirement pay (Males, 1993) unit 10,000Yen(equivalent to— month's wage)

	University graduates		Senior high school graduates		Junior high school graduates	
Average	2,462	41.9	1,159	35.7	1,148	35.9
Corporate scale						
30-99 employees	1,048	21.8	919	28.4	624	22.7
100-999	1,854	34.3	954	29.6	1,000	30.9
1,000-	2,778	45.4	1,439	43.8	1,529	45.0
Length of Service						
20-24 years	1,285	24.7	601	21.1	623	22.0
25-29	1,693	30.9	970	29.7	954	30.9
30-34	2,504	41.3	1,333	40.3	1,239	38.5
35-	2,848	48.0	1,682	47.0	1,602	45.3

1. LEARN:LINE - AN EDUCATIONAL ENVIRONMENT ON THE WEB

Wolfgang Weber
Landesinstitut für Schule und Weiterbildung
Referat Z2, Paradieser Weg 64, 59494 Soest, Germany Phone: +49 2921 683-235, Fax: +49 2921 683-388
E-mail: wolfgang.weber@mail.lsw.nrw.de

ABSTRACT

On the basis of the "Proposal for the Pedagogical Role of the NRW-Educational server", learn:line was developed as a platform to the exchange of information, as well as mutual communication and co-operation. learn:line officialy started on February 17th, 1997 on the Web (http://www.learn-line.nrw.de).

Work areas relating to particular topics are characteristic of the NRW-Educational Server. They represent a kind of learning arrangement and provide an infrastructure for encouraging learning. Within a work area users will continually come across a selection of the following modules: media center, notice board, foyer, seminar room, conference room and work room.

Such work areas can be used to help the planning and analysis of the educational process, to increase co-operation between teachers and with others, to support existing and to try out new forms of further education and consultation, and in particular, to support learning processes - i.e. as a new medium for specialist and interdisciplinary learning.

The paper shows - in two examples - how, by using this new medium, a higher quality of learning and working in schools can be achieved - by teachers and pupils: 'Learning with new media' - a work area especially for teachers need and 'Young People' - a work area especially for pupils' need.

Keywords

Collaborative Learning, Communications, Internet, Learner centred Learning, Open learning

1. Introduction

In June 1996 the *Landesinstitut für Schule und Weiterbildung* published the "Proposal for the Pedagogical Role of the NRW-Educational server" (LSW, 1996). Developed on this basis learn:line (http://www.learn-line.nrw.de), the North Rhine-Westphalian Educational server, officially started at 17th February 1997. Learn:line is designed as a platform to the exchange of information, as well as mutual communication and co-operation. As is testified to by all participating parties, the true value for learning is only seen once these three processes are brought together and the building of a "virtual house of learning" becomes possible.

Participants were aware from the very start that the possibilities now on offer can be used e.g.

- to help the planning and analysis of the educational process,
- to increase co-operation between teachers and with others,
- to support existing and to try out new forms of further education and consultation,
- and in particular to support learning processes - i.e. as a new medium for specialist and interdisciplinary learning

2. Work areas - characteristics of learn:line

Work areas relating to particular topics are characteristic of learn:line. They represent a kind of learning arrangement or provide an infrastructure for encouraging learning. According to our intention to learn and teach within meaningful and specialised contexts, each work area concentrates on a particular topic.

Figure 1: A work area.

Within a work area users will continually come across a selection of the following modules: media centre, notice board, foyer, seminar room, conference room and work room.

- In the *media centre* information and materials are to be found that are fundamental to the work area. Or links to other sites will be opened that seek to make others think about and contribute to work on the topic. This could involve the use of texts or diagrams, but also perhaps audio or video cassette recordings, computer programs etc.

- The *notice board* can be used to ask questions on the topic, for example, or to provide answers to questions that have already been asked there, or to come into contact with others. The *notice board* acts as a kind of "information exchange" for the work area.

- The *foyer* is there to help with the organisation of projects and to act as a platform for those people who wish to contribute something to the topic. Here, people can make progress reports, present the results of their work and lay these open to criticism.

- The *work room* can be used for working together on documents, or to collate materials worked on by separate parties.

The *seminar room* and *conference room* are more like "meeting points" and, therefore, require that the participants are at their computers at the same time.

- In the *seminar room,* for example, different groups can meet up for so-called on-line conversations (chatting room) where they discuss questions and problems relating to the topic.

- In the conference room video conferences relating to the topic can take place.

Figure 2: The learn:line-homepage (10.06.1998).

On February 17th, 1997 the NRW-Educational Server, now named learn:line, officially started on the Web (http://www.learn-line.nrw.de).

Under the heading *Fächer* (subjects) there are different work areas available e.g. for foreign language learning, mathematics, biology, chemestry, physics, history, geography, economics. Under *Themen* (topics) you will find work areas for interdisciplinary learning (see Figure 2).

From the following **two examples** it will be shown how, by using this new medium, a higher quality of learning and working in schools can be achieved - by teachers and by pupils.

3. A work area especially for teacher's need

Under the heading *Themen*, interested parties can gain access to the work area *Lernen mit Neuen Medien* (learning through new media). Teachers in particular, who e.g. want to arrange a media corner in their classroom for a specific topic or subject, can obtain information here about new media available on the market for learning.

Via the *media centre* they can log on to the database, SODIS (Software Documentation and Information System). By carrying out the necessary research they can look at the new medias currently on offer. They can also call up detailed reports for the individual documented media.

In this work area, however, particular attention is paid to the exemplars - the new learning media that the examiner is convinced will improve the quality of work and learning at school. These very media can support teachers who base their lessons on concepts developed by the latest academic researches on learning processes. They also support those teachers who consider a pupil's interests and previous experiences to be the most important aspects of the learning process and who aim at equipping the pupils with basic competencies in and across the curriculum and the basic motivation for a lifetime of learning

Whether now organized by subject or type, in any case more diverse additional information will be accessible in *media centre* examples, supplementary literature, pointers to other work areas which use/discuss the use of these media etc.

On the *notice board* questions are to be found which have come up from the use of these new media, as well as other people's tips and suggestions. In stages, opportunities are taken advantage of to communicate and to exchange ideas and experiences with one another. In the *foyer* teachers report on their initial experiences with these new media.

This learn:line work area could increasingly develop into a kind of "meeting point" for the employment of new media, via which those people interested in exchange information, ideas and experiences with one another, provide each other with stimulus, mutually benefit from each other's findings and co-operate with each other.

4. A Work Area especially for Pupils' Needs

This second example will show the use of learn:line in English lessons. Learning to speak a foreign language can best be done in a classroom situation in which each pupil determines the lesson's topic within a set framework and decides on suitable exercises according to his/her individual interests, preferences and previous experiences. Each pupil should then be allowed to work independently. Instead of just using the language in fictitious role-playing situations, they should also try "real life situations". For this, chances to speak and to write are needed - real communication partners and the opportunity to really exchange views and experiences with each other. The planning and carrying out of a school trip to a partner school abroad, for example, is a typical, yet rare or even a one-off opportunity for the individual class.

In such open teaching periods, pupils get into small groups, divide work up between themselves and work towards creating a final product - that is to say, the results of the lesson are visible products which hold some significance for the youngsters and which may also be acknowledged outside the classroom. Good examples include newspapers, information brochures, guides for partner schools, small theatre productions etc.

The teacher is no longer the focal point of the pupils' attention and rather than being the provider of information and telling the pupils where they should be heading, he/she should merely act as an advisor to his/her pupils. This places great demands on teacher's subject related knowledge and requires a large degree of flexibility. The preparation time and effort needed for a pupil-orientated group lesson is usually greater than that required for a conventional teacher-centred lesson. This is because the teacher cannot know in advance which aspects of the lesson will interest the pupils, to what degree the pupils will require help, or even if the pupils will show any interest whatsoever.

In open teaching periods, it is absolutely essential to make available a wide range of authentic materials which deal with as many different aspects of a particular topic as possible and also take into account different people's interests and allow the individual to follow his/her preferred learning path. In addition to this, the level of work achieved by different groups will vary. Therefore, materials in language of varying difficulty should be provided.

After the project has been agreed upon, all participants (pupils and teachers alike) create a pool of material on the topic: English literature, newspapers, magazines, information leaflets from foreign institutions and firms etc. Authentic multi-media material is increasingly being offered on CD-ROM - e.g. encyclopaedias in the English language. And now, learn:line is available on the Web.

Here, one possible scenario : Let us imagine the classroom situation in a year 10 class. In a class discussion the pupils decide to set to work on the project "Freetime, Lifestyle, Worries and Problems of Young People in GB, USA and Germany". Different groups are formed to work on the various aspects according to pupils' interests. The objective could be to pinpoint national similarities and differences in order to analyse one's own way of life in the light of this background information. The individual groups will present their results to the others at the end of the project period and will stimulate a concluding all-in group discussion.

Perhaps we find there is a group which has not yet come up with any suitable ideas on a particular topic. "Young people's problems, that sounds interesting" might be the vague idea of the group members. So, stimulus is now needed to put this group's topic in concrete terms as well as to keep the discussion within certain boundaries. The teacher has spotted the situation and ensures that the group gets access to the on-line computer for a specified length of time at the beginning of the group work phase.

The youngsters are familiar with "Smiley" (the logo of learn:line). They know that on the learn:line homepage there are links to websites on various subjects and topics, and by various institutions. They opt for a look at the usual offer available in learn:line under the slogan, "We 'll look for something for English!". Under the heading *Fächer* you will find the work area - indicated by a red box alongside the heading - named "Young People". By clicking you reach the front page of the work area, where you can read the summary which gives an overview of the content and objectives of the work area .

The juveniles know that the basic information on each topic is put in the media centre. On the first page here they find a potpourri of various aspects - for example, "Alcohol in the Family", "Inline Skating", ... and "Reading and Writing". A click on the last entry brings them to a page where various electronic magazines in English language are listed on the Internet, which are specifically concerned with young people and which for the large part have also been written by young people.

Each entry is also accompanied by a small piece of commentary in which the 'moderator' of the work area summarizes the entry's contents as well as assessing its quality and its suitability for use in the classroom. This service enables the user to evaluate whether or not the entry is suitable for its intended purpose. In this way, finding one's way about the Internet - a veritable 'bazaar' of innumerable possibilities- is made that much easier and the time needed to assess the quality of a particular entry is reduced.

Using the available commentary, the youngsters do, of course, discuss the way in which to proceed. Working with the computer, therefore, leads to a situation in the classroom in which the pros and cons of the material on offer are discussed by the pupils. They learn how to argue, how to consider their own position and how to react to the arguments of others. In doing this they build up their own knowledge while improving their ability to work well in a team situation.

The group finally decides on an entry that has the title "Children's Express" (CE) on the basis of the commentary belonging to it - a children's magazine, which is financially and ideologically backed by UNICEF.

Every month, young editors (13 years old plus) do research on various topics. The quality of language is extremely varied according to the age and ability of the author and therefore also gives younger pupils the opportunity to look critically at authentic texts and discuss these with native speakers. Following a discussion on the wide topic area, the group decides to analyse in greater detail a special section in the March issue with the title, "CE's Special Report on Child Labour in Bangladesh".

In these articles the pupils have access to materials that are authentic from both a language and content point of view and that are concerned with the real life situations of people of their own age, thereby affecting the reader and encouraging the pupils to make a stand and undertake work on associated further activities.

In our case the group members could show to what extent they have been affected by writing an e-mail to individual authors or by sending in a letter to the magazine which can then be read by all readers of CE. With the help of the Internet, communication possibilities extend far beyond the boundaries of the normal classroom. Reading has lead to the group undertaking research themselves into whether there are young people in Germany, in GB and in the USA who are also forced to labour. They want to record their results in the English language on their own websites. In this way interested parties from Great Britain and the USA can understand and, if need be, add to the information.

To obtain their own research material the group can, amongst other things, access German and foreign newspapers on the Internet. On a professionally laid-out index page under the heading *"Anbieter/Institutionen"* (provider/institutions) in learn:line, over one hundred newspapers from all over the world are referred to, which have offers on the WWW. Such services that already exist on-line which help you find your way about the Web are being made accessible to learn:line.

Learn:line also refers to individual American and English newspapers under the heading "*subjects/ learning areas*", as these can particularly enrich the English lesson. Here, each reference comes complete with a commentary which, amongst other things, tells you whether or not you have to pay for the entry and whether or not there are archives available so that past articles can be retrieved. Furthermore, the commentaries contain tips on teaching methods when using the entries.

The *foyer* in the work area "Young people" is the place where young people can have their pages published worldwide and where they can lay these pages open to discussion. This is how they get themselves heard and get some publicity for their work. By creating their own pages on the Web and exchanging opinions with other readers, the pupils' linguistic ability will improve and they will also learn more about the media.

The *notice board* acts as a platform on questions to do with people making their own contributions to a work area. It is easy to use, so "beginners", too, can quickly find their way about. The creator of the work area structures and takes care of the *notice board* as well as the *foyer,* makes suggestions for further contributions and, if need be, offers advice to the user.

In another letter our group draws the CE readers' attention to their own entry in learn:line. In *notice board* the group puts forward questions and theories for discussion. They also hope to receive contributions from the USA and GB, and perhaps also from other websites created there by others.

During the lengthy group work period, short plenary sessions take place regularly. The groups then inform their classmates of the progress they are making, get advice on any problems that have come up and discuss any suggestions made by others.

5. Learn:Line 1st Just Beginning...

The above example is (as yet) a made up one. Learn:line has only officially been on the Web since 17th February 1997. However, one thing is clear already: no other medium for the foreign language lesson is in a position to offer opportunities like this for receiving up-to-date authentic texts and for communication between genuine partners with such little effort. The wide range of materials on the Internet, the references to interesting entries and the stimulus given to pupils encouraging them to work actively and creatively on the learn:line work areas take away much of the burden on a teacher by providing for a classroom situation where the youngsters work together in small groups. In this way, learn:line supports those teachers who base their lessons on concepts developed by the latest academic researches on learning processes.

If we succeed in extending the learn:line project with regard to the varying interests and topics of educational institutions, and if pupils as well as teachers learn how to use these new possibilities competently, then new opportunities will really begin to present themselves in the field of learning and work in schools, in institutions of further education and in professional education and training.

6. References

Landesinstitut für Schule und Weiterbildung (LSW) (ed.) (1996) Vorschlag für die pädagogische Konzeption des NRW-Bildungsservers. LSW, Soest

7. Biography

Wolfgang Weber was born in 1954, and studied mathematics and biology at Bielefeld University between 1973 and 1979. He was a teacher at Gymnasium and Gesamtschule between 1979 and 1990, and made a study of computer science beetween 1988 and 1991. From 1990 to 1997 he was deputy head of the Advisory Centre for New Technologies at the State Institute for Schools and Further Education of North Rhine-Westphalia, Germany. Since 1996 he has been project manager of learn:line, the North Rhine-Westphalian educational server. Since 1997 he has been head of the Advisory Center.

2. NETWORK-CENTRIC WORK - IMPLICATIONS TO PROFESSIONAL IT EDUCATION

Mikko J. Ruohonen
University of Tampere
P.O. Box 607, FIN-33101 Tampere, Finland
Tel: (358) 3 2156111 Fax: (358) 3 2156070
email: mr@cs.uta.fi

ABSTRACT

Telework, telelearning and telecommuting are current buzzwords in the modern information society. Information and communication technology (ICT) gives us many options and challenges to transform work and learning processes being independent of time and place. However, some findings indicate that people are still moving to city centres despite teleworking and telelearning opportunities. Division of tasks and processes, support of management, technological problems, location of telework sites and acceptance of new technology are some of the inhibitors. The following study focuses on three research areas. First, it examines the quality and level of ICT used in households of Finnish business people; secondly, the current state and growth of networking in office and at home; and thirdly, the related service and financial issues hindering the implementation of network-centric technology and processes. The sample represents the views of Finnish small and medium size enterprises' managers which actually may gain the most from telework and telelearning. Results indicate that the emerging network technology should fit with the current technology used in households and with no major barriers, either technical or social. On the other hand, the services and content of network-centric working and learning should be clear and visible.

Keywords

Higher education, professional development, implications, organisations, open learning, visions

1. Introduction

New technology-intensive ways of working and learning offer a flexible way to arrange work and learning processes in the information society. On the other hand it puts pressure in providing technology and applications which fit with the work and learning routines, workplace and household facilities and furthermore, with management procedures. This new way should be independent of time and place and includes normally a high intensity of information and communications technology (ICT) use.

ICT involves use of computers, facsimiles and other teleoperator network services. The advertised benefits of telework or telelearning are related to decreasing load of traffic, environmental issues, quality of life, flexible control and improved reward systems for employees. Especially in the European Union area telework projects are favoured while it provides possibility to balance regional equality.

In this report first results of diffusion drivers in the Finnish small and medium size enterprise (SME) environment are reported based on a large survey of telework technology at households. SMEs provide a great potential to be flexible in their operations and joint processes, while larger organizations seem to be monolithic and also heavily tied to the traditional office buildings. SMEs can gain some competitive advantage from designing their work and training in a more flexible and virtually effective way. The results give an excellent view to evaluate the role of education in the forthcoming work and learning process environment.

2. Theoretical background and concepts

2.1 Definition of telework

Telework is difficult to define while it is a evolving concept. However, one of the best definitions and also a complex one is from Gray et al. (1993): "teleworking is a flexible way of working which covers a wide range of work activities, all of which entail working remotely for an employer, or from a traditional place or work, for a significant proportion of work time. Teleworking may be on either a full-time or part-time basis, the work often involves electronic processing of information, and always involves using telecommunications to keep the remote employer and employee in contact with each other." A more simpler definition is "a form of ´flexible´ work which involves distance work, remote work or telecommuting which is dependent upon the use of information and communication technologies" (Moon & Stanworth, 1997).

2.2 *Innovation diffusion theory and telework*

In Finland, in the country of highest percentage of Internet access and well-developed telecommunications infrastructure (Goodman et al., 1995), telework is not very well dispersed and the latest surveys on labour movements from rural area to attractive city areas seem to be contradictory to objectives of telework objectives (Talouselama 30/97). Although our analogical telephone networks are almost 100% converted to digital ones, a faster Integrated Digital Service Network (ISDN) is not well diffused in Finland. Previous surveys indicate that 3-5 % of households have an ISDN access to the telephone network. This might be due to many factors such as pricing of ISDN services, learning potential of users or technological compatibility. Innovation diffusion theory is suggested to fit well in this research while adoption of telework practice is mostly voluntary-based innovation. Needs to invest in ICT equipment at home or correspondent remote office are mostly evaluated from the perspective of personal or family use.

The innovation diffusion theory (Rogers, 1983) assumes that a potential adopter engages in mental evaluation of the innovation, and that the likelihood of an adoption decision increases when the innovation promises to have a strong relative advantage over alternatives (relative advantage), is highly compatible with existing practices (comprehensiveness), is not too complex, (complexity), can be tried out (trialability), and the results of the innovation can be observed (visibility).

A new technology-based innovation such as telework demands redesign of routines and activities from the user community. Users need to learn the new system innovation and upgrade or transform their knowledge on using the system in the context of their work. Normally when teleworkers (or telelearners) need to buy the technology by themselves, costs of the new innovation are a major inhibitor of diffusion (relative advantage). If the voluntary user needs to put more money to get seemingly similar services from this new innovation (such as an email service) he or she will not probably adopt the innovation. It might also be that the telework technology is too complex and difficult to implement and use (comprehensiveness, complexity). In the same time management procedures need to support new work design and arrangements in order to foster the change process (trialability, visibility) It is clear that telework needs to be based on trust and not on control. Reward and performance evaluation systems need to converted to fit in this new situation.

3. The Research Process

A mail survey was executed in collaboration with a major Finnish teleoperator company Helsingin Puhelin (which belongs to a major Finnish teleoperator pool FINNET Group), a communications systems company Teleste Communications Ltd (later on called Miratel Ltd) and a business people association the Junior Chamber of Commerce Finland which was the sample group of the survey. The mail survey was sent on December 1996/January 1997 and replied questionnaires were analyzed during Summer 1997.

From 4500 sent questionnaires 875 people replied i.e. the reply rate was 19,4%. The reply rate is acceptable and reasonably high considering the obvious time restrictions of the respondent group.

The objectives of the study were exploratory i.e. we observed the group's opportunities and willingness to apply telework, use of information networks and their intensity of use. Especially we were interested in the level of technology investments in households (computers, network devices and access services), the needs for information society services and sensitivity to acquire new technology to this purpose.

3.1 Sample

The age of the respondents varied between 30 and 40 (a biased sample due to the association's rules). The study follows the principles of convinience sample due to the nature of the study. Although the sample is biased by age its quality is excellent involving respondents from business organizations. Educational level was relatively high, mainly respondents with a university degree. Despite this fact the sample involves a large amount of SME entrepreneurs. Organizational position was either in manager or executive level, work tasks or functions were usually related to either administration, marketing or sales.

Most of the respondents' companies belonged to the SME group which means an organization with a turnover of less than 40 Meuro (about 45 Million USD) and balance sheet total of less than 27 Meuro or employees less than 250. The sample is very unique while it is usually difficult to find business people oriented studies where respondents represent highest decision making level (i.e. managers or executives).

3.2 Preliminary results of the study

Due to the space limits and the on-going research programme the first set of descriptive statistics is reported in this paper

3.2.1 Technological environment. The first set of questions examined the amount and quality of ICT technology in households and the level of experience in using ICT. This related to comprehensiveness and complexity to adopt an innovation. The respondents described themselves as experienced or at least having a good fundamental knowledge on ICT. They use computers daily in their work. We can conclude that these people are qualified to evaluate the benefits of telework and ICT technology.

One of the most interesting findings was that almost 80% informed to have and use computer at their homes. This is a very high figure while the average of home computer penetration in Finland is near 35 percent according to the latest surveys for all households. The computers were quite new while most of them were either Pentium or Intel 486 processor-based computers. Survey participants informed that almost all family members are using the home computer. About 31% replied that their computer is used by three of more of the family members.

This might have far-reaching implications to organize telework and learning activities at homes. We may ask do the families need several computers or even a home network with a server and clients with multiple access to the network? This might put challenges to ICT home sales and consultation, teleoperator and network service providers and digital media services.

3.2.2 Organizational support. The second set of questions dealt with organizational support for applying telework as one part of work practice (relative advantage, partly trialability and visibility). According to survey results, companies support telework quite actively, almost 50% of the respondents informed that their employers support telework arrangements. However, we must be careful in interpreting the results while the whole concept of telework is very fuzzy. Most of the organizations doing already telework were SMEs. Most of the previous studies do not indicate that companies are favouring telework arrangements, vice versa, rather being skeptical and wanting to keep control.

3.2.3 Telecommunications facilities and usage level. The third set of questions was about telecommunications facilities. Half of the home computers involved also a telecommunications device (a modem or equivalent). Most of the devices were high-speed modems (over 28 000 bps, but only 3% of them with an ISDN access device). Most of the respondents replied their telecommunications device to be slow or moderate when asked about their view of data transfer speed. Less than 25% indicated that the speed is satisfactory.

We must note that most of the teleconnections were typically done couple of times per week and lasting in average not more than 15 minutes. This means obviously that home computer systems are used for reading and replying email messages and/or doing remote banking which is a very common practice in Finland (about 400 000 active users of the population of 5 million people). We can say that the level of using extensively network services is still waiting, this might be mainly due to slow supply of digital contents in the network.

3.2.4 The use of Internet network in office and at home. The use of Internet network services for work and business activities was surprisingly low remembering the highly advertised image of Finnish Internet diffusion. Less than half of the participants used Internet in their offices and at homes less than 20%. Outside the work tasks in office about 30% of the people indicated to use Internet. Although there is a high interest to find something from the Internet, the research group also identified a group which has never used Internet and is reluctant to use it in future. This is very surprising while the object group had a very good facilities to do networking. It might mean that the relative advantage of doing telework or other activities such as learning and education is in its embryonic phase.

4. Educational implications

This survey indicates a number of paths for developing learning and education activities for network-centric organizations. The next analysis is based on the earlier study on opportunities and limitations of IT-induced learning and education (Ruohonen, 1998).

4.1 Learners and other stakeholders in the network-centric context

Telelearning, teleteaching and other equivalent approaches face the problem of user abilities. New ways of working and learning are not just related to high level investments in computers and networks. Personal experiences of the author suggest that if educational processes need to change also learning processes need to be transformed. A typical learner say, in a university or a vocational institute, is used to follow certain standard flow of education.When this flow is changed radically by using networks, interactive chat channels and email groups in addition to digital document supply centers the learners need to change their learning processes, too. Other stakeholders of the whole process such as teachers, administrators, digital contents providers, telecommunication services and publishers need to be aware of the emerging community's way of learning. In terms of innovation diffusion, we might say that people need to see the relative advantage of teleactivities before changing their daily practices.

4.2 Interactive technology as a tool for network-centric education

Much of the technology provided nowadays is far too sophisticated and expensive. Transmission of "a talking head" to another city or even a country does not much raise the quality of education but it surely raises the costs of it. Naturally, if this is the only way to deliver something (i.e. teaching resources are scarce and/or not available with some other way), it works well. However, surprisingly often the latest interactive technology needs also support personnel while teachers and students can not cope with these new ICT applications. New technology might be difficult to use both for teachers and students or it is far too complex and managed only by "teaching support engineers". Therefore it is very important to evaluate the level of teaching and learning tasks and use "fit" technology to execute them. Very often just an email or World Wide Web access and maybe some simple videoconferencing through workstations may do the same as a hard-core teleteaching studio with an optical fiber network, video servers, digital documents and multiple camera systems (see for an example, Newman, 1998).

4.3 Mastering the subject knowledge for network-centric education

The type of material covered during teaching sessions can be factual, procedural, conceptual or exploratory in nature. Leidner and Jarvenpaa (1993) have noted that procedural and exploratory knowledge contents dominated computer-based education sessions more that conceptual or factual knowledge which were more typical in traditional lecturing. It is obvious that, for example, computer algoritm education and many of the engineering education topics fit well with the network-centric education ideology. However, how do we teleteach strategic management through networks or handicraft design? This type of knowledge might demand several channels of knowledge transfer and it puts pressure to analyze the nature of courses in the network-centric context.

4.4 *Prevailing education strategies and rules*

Transformation processes can be ruined by administrative policies or standards of doing things "in the good, old way". For example, telelearning and remote evaluation may put more extra work and costs to traditional schools and training institutes. Some administrative rules might inhibit, for example, remote examination or arrangements in contradiction with the master teaching plan of organizations. It starts from the educational policy level where you put your grand objectives for information society. The most dangerous is sectorial thinking in the age of networks, both social and technical networks. We should remember that teleteaching and similar arrangement may exist just for decreasing unit costs i.e. to copy the same standard lecture to multiple sites and having that way cheaper education per student. If we are looking added value from these experiments we need to redesign our educational processes and structures which makes the education game political.

4.5 *The nature of learning communities*

In the global context we are facing a new challenge which is related to multi-cultural communities both in our own institute or country and across the borders. In the current and future working life people need to collaborate and run teams which are very diverse by home country, religion, culture and habits. It means that already in our educational system we need to practice these diverse contexts. This is very well boosted by network technology and global virtual teams which can learn and work globally (Knoll and Jarvenpaa, 1995). However, it also demands networking of teachers, professional communities and even institutes to set up these learning and education networks. This is beyond just technical issues while people networks must work, too. Communities of practice, business or some other interest areas seem to be the key for teleteaching and telelearning activities.

4.6 *Networked, open learning environments*

The traditional way of sharing duties or workload is changing dramatically. In the management of education you need to analyze carefully which phases of the whole process belong to your core competencies. This differs when comparing different educational levels, primary, secondary and tertiary. It is, however, clear that outsourcing and insourcing effects are evident also in the field of education. You might need to plan your course in collaboration with some foreign institution to face the challenge of unification of education. You might also co-operate in allocating time or place of teaching and also financial resources put to your joint course or program. Finally you need to evaluate probably with same standards. In addition to that all the supporting processes can be re-evaluated such as examination procedures, case and exercise control, teaching/learning material production, students services, add-on course supply, industry projects and connections, job search and research & development projects. This makes also educational cluster more competitive, via networks virtual institutions and companies can compete about the same audience and customers.

5. Discussion

Based on the survey to Finnish business people and previous work on IT-induced learning and education implications for network-centric learning and education were discussed. Much of the technical problems have been solved at least in developed countries, however, it seems that many social and cultural issues are more complicated.

In the network-centric context of education educationalists, teachers and all other stakeholders need to evaluate the situation holistically. Technological determinism is not viable option while many of the transformation processes are not related to technology as your survey also indicates. The use of telecommunications for work and other activities was at a reasonably low level despite the good level of ICT equipment in use.

Learning and education in network-centric environment is, however, a very challenging and potential area for training business people which are normally unable to participate in educational activities during office hours. On the other hand it seems that markets are open for those players which can provide good quality education via networks.

6. References

Goodman, S., Dedrick, J., and Kraemer, K. (1995) *Little Engines that could: computing in Small Energetic Countries.* Communications of the ACM, **38**(5), 21-26.

Gray, M., Hodson, N., and Gordon, G. (1993) *Teleworking Explained.* Wiley, Chichester.

Knoll, K. and Jarvenpaa, S.L. (1995) *Learning to Work in Distributed Global Teams.* (http://uts.cc.utexas.edu/~bgac313/hicss.html, 4.6.1998)

Leidner, D.E. and Jarvenpaa, S.L. (1993) The Information Age Confronts Education: Case Studies on Electronic Classrooms. *Information Systems Research* **4**(1), 24-54.

Moon, C. and Stanworth, S. (1997) Flexible working in Europe. The case of teleworking in the UK, in *Quaderni di Psicologia del Lavoro Vol. 5: Feelings Work in Europe* (eds. F. Avallone, J. Arnold and K. De Witte), 337-344.

Newman, W. (1998) Principals, information technology and leadership - coping with professional development despite isolation, in *Capacity Building for IT in education in Developing Countries* (eds. G. Marshall and M. Ruohonen) Chapman & Hall, London.

Rogers, E.M. (1983) Diffusion of Innovations. The Free Press, New York.

Ruohonen, M.J. (1998) Opportunities and Limitations of IT-Induced Learning and Education, *in Proceedings of the LeTTet '98 and MaTILDA '98 Joint conference* (eds . J. Multisilta and J-P. Niemi), Publications of the Pori School of Technology and Economics, Series A:18, 23-34.

Talouselama 30/97: Alkoi joukkopako kaupungeista: muuttoliike. Talouselama **30/97**. (Finnish business journal).

7. Biography

Mikko Ruohonen is a Professor at the University of Tampere, Department of Computer Science and a Docent of Information Systems Science at the Turku School of Economics and Business Administration. Dr Ruohonen's interest areas are business strategy and information management, management participation in strategic information planning, knowledge management and IT/IS education. He has published three textbooks, two chapters in international textbooks and more than 90 articles in informations systems research field. He is a Full Member and a Vice Chair of the IFIP Working Group 3.4.

3. PLANNING GUIDELINES FOR NEXT GENERATION BUSINESS SIMULATION

Timo Lainema
Turku Centre for Computer Science and
Turku School of Economics and
Business Administration
P.O. Box 110, FIN-20521 Turku, Finland
E-mail: timo.lainema@tukkk.fi

ABSTRACT

Although the benefit of using business games is generally approved it is questionable if the present games serve the learning process as effectively as possible. The present state of computer environments and programming languages offers tools with which the games could be developed to serve as even more effective tools of teaching the rules of businesses. While the world around businesses is changing with growing speed the business game processing methods are still quite the same as 25 years ago. The purpose of this paper is to introduce some advanced business game techniques and operation models. By applying these new techniques, business games would serve the learning more effectively compared to the traditional techniques.

Keywords

Games, Simulation, Industry Training, Professional Development

1. Introduction

The competitive environment around most businesses and companies is changing with accelerating speed, i.e. competition is becoming worldwide, new products are developed faster, new producing technologies are emerging and new delivery channels are available. Organizations are in the midst of whole new challenges and are seeking for better competitive position and productivity. *Attaining such improvements in productivity would be a significant challenge under normal circumstances, but the process is made significantly more complex by the volatile environment that is becoming more evident and is expected to continue to increase into the 1990s. In this highly unpredictable environment, novel approaches to attaining high levels of productivity must be pursued* (Madnick, 1991).

There is also a demand for training methods that describe the characteristic of the recent and future competitive environment. Regardless of the level of productivity improvement desired, people as decision-makers and as responsible for task execution need to understand thoroughly what they are part of in order to be able to cope with every day tasks.

Compared to spoken information business games are good in that they are visual by nature. In business games players learn and become better problem solvers, allowing them to master successively more complicated tasks and to transfer expertise (Porter, 1995). Saffo (1997) has noted: *In the next decade, the most important new sense-making tools will be those that help people visualize and simulate. Visualization techniques reduce vast and obscure pools of data into easily comprehended images. And simulation systems will become intellectual training wheels for executives, allowing them to experiment with strategies in the forgiving world of cyberspace, in much the same way that pilots in the Gulf War ran practise missions before flying the real thing.*

In the future the use of management games will be at least as common as today (Elgood, 1996): *Technological development will certainly not slow down, and one will be able to simulate more situations with greater realism and greater ease. Work will be seen as an activity that should be rewarding in itself, and enjoyable, and therefore something to which game-playing can reasonable be linked.*

2. Modern Business Decision-Making Environment

Business games offer the participants knowledge on how the decisions carried out affect the business environment and thus prepare the participant to learn more about decision-making by experience. The game used should hereby describe the actual decision-making environment of the organization.

2.1 Changes in the significance of time

Traditionally strategic decisions have been long range decisions, and operative decisions have been every-day-like, executed often by a sudden change or need in the business environment. Today, the world is changing more rapidly than ever, mainly because of technological development. The speed of change reflects, of course, on the way operational decisions are carried out, but it also reflects on the way strategic decisions are made.

Some years ago the strategic planning process was seen as a planning tool with which (Näsi, 1991) the environment is forced to bend if the company only knows its planning procedures properly We are dealing with an ideal world: Information is available, the company has money and resources to create and shape things; the CEO and the secondary management have time to discuss the matter; they are also capable of understanding all the preconditions of good decision making and the connections.

Nowadays, the future is very difficult to predict, but it is also realized, that mastering the future does not necessarily demand predicting. The faster and more effectively we can react to changes, the less we need to predict them.

Näsi (1991) states that the development of the traditional strategic thinking has moved from the strategic planning and portfolio management stages to a new stage which he describes as strategic gameplaying stage (Näsi, 1991, p. 35) the central task of a strategist is to make good moves on the play ground. The key to the third stage is to view strategic thinking as gameplaying... The limits of the ground or board are more undetermined, the rules are only partially known and can change and the player must create and develop the alternatives - by him/herself.

In this turbulent competitive environment the customers expect shorter times of delivery, accurate deliveries and fault free products. The speed of reacting market changes has become an essential competitive factor. Very likely this development will even become more rapid in the near future, because the technical evolution is enabling shorter production development periods, new product innovations and new ways to organize customer communication and transactions.

A company mastering time has several new characteristics compared to a conventional company (Kanerva, 1991): it develops integrated functions and operates without function boundaries in accordance with process workflow. Experts and users work together both in planning and implementation. Flow of information is emphasized and information passes fast through the organization.

Because of the fast decision-making the present batch-processed business game methods do not describe the environment of the decision-making well enough.

2.2 Holistic business environment and stakeholder thinking

The demand to understand the overall business structure is becoming more and more current. By the growing speed of environmental changes also the employees must be able to change their way of thinking and working. The general knowledge on how a company works helps the worker to adopt new behaviour.

Besides of understanding the internal business function activities the employees must have understanding on what kind of interest groups the company has. Any business operates in the middle of different stakeholders. In order to be able to carry out stakeholder thinking the company decision-makers must have understanding on what stakeholder groups a company has and what are the demands and expectations of the stakeholders.

3. Advanced Business Game Techniques

The purpose of using business games is to promote learning. The better the participants learn by playing the business game the better the game is. This paper puts forward four propositions on business game techniques. By applying these propositions the business game learning may be further enhanced.

3.1 Proposition 1: the ability to configure the game environment

For the learning itself it is important that the business model adequately resembles the real world environment of the participants. Learning is deeper if the business model is realistic compared to the real environment. This means that the game model must be dynamic and can be tailored according to the purpose and the target of the learning project. Thus, the game environment should be configured for the players to describe their own business environment.

The real business environment can be divided in two parts: the internal business environment and the external business environment. The internal business environment includes the structure of the business unit under decisions during the game. For example, configuring the internal business environment includes the structure of the manufacturing process inside the business unit.

The external business environment includes the capital market, the market of production factors, the customer market and the competitors. E.g. the sales market must include great flexibility in order to be able to imitate the structures of real world markets.

3.2 Proposition 2: real-time processing

Present business games are not realistic in the way they are executed. Present business games work in a batch-processed manner which quite poorly adapts to the real world business environment. Batch-processed simulation works in a way where all the decisions from all the competing companies are first made for the whole season to be simulated. Then the simulation phase takes place and all the decisions are processed as a batch, all decisions being equal in the processing.

The problem with the batch-processing method is that world very rarely works in such a sequential order. There are hardly no business areas where the decision makers first enter all their decisions for the next term, then rest during all the actual term, and enter again the business in the end of the term to analyze the term results and to prepare the next budget.

To take one example, there are very few business branches in which a company sets the price of its product for the whole next term before the term even has begun and then keeps to that selling price during all the term. The batch-processing model does not give the decision-maker the possibility to change the decisions according to the competitor's actions.

The disadvantages of batch processing are obvious (Lawrence, 1997): *The result of this is simulations that severely limit the management experience. Participants cannot afford to test strategies and plan contingencies since they are tied to their decisions for the entire period. This can often be unrealistic. ...In general, such business simulations tend to lock their participants into a particular approach towards decision making which reduces their potential value. The acute lack of flexibility discourages creativity which is often a trait which should be emphasised in management training.*

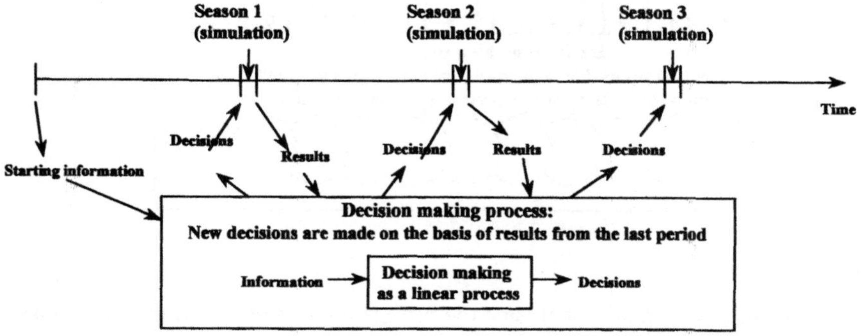

Figure 1 The batch-processing business game environment.

Proposition 2 means that the next generation business game model should work the same way as the normal business environment works, i.e. decisions making and having results from decisions made should happen in real-time mode when so also in the real-world environment. Real-time mode means that decisions are made continuously, especially when there are situations, which need instant reaction.

For example, a better way to describe the problem setting of pricing is a real-time model in which the customer market and the competitor actions are changing continuously. In a real-time model decisions are made as soon they are needed or at least as soon as the decision-maker notices that the market situation needs actions from him. And pricing is just one example - in fact most decision-making areas work similarly and are time bound.

Batch processing can never describe the time-dependent environment realistically because:

1. the faster decision-makers do not benefit anything from being faster because the batches of decisions of all the companies are processed simultaneously
2. if the batch-processing frequency is accelerated, the slow decision-makers drop totally out of the decision-making process. In real world slow decision-makers are able to do decisions, although the amount of decisions may be less than with the faster ones.
3. it would technically be possible to implement a time measuring mechanism to batch processing. But a solution like this would be very difficult to implement because the model should measure the decision-making time of every single decision. Furthermore, this kind of measuring of the decision-making time would be unrealistic, because the decisions made will still not trigger any immediate responses.

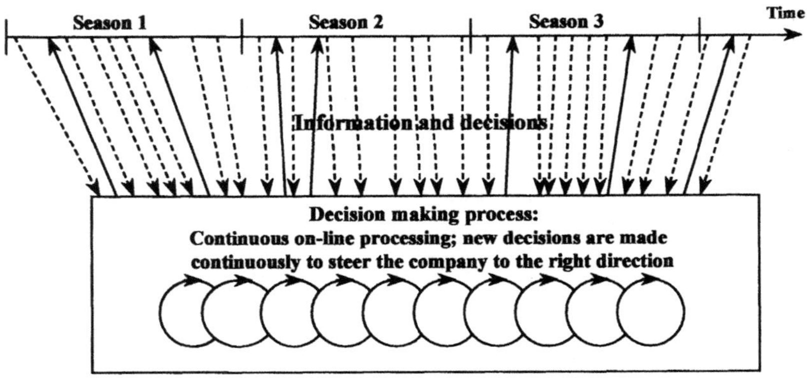

Figure 2

To sufficiently realistically represent the turbulent business decision environment the significance of time must be included. This is accomplished by building a business game, which includes internal time - a game which works as normal business environment so that different business events and decisions are processed, decided and executed in virtual real-time. In real-time simulation all the processes take place continuously. The participants who steer the company see all the market events and internal processes on-line. What ever happens – reactions can be carried out instantly.

3.3 Proposition 3: the overall business environment

There is a demand on business games covering the total business activities area. In the present business world workers with different background must have the ability to understand the purpose, the goal and the business idea of the company or organization they are working in. This demand is even more current when the companies follow cross-functional team working and process thinking. Thus there must be tools to teach the workers how a company works as a whole and what the purpose of each business function within the whole structure is.

3.4 Proposition 4: selectable decision-making levels

From the learning stand of point the business game model must not be too complicated. The game model must be realistic enough compared to the real world but still it must be simple enough for the participants to learn it in a few hours.

Research from empirical studies on simulations used for improving manufacturing operations (Räsänen, 1996) point also out that: *We also recognised that building an overly detailed simulation model results in a very time-consuming model-building and lengthy simulation exercise periods. An overly detailed simulation model also has a tendency to block people from perceiving fundamental cause-effects included in an actual manufacturing environment.*

From this can be derived proposition 4: the decision making level in the game in each particular business function can be selected according to the group taking part to the game and by the objectives of the game. Every business decision function includes from 2 to 3 different decision making levels. The first level is a general level in which can be done decisions in a very general manner. Gradually on the second and third level the decisions to be made become more demanding.

With these different functional decision making levels the game can be used to teach very different kind of groups of participants. Or then the game objectives can be emphasized on certain functions and leave the rest of the functions with less attention. On the other hand the decision levels in each business function may be changed during the game. So it could be possible to introduce new decision making aspects during the game when ever the game operator sees that the participants have learned the basics of a business function and are ready to be presented new decision making problems.

4. References

Elgood, Chris (1996). Using Management Games. Gower Press.

Kanerva, Hannu (1992). Aikaa hallitsevan organisaation rakentaminen. In "S.A.M.I Vuosikirja 1992 - Aika kilpailutekijänä". Strategic Analysis & Management Inc. Oy (S.A.M.I.), 1992.

Lawrence, P. J. (1997). Business Simulations: dynamic, computer based case studies for management development, in The Place of Information Technology in Management and Business Education (edited by Barta, B, Tatnall, A. and Juliff, P.), TC3, WG3.4 International Conference on the Place of Information Technology in Management and Business Education, Chapman & Hall

Madnick, Stuart, E. (1991). The Information Technology Platform, in The Corporation of the 1990's - Information Technology and Organizational Transformation (edited by Michael S. Scott Morton), Oxford University Press.

Näsi, Juha (1991). Arenas of Strategic Thinking. Liikesivistysrahasto, Helsinki.

Porter, D. B. (1995). Computer Games: Paradigms of Opportunity, Behaviour Research Methods, Instruments & Computers, Vol. 27, No. 2, pp. 229-234.

Räsänen, Hannu (1996). Simulation for Improving Manufacturing Operations. Report no 170/1996, Helsinki University of Technology.

Saffo, Paul (1997). Looking Ahead: Implications of the Present, In Harvard Business Review, September - October 1997

Scott Morton, M. S. (1991). The Corporation of the 1990s, Information Technoly and Organizational Transformation (ed. Scott Morton), Oxford University Press, Inc.

4. DATA COMMUNICATION AND DISTANCE LEARNING METHODOLOGIES FOR TECHNICIANS TRAINING

I. S. Zilberstein,
Director School of Technology,
the Open University of Israel
16 Klausner Street, Tel-Aviv, Israel
Tel: 972-3-6423236, 972-3-6460191
Fax: 972-3-6460068
E-mail: israel_z@cet.ac.il

B. Z. Barta,
Centre for Educational Technology
16 Klausner Street, Tel-Aviv, Israel
Tel: 972-4-850-9569
E-mail: ben@barcode.co.il

ABSTRACT

Within the continuous efforts of the School of Technology of the Open University in Israel to improve the teaching/learning process, new methodologies were adapted: use of engineering and simulation software and the use of data communications for distance learning (DCDL). The DCDL system uses for educational purposes most of the facilities available on the web. The educational, training and social aspects of the rationale for using DCDL are shortly mentioned. Examples of application in electronics studies and the data collected during the first, limited scale implementation of the system are described.

Keywords

Distance Learning, Vocational Education, Electronics, Methodologies, Courseware

1. Introduction

The School of Technology of the Open University of Israel was established some 11 years ago, as a nation wide distance learning system for training **Technicians and Practical Engineers.** Technician is one year post secondary level and Practical Engineer two years.

The School developed about 20 courses in each of 3 Engineering fields: **Electronics, Software Engineering, and Industrial Management.**

A technician must complete 13 courses for the diploma and a Practical Engineer 18 courses.

Each course used until recently all or most of the following learning methodologies: Self Study written units, Home laboratories, Software for home use, Group sessions at study centers, Weekly telephone assistance, Home assignments and practical work, Final exam in each course.

2. New Methodologies

Updating the study methods and means in recent years involved two main directions:

1. Intensive use of Engineering and Simulation software
2. Introducing Data Communication for Distance Learning (DCDL)

The first updating direction includes the use of applications, simulation and system analysis packages which were adapted for educational purposes from points of view of complexity, user friendliness, and course content.

Some examples are: Access for the courses: 'Data Bases' and 'Information Systems'. EWB and TESS for studying some courses in Electronics and Communication Systems. The simulation packages being used in Electronics and Industrial Management courses are sometimes very good substitutes for laboratory experimentation and fault finding conducted previously on real hardware training systems. In addition, the software packages have broader and deeper analysis and experimentation possibilities than the hardware training systems.

The computerized activities with these packages are conducted in some cases on the personal computers of students at home and in other cases on networked computer classes at study centers spread all over the country with tutors guidance and assistance.

The considerations involved in using these software packages either as networked computer classes at study centers or as stand alone are:

1. Availability of course material for self study and how much tutorial assistance will be needed for the work with the package, or else the difficulties or even unavailability of materials for home use and tutoring.
2. The amount of the pedagogic contribution of team work in a networked class.

3. Availability of home computers and availability of computer classes in a particular student location.
4. Price of the package for single user versus site license in the classes.

3. Data Communication For Distance Learning (DCDL)

3.1 Main features

The DCDL system was introduced in the past few years in several Open University academic courses, and we at the School of Technology are preparing to use the system in a few courses, beginning in March 1998. Every student receives a Modem (if he doesn't have one), a communication software package, an e-mail address, and basic operation instructions, in order to connect to the system.

The main features of the DCDL system are:

1. **E mail correspondence** - students between themselves, students and tutor, students and tutor with their instruction manager at the School of Technology. Messages from the course tutor or instruction manager to the students are about: course operation, supplying additional material, learning procedures, exercising new Internet relevant sites, etc.
2. **Discussion groups** or asynchronous conferences, between the students and with the tutor. The tutor will pose a problem to all the students via e mail and the students will discuss options and solutions. 'External' guest experts will also pose issues for discussion. The possibility to connect students to various news groups available on the net will also be studied.
3. **Opening an Internet site for the course** and using it for guided access as well as personal access to Internet resources dealing with the technological topics of the course. A FAQ facility is also investigated. Questions raised by students in the past alongside misconceptions expressed by students will be presented in a FAQ file.
4. **Interactive self study courseware** that integrates Internet possibilities in the computer based learning. It will be described in more detail further on.

Features 1 and 2 of the above and in some sense 3 are technical possibilities supplied by the system for learners and teachers. Some aspects of feature 3 and mainly feature 4 are those containing reach pedagogical and instructional content.

3.2 The Rationale for DCDL

Using DCDL for our training system has several goals, professional, pedagogical and social.

Any recently trained professional in Electronics, Informatics and many other areas, has to be able to use the Internet facilities in his daily work. To be able to browse for information and technical data, purchase, make bids and proposals, etc.

Another development, gradually introduced by Industry is that of team work based on data communications, having team members working from disperse locations.

Starting to use such facilities while being educated, will not only augment the educational process but will have the graduates better prepared for their future professional activities.

Pedagogically, the use of DCDL promises to be a valuable add-on to the other methodologies and materials already in use. It is the most efficient way to provide updates to existing written materials or educational software available at students' homes. It allows to work from the home computers, interactively with centrally located packages, to get tutor's interaction, on line while working with the package. Additional materials and support can be provided to individuals and groups according to their specific needs - at a level of interaction, presentation quality, and speed of distribution which cannot be obtained with any other conventional learning means.

From the social point of view, one of the problems of distance learning is the lack of daily and easy contact with the tutors and with other students. Efficient data communication using all the facilities provided by the Internet, is a good and cost-effective substitute to face to face contact. It gives the feeling of belonging to a group and of having its support, even if students get to the system from different places and at different times.

Having these issues in mind, the presently developed courses, as described further on, will provide the opportunity to test these approaches and to evaluate their efficiency.

4. Applying DCDL In Electronics Studies

The DCDL method is introduced experimentally in 2 Electronics courses: 'Beginners Electronics Circuits' and 'Advanced Electronics Circuits'. We chose a main topic of Electronics Circuits in which students have difficulties and which is included in both courses at different levels: 'Operational Amplifiers and their applications'. In addition to opening the Web site for these courses and using the correspondence and e mail facilities, we are developing courseware which presents the material to be learnt in a staggered manner. In each stage only the minimal information needed for that stage is presented, and the student is asked for interactive response in order to proceed. The distant computerized learning system presents problems at various levels and the student can ask for clues, and/or receive partial solution and/or receive the complete solution. The basic exercises and problems posed are suitable for the beginners course while the problems including industrial applications and circuit analysis are suited to the level and complexity of the advanced course. The system also includes summaries and abstracts of the basic concepts and principles of the Electronics topic involved. The student can access them when he feels the need for it.

The integration of the Internet resources and learning possibilities in this system will be done in several ways:

1. **General links in the courseware** to sites teaching relevant Electronics topics, for enrichment and further study of the topic.
2. **Specific links in the self study units of the courses** - these will include specific explanations and/or instructions regarding proper pages of Internet sites, in which relevant material is presented.
3. **Internet tasks** - some assignments and problems in the courseware and in other distance learning means of the Electronics courses need Internet resources in order to reach proper solutions. Knowledge of how to access and retrieve information from one or more sites and data bases is needed.
4. **Group project assignment** - these are large assignments intended for collaborative work of 2-4 students who have to use the correspondence and discussion capabilities of the system as well as Internet resources and data bases in order to accomplish the project. The projects are taken from real life problems that need investigation and analysis before beginning solving them. This investigation should be done by team work using the DCDL system. The team has to work together to find a proper solution, analyze it, and prepare a proper report on it.

Some examples of the Internet tasks and assignments are following. Our comments in parentheses explain the underlying instructional considerations:

1. What is a Darlington circuit and what is it used for?
2. (This type of circuit has not been studied yet so this is an investigation task in which the Internet resources and the specific links given in the course site must be explored.)
3. Detail the differences between an ideal Diode (operational Amplifier) and a real one. Use up-to-date data of Semiconductor producers, such as Philips, Motorola, etc. (Here, the student has to deal with real life situations of finding data files of components and electronic devices, using the Net.)

An example of the learning software integrated

Problem

A waveform has a positive amplitude of (V_1) and a negative amplitude of ($-V_2$). Use two peak detectors and design a circuit, in the output of which we will get a DC voltage of ($V_1 + V_2$).

Links are available to:

1. clue

2. partial solution
3. full solution
4. basic concepts
5. instructor's help - on line or off line,
6. FAQ related to the problem.

An interesting and further reaching instructional idea which we consider to incorporate in future courses is to use a software simulation package which is available on the Net and actually 'build' the circuit that solves the problem, connect the input voltage and investigate the output voltage. The packages on the Net, we refer to are demos or student versions of large packages used in industry but they will suffice for the circuit complexity of the course.

In order to increase student's motivation and willingness to use the system, we chose to teach by DCDL such subjects that are included in the final state examinations for the Technician/Practical Engineer diploma.

We intend that the development teams will update the courseware according to the feedback from its operation as well as the changes in the curriculum and the state examinations.

5. Usage Statistics

First run-in implementation of DCDL for the electronics course, started in March 1998 with a limited number of students — the main goal being to debug the system and to get a rude first evaluation of the way students use it.

The course is taken by a group of 25 students which were offered to access the system on a volunteer basis. They have been allowed to use the system as they wish, with the option to accomplish some web-based assignments instead of the regular assignments included in the course.

Weekly data has been collected on the access of the various system facilities, the assessing sites and the frequency of students' accesses. Comments and suggestions of the students have been collected as well. Some of these get immediate response and full analysis is to be done at the end of the semester. About 10 students are accessing the site weekly.

Some 150 pages are requested weekly with no fixed patterns of usage on the different days of the week. It is clear that the peak of the request is not on weekends only but one of the week days randomly.

About 20% of the pages requested are from the news groups; 30-40% from exercises and assignments; about 5% are requests to other sites accessed through our system. The rest splits between general information about the site, timetables, etc.

From this preliminary data, we can conclude that the system is operating correctly and that some of the students find it useful and access it regularly. There is as yet no evaluation of its benefits to the learning process.

It is not yet clearly known why some of the students did not use the system. It may be caused by the habit to use printed material or by the limited access some may have to the computer. This fact will be investigated in future runs of the course.

6. Summary

The DCDL as described so far, will be used for several semesters as an additional methodology to the self study written material which is still the main learning method and to the other conventional distance learning methodologies. We intend in the future to put more and more weight on the DCDL and the use of simulation software instead of the written material and the hardware laboratories. The more the availability of computers, software packages and Internet access of the students increase, the more pedagogic emphasis will be on DCDL and similar methodologies as well as the intensive use of 'Virtual laboratories' through simulation and analysis software.

By the beginning of August we will have some conclusions from the first run of the DCDL in the several School of Technology courses and these will be presented at the Working Group conference

7. References

Zilberstein, I. and Barta, B.Z. (1992) Using Software and Hardware in Distant Training System for Computer Professionals, in *Proceedings of FIE Conference*, 755-762, Vanderbilt University, U.S.A.

Zilberstein, I.S. (1993) Implementation of Computerized learning methods in secondary electronics education, in *IFP Transactions A~35* (ed. B.Z. Barta, Eccelston, Hamblish), IFIP Working Group 3.4, Soest.

Zilberstein, I. (1997) Assessment Methods in Distance Learning Post Secondary Technology Education, *Proceedings of PATT-8 Conference*, (ed. Ilja Mottier and Marc J. de Vries), Shweningen, Netherlands.

8. Biography

Israel S. Zilberstein

Born 1946, received B.Sc. in Electrical Engineering 1967. Since 1970, Project Director and since 1976 Head of Technology Education Division of the Center for Educational technology (CET) in Israel as well as Head of Vocational Training through self study methods at the Open University of Israel. Since 1983 Head of Development of the School of Technology of the Open University. Since 1996 Director of the School of Technology. Participated and presented at IFIP WG3.4 Conferences in 1984, 1990 (with the WCCE), 1991, 1993 and also at FIE 1992 Conference in USA, UNESCO, 2000+ Conference 1993 in Paris, IRNTED 1994 Conference in Italy, IOSTE 1996 Conference in Canada, JISTEC 1996 in Jerusalem, PATT 8 1997 in the Netherlands. Participated in Committees for Technology Education development and Telecommunications training at ORT STEP/LEAP 1995, 1996 and 1997 in South Africa.

Ben Z. Barta

Born 1931, Ph.D. from Technion Israel. Consultant on Internet Working and Computers in Education. Retired. Chief Inspector for Computers in Education in the Ministry of Education, Israel, in charge of the coordination of R&D projects and the implementation of computer education activities in the Israeli school system. Chair of IFIP's Working Group on Information Technology in Educational Management. Chaired IFIP's Working Group on Training and Education of IT Professionals. Chaired several Working Conferences, published and edited in the areas of teaching of Informatics and of computers in education.

5. EDUCATIONAL EFFECTIVENESS OF AN INTERACTIVE MULTIMEDIA COMMUNICATIONS ENVIRONMENT

K. Maeda†, R. Aibara‡, K. Kawamoto†,
M. Terauchi†, and S. Otsuki†
†: Hiroshima City University, 3-4-1, Ozuka-Higashi, Asa-Minami, Hiroshima, 731-3194 Japan
TEL: +81-82-830-1655, FAX: +81-82-830-1792
E-mail: kaori@ipc.hiroshima-cu.ac.jp
‡: Hiroshima University, 1-4-2 Kagamiyama, Higashi-Hiroshima 739-8526 Japan

ABSTRACT

The goal of this study is to consider an effective environment to instruct and learn how to use interactive multimedia communications on the Internet. In this paper, we describe several experiments of interactive distance learning. In our experiments, we used a high-speed ATM network with Internet collaboration (video, audio and whiteboard combined), called as the Mbone (Multicast Backbone) tools and present the results of the questionnaires on distance learning to evaluate its effectiveness. We show good evaluation to our proposal environment to keep quality as ordinal lectures for learners and teachers from these results. Also, we get positive results for distance learning in the viewpoints of effective experience to learn on networks and familiarity with distance learning. This means that interactive distance learning is effective not only to solve time and geographic restrictions but also to learn/instruct multimedia communications. Finally, we discuss a new literacy education defined as Multimedia Communications Literacy (MCL) which is different from the existing computer or network literacy. The MCL must be required for teachers and learners to attend distance learning, and for everyone communicating on multimedia networks.

Keywords
Distance Learning, Video Conferencing, Multimedia, Internet

1. Introduction

Increasing availability of higher-speed networks, two-way digital telecommunication facilities has introduced opportunities for interactive multimedia communications. Using the Internet has become a part of daily life for people in various fields in the world. From these changes, multimedia data such as images and voice can be transferred to several recipients all over the world by multicasting to transfer data across networks. The first such applications have come into widespread use on the Internet using the Mbone (Multicast Backbone), a virtual experiment network (Macedonia, 1994). Many applications such as videoconference or broadcasting are being done experimentally on this network. Using this kind of network, interactive multimedia communications will be necessary, especially for professionals in a cyber space as a basic way to communicate in the world. However, there is no good way to learn how to use interactive multimedia communications on the Internet. Distance learning is one of options given in the high-speed networks such as fibre-based terrestrial networks and satellite-based networks (Quemada, 1996) (Kondo, 1996). We focus on interactive distance learning as an environment to instruct and learn how to use multimedia communications on the Internet.

In this paper, we investigate an effective environment to instruct and learn and propose an environment of distance learning. We emphasise its educational effectiveness. First, we present the experimental environment using a high-speed ATM (Asynchronous Transfer Mode) network and the Internet collaboration (audio, video, and whiteboard combined) as the Mbone tools for distance learning. We show the results of the questionnaires to the learners on the effectiveness of distance learning (Maeda, 1997) and discuss their evaluation to our proposal environment to keep quality as ordinal lectures for learners and teachers. Through the experiments, we found an importance of a new literacy education which is different from the existing computer or network literacy. Then we discuss on a new literacy education defined as Multimedia Communications Literacy (MCL). Finally, we offer conclusions on the educational effectiveness of an interactive multimedia communications environment and describe the future problems.

2. Experiments for Interactive Distance Learning

2.1 Outline of Experiments

The purpose of our experiments is to investigate an effective environment to learn how to use multimedia communication tools on the Internet. Two sites, i.e. the teacher and the learners, in the experiments are connected by the ATM backbone providing total bandwidth of 67Mbps. We used the Internet collaboration tools (audio, video and whiteboard combined) for the six times of lectures described below and a remote camera control mechanism designed for this purpose. Figure 1 shows a typical snapshot window in a teacher site. The following are details of the tools.

- Video: **vic** (Video Conference) (McCanne, 1995).
- A user transfers his images through a camera to remote sites and receives all images from remote sites. Transfer speed, frame rate and compression format can be specified by each user.
- Audio: **vat** (Visual Audio Tool) (Jacobson, 1995).
- A user transfers his voice through a microphone to remote sites and receives voice from all remote sites. Transfer control is the same as a **vic**.
- Presentation tool: **wb** (White Board) (Jacobson, 1993).
- Presentation slides of course materials are displayed on a **wb** window. A user can operate for turning slide pages and additional writing and drawing in real-time on his window using optional buttons. These controls are transferred to remote sites. A **wb** provides a clear images (PostScript format images) of teacher materials rather than analog NTSC images captured by a camera.
- Remote camera control: a WWW browser with CGI.
- A teacher can see images of any location in a learners' room. He can change his view (right/left, up/down, and zoom) by clicking the buttons on a WWW (World Wide Web) browser window. An operator can choose two levels of moving or zooming degrees. This window is created as a Netscape browser by CGI (Common Gateway Interface). Using this function, a teacher can easily get reactions of learners, e.g., all learners or a specific learner.

A teacher operates these tools on his own workstation (in short, WS) by himself. All learners are in the same room at a remote site. Situations of learners' sites are different in six experiments as the following and the detail is in Table 1.

- Case 1, 2, 5, and 6:
- All learners can see clear images of a teacher and course materials on his own monitor (19 or 17 inch), but they cannot operate the collaboration tools and a teaching assistant operates instead of them.
- Case 3:
- The number of WSs for the collaboration tools is equal to the number of the learners. Different from other experiments, each learner can operate all tools on his own WS with its camera and microphone himself by multicasting.
- Case 4:
- Tool operation style is the same as the Case 1,2,5 and 6. The difference from Case 2 above is a big screen (over 200 inch). Learners see images on a shared big screen projected by a high resolution video projector (over 1000 TV lines and 2300 lumen).

2.2 Results and Discussions

The total number of learners is 246 through the six lectures. We prepared questionnaire sheets including 20 or 22 items for the learners. The major 15 questionnaire items and the evaluation results are shown in Figure 2. The vertical axis of Figure 2 means the normalized average of each item. The value 1 corresponds to good evaluation on a question item. Figures 2(a), 2(b) and 2(c) show the difference among three types of the learners, the difference between two display types and the difference on tool controllability, respectively. We also prepared questionnaire sheets including more than 20 items for the teachers.

2.2.1 Learners' Evaluation There is not a typical trend depending on the learners' type in Figure 2(a). The difference in items 4 and 5 might be caused by familiarity with computers and networks. Notable difference of display types is items 8, 9 and 10 as Figure 2(b). This means that an individual monitor is not always the favourite for learners. A more important factor is high-resolution. The difference of tool controllability is not so remarkable as Figure 2(c). According to the results, average scores of the learners' evaluation are higher than the median (0.5) except for the items 3 and 10. The learners' impression on the quality of images (both of a teacher and presentation pages) and voice is acceptable as an ordinal class. Moreover, distance learning itself was very attractive to them. The style of distance learning is effective for reinforcing attention and understanding of subjects on the network, computers and related things even though they did not directly operate the tools.

2.2.2 Teachers' Evaluation In all experiences, the teachers are familiar with computers and networks in their daily life, so operations of Mbone tools are not hard for them. Also, to prepare the on-line course materials used on **wb** is easy for them. However, operations of these tools and preparation of on-line course materials are not so easy for teachers in general. This is a remarkable problem to be solved in the future.

A feedback of learners' reaction in distance learning is important while lecturing as well as a discussion period. For this purpose, controlling a remote camera is required. The mechanism described above is simple and convenient, however an improvement of its user interface is expected.

Teachers' impression on the educational effectiveness of distance lecture is the same quality comparing with ordinal lectures. The distance lecture has advantages such as clearness of providing course materials by using high resolution display and presentation tools, even though quality of video images is relatively lower than TV. Concentration of participants' minds on the lecture seems to be same as or higher than ordinal lecture according to the results of the questionnaire to teachers and learners. To precisely evaluate the educational effectiveness of distance learning, we are planning to do comparative experiments, for example, lectures of the same topics for different members but similar situation by the ordinal lecture style.

3. Multimedia Communications Literacy

Through our experiments, we found a new literacy education for multimedia communications which is different from the existing ones. Computer literacy is used as the concept to learn how to use computers. Network literacy is to learn how to use the network services based on the Internet such as E-mail and WWW. Here we define Multimedia Communications Literacy (**MCL**) as a literacy to communicate interactively using various media such as video, audio and remote control devices simultaneously. The definition of **MCL** is natural in the next generation of computer and network literacy using high-speed networks and interactive multimedia communications. We need network literacy because of their effects all over the world and instantaneous propagation of information. The MCL is needed supposing that we can easily send and receive multimedia data by multicasting or broadcasting on the Internet in the world. There are several differences between the MCL and the existing network literacy. A bandwidth of connections must be recognized to use multimedia data such as images and audio data on networks. Interactive operations of collaborative multimedia tools should be acquired. The necessity of the **MCL** is to learn these additional points to the network literacy.

Here, we show the following points as teaching subjects of the **MCL**.

- How to operate multimedia communication tools,
- How to use network resources and information resource, and
- Ethics on multimedia networks.

To teach the first two subjects, we show the effectiveness of an environment for distance learning in the previous section. The MCL must be required for teachers and learners to attend distance learning, and for everyone communicating on multimedia networks including the Internet in the near future.

4. Conclusion

We emphasise the importance of multimedia communications on the Internet as the necessity for research work of the professionals in a cyber space. Some educational environment should be provided to be familiar with multimedia communications. Then we consider an effective environment to instruct/learn how to use multimedia communications through the experiments. From the experiments results, we show good evaluation to our proposal environment to keep quality as ordinal lectures for learners and teachers. Also we get positive results for distance learning in the viewpoints of effective experience to learn on networks and familiarity with distance learning. This means that interactive distance learning is effective not only to solve time and geographic restrictions but also to learn/instruct multimedia communications. Finally, we introduced a new literacy education called as the **MCL** to use multimedia communication methods on the Internet as daily tools. By learning the **MCL**, learners can consider effects of multimedia communication tools all over the world on the Internet. At the same time, they can learn convenience of interactive multimedia communications. As a future task, we should consider a training method for teachers to teach the **MCL**.

5. References

Macedonia, M. and Brutzm, D. (1994) Mbone Provides Audio and Video Across the Internet., IEEE *Computer*, **4**, 30-36

Quemada, J., Miguel, T., Azcirra A., Pavon S., Salvacuha J., Larrabeiti D., Robles T. and Huecas, G. (1996) ISABEL: A CSCW Application for the Distribution of Events, *Multimedia Telecommunications and Applications (Lecture Notes in Computer Science 1185)*, *Springer*, 137-168.

Kondo K., Suzuki R., Uto Y., and Igata A.(1996) A Comparison Experiment of Compressed and Wide-Band Pictures for Educational Purpose, *Trans. of the Institute of Electronics, Information and Communication Engineers* D-II, **Vol. J79-D-II, No. 10**, 1734-1740 (in Japanese).

Maeda, K., Aibara R., Kawamoto K., Terauchi M. and Otsuki S. (1997) An Environment for Multimedia Communication Literacy, *ED-MEDIA/ED-TELECOM 97*, 653-658.

McCanne, S. and Jacobson, V. (1995) vic: A Flexible Framework for Packet Video, *Proc. ACM Multimedia'95*, 511-522.

Jacobson, V. and McCanne, S. (1995) On-line document available at URL http://www-nrg.ee.lbl.gov/vat.

Jacobson, V. and McCanne, S. (1993) On-line document available at URL http://www-nrg.ee.lbl.gov/wb.

6. Biography

K. Maeda received her B.L.S. degree from Hiroshima University in 1982. She worked at the faculty of engineering in Hiroshima University from 1982 to 1989 and at Radiation Effects Research Foundation from 1989 to 1994. At present she is an assistant professor of Information Processing Center, Hiroshima City University. Her research interests include computer networks and multimedia communications for education.

R. Aibara received his B.E., M.E., and doctorate in system engineering from Hiroshima University, in 1981, 1983, and 1986, respectively. He was an associate professor of Research Center for Integrated Systems, Hiroshima University from 1989 to 1994. At present he is an associate professor of Information Processing Center, Hiroshima University. His research interests include multimedia network architecture, computer architecture, real-time computing, and neuro computer architecture. He is a member of IEEE Computer Society.

K. Kawamoto received her Bachelor and masters of Education degree from Tokyo Gakugei University in 1989 and 1992, respectively. Since 1994 she has worked for Hiroshima City University as a research associate of Information Sciences. Her research interests include communication and learning process of cooperative learning through the Internet.

M. Terauchi received B.E. and M.E. degree in 1984, 1986 respectively from Kansai University. He finished doctoral program in 1989 at Hiroshima University. From 1989 to 1994, he was a research associate on the faculty of engineering at Hiroshima University. In 1994 he joined Hiroshima City University. His research interest includes intelligent systems, computer vision, human computer interface and distributed processing. He is a member of ACM, IEEE, AIED and other academic societies.

S. Otsuki received her B.S. degree from Kyoto University in 1955 and her doctorate from Kyushu University in 1971. Since 1956 she has worked for Kyoto University, Nagoya University, Kyushu University and Kyushu Institute of Technology. At present she is the Dean of the graduate school of information science and faculty of computer science, Hiroshima City University. Her research interests include integration of intelligent and multimedia architectures, especially for educational systems.

6. EMPIRICAL STUDY ON EFFECTIVENESS OF HDTV IN DISTANCE EDUCATION

Hiroshi Kato, Mitsushige Iwamoto,
and Hideki Asahi
C&C Media Research Laboratories,
NEC Corporation
4-1-1, Miyazaki, Miyamae-ku,
Kawasaki-shi, 216-8555, Japan
Phone: +8-427-44-7527, Fax: +8-44-856-2235,
E-mail: kato@ccm.cl.nec.co.jp

ABSTRACT

A distance learning experiment was conducted to examine differences in learning performance and to obtain subjective evaluations of three types of learning methods: face-to-face (LIVE), distance learning using high-definition television (HDTV), and distance learning using normal TV (NTSC). Five sites were used for HDTV and six sites for NTSC, where the same lecture was watched at the same time. There were 74 voluntary participants for the LIVE lecture, 144 for HDTV, and 139 for NTSC. Based on pretest, posttest, and questionnaire results, the authors found that, as far as the learners' performance level is concerned, the LIVE method is more effective than the others, while there was no significant difference between HDTV and NTSC. It was also found that HDTV is better at showing the atmosphere of the lecture, and motivates learners more than NTSC. Third, HDTV still has difficulty in showing a high-resolution computer screen, though it is perceived better than NTSC. As for other points, HDTV's image quality is satisfactory to learners as a whole.

Keywords
Distance Learning, Communications, Multimedia, Satellites, Video Conferencing

1. Introduction

Recent advancements in communication technology have made distance learning systems more economical and more efficient. Since distance learning systems allow learners to attend lectures by eminent lecturers with less transportation costs, they have become popular with universities (e.g. Shimizu et al. 1986, Tanaka 1993, Yamasawa et al. 1991) and companies (Shiratori 1988).

In these systems, TV-based teleconference systems are utilized. The image quality from current TV standards such as PAL and NTSC, however, is not clear enough to show characters on a white board or on a computer screen legibly. Therefore, high-definition television (HDTV), which has approximately twice as many scanning lines (1125 lines) as compared to NTSC (525 lines), is expected to be a core technology for the next generation of distance learning systems.

Shimizu and Shiroma (Shimizu et al. 1989, 1990, 1995) investigated distance learning using HDTV, and found that HDTV was evaluated better than NTSC on two points: 'atmosphere of the lecture' and 'quality of the image.' In these experiments, however, learner's performance was not examined. This is probably because the content of the learning was different for NTSC and HDTV, so learner's performance levels could not be directly compared.

Although it was not a case of distance education, Iimori et al. (Iimori et al. 1991, 1993) conducted experiments using video programs for school education to examine the differences in cognitive performance and impressions between HDTV and NTSC. They showed subjects a short (approx. 15 minutes) video program produced for broadcasting, and performed recognition and memory tests concerning the contents of the program. In one of their experiments using a drama program, students watching HDTV achieved higher performance in understanding and memory tests, but in another experiment using a verbally explanatory program, no significant difference was found in understanding and memory test (Iimori et al. 1993). However, we should be careful in assuming that these results would be the same in the case of distance learning, because distance education includes some other factors such as difference in instructional method, the possibility of interaction with a lecturer, and the sense of simultaneous presence with a lecturer and other learners at other sites.

In our experiment, we used a three-hour lecture given live and transmitted at the same time through an NTSC-based distance learning system and an HDTV-based distance learning system. We conducted pre- and posttests concerning the content of the lecture and a questionnaire for learners' subjective evaluations of the three learning methods in order to analyze the differences in learners' learning performance levels and motivation, impressions, etc., respectively.

2. Experiment

2.1 Distance learning system

The lecture was held at a central lecture room in Tokyo. HDTV signals of the scenes were transmitted from an up-link van parked outside the room to five remote sites via the JCSAT-1 communication satellite (Figure 1). The video and audio signals were transmitted by MUSE and B-mode stereo, respectively. On the other hand, common TV (NTSC) system was based on NESPAC; NESPAC is a commercial two-way distance learning system employing a communication satellite (Shiratori 1988). The NTSC signals were transmitted to the Tokyo NESPAC site via a microwave link, and to six remote sites via JCSAT-1. The source signal for NTSC was generated from an HDTV signal with an HDTV-NTSC converter, so that the lecture was the same for all remote sites.

The equipment used in the experiment included video cameras, a document camera, a monitor screen (1280×1024) of an engineering workstation (EWS) down-converted to HDTV, and an HDTV (Uni-hi) VCR.

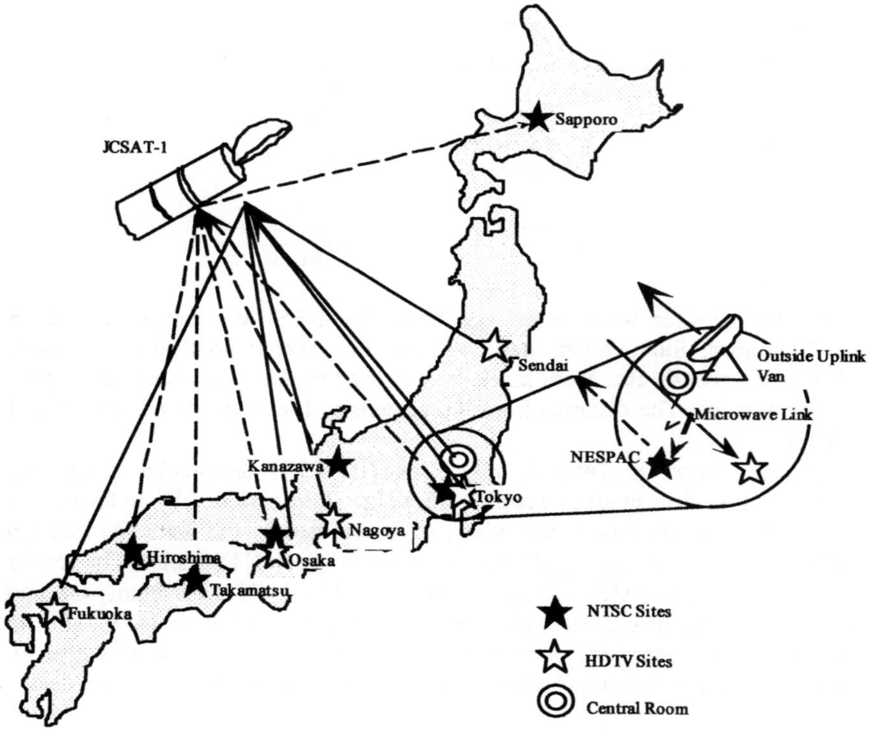

Figure 1 Distance learning system used in the experiment.

2.2 Learning conditions

The major factor in the experiment was the types of learning methods. Based on the learning methods, conditions were divided into three categories: face-to-face learning, distance learning using HDTV, and distance learning using NTSC. We refer to these conditions respectively as 'LIVE', 'HDTV' and 'NTSC'. Table 1 shows the condition, number of subjects, size of the monitor screen, and room configuration at each site.

Table 1 Overview of the experiment design

Condition	*Location of sites (city)*	*Screen size (inch)*	*Room configuration (The # of seats per desk * the # of desks per column) for the first column + (...) for the 2nd + ...*	*Number of subjects (# of missing values in pre/post-test)*	
LIVE	Tokyo	110	(3*9)+(10*9)+(3*9)	74(1)	74(1)
HDTV	Sendai	54	(3*4)*3	19(0)	144(5)
	Tokyo 1	61	(3*3)+(3*6)*3	62(0)	
	Nagoya	54	(3*5)*3	15(2)	
	Osaka 1	54	(3*4)*3	31(2)	
	Fukuoka	54	(3*4)*3	17(1)	
NTSC	Sapporo	70	(3*4)*2	19(0)	139(6)
	Tokyo 2	70	(3*5)*3	9(1)	
	Kanazawa	70	(3*3)+(3*4)*2	31(2)	
	Osaka 2	46	(3*6)*3	41(0)	
	Hiroshima	70	(3*5)*3	31(3)	
	Takamatsu	70	(3*4)*2	8(0)	
				Total	357(12)

All of the remote sites were lecture rooms for the NESPAC distance education system. Therefore, illumination, desk arrangement, screen configuration (every room had two screens), etc., were carefully designed so that every seat had a good view of the screens. The distance from the screens to the first row of seats was 2 through 3 m.

However, as shown in Table 1, only Osaka2 (NTSC) had smaller screens in relative to its room size, so let us examine if it affected the results. >From the results of the questionnaire items on screen view, as determined by the items Q4 through Q12 (Figure 4), there was no significant difference between NTSC sites. The results of analysis of variance (ANOVA) are shown in Table 2. Of these items, Q8 and Q11 were nearly significant, but Osaka2 was the fourth best of all six NTSC sites in both items, so the screen size in this case was determined not to have mattered. Consequently, we decided that Osaka2 did not have to be eliminated from the data.

Table 2 Results of ANOVA for NTSC sites

	Q4	*Q5*	*Q6*	*Q7*	*Q8*	*Q9*	*Q10*	*Q11*	*Q12*
df	5/ 131	5/ 131	5/ 132	5/ 133	5/ 133	5/ 132	5/ 133	5/ 132	5/ 132
F	1.49	1.61	1.84	1.75	2.06	.733	1.39	2.27	0.78
p	.200	.162	.108	.129	.074	.600	.232	.051	.566

HDTV monitors were installed 0.5 through 1 m in front of the front seats, so the screen was nearer to the learners than the NTSC screens, so as to compensate for the smaller screen of HDTV monitors. In the HDTV condition, only Tokyo1 had two HDTV monitors. This is why the width of the room was a desk-width longer than the other rooms. In the same way, the screen size at Tokyo1 was seven inches bigger because the depth of the room was one or two desk-depths longer. The viewing conditions of HDTV remote sites were thus controlled.

2.3 *Subjects*

All of the subjects were employees of NEC or affiliated companies aged from 20 to 35. All of them were voluntary applicants for the following learning course specially provided free of charge, which was announced in an ordinary manner as employee education program. In Tokyo and Osaka, both distance learning systems were tested in the same buildings, so subjects are distributed randomly in two sites of Tokyo and Osaka each before the actual experiment. The numbers of subjects at each site are shown in Table 1.

2.4 *Lecture*

The theme of the lecture was 'Introduction to GUI (Graphical User Interface).' This theme was selected because it requires high-resolution image (1280×1024) of computer operations to be shown on a monitor screen.

The lecture was performed for three hours, including short breaks, in the afternoon on February 22nd, 1993. A brief question-and-answer period was taken at the end of the lecture. The questioner's image from a remote site was transmitted to the central lecture room in NTSC, and then distributed to the other sites.

2.5 *Apparatus*

(1) Pretest and posttest. Pretests and posttests were designed to investigate the performance of the learners under each condition. The pretest consisted of 13 items directly related to the content of the lecture. The posttest included all items of the pretest and three questions on learners' prior knowledge of the theme. Three minutes were given to take the tests.

(2) Questionnaire. A questionnaire was designed for learner's subjective evaluation of various aspects of the experiments. It consisted of 32 items for LIVE, and 36 items for NTSC and HDTV. The items included questions about installation of the monitor screen, legibility, audibility, impressions of the lecture, quality of the lecture, and familiarity with the lecturer. The items are listed in Figure 4.

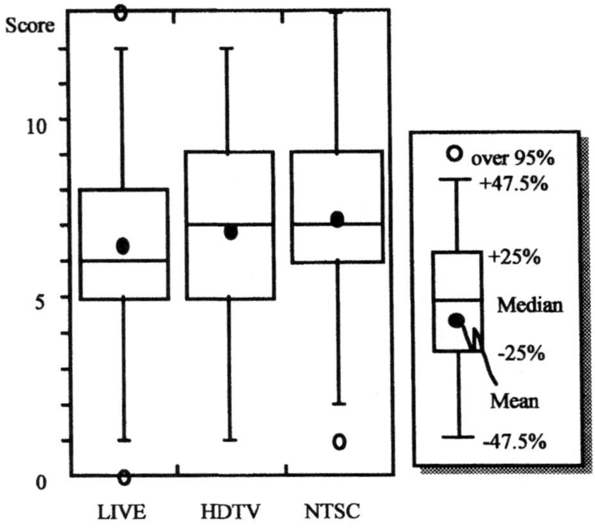

Figure 2 Mean of pretest scores of each site.

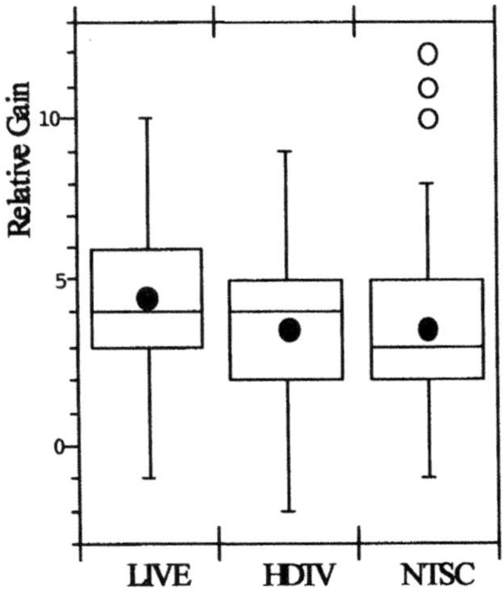

Figure 3 Distribution of relative gains of each condition.

3. Results and discussion

3.1 Equality of learners regarding subject matter

The learners' equality among conditions in terms of their prior knowledge on the lecture subject matter is discussed. Figure 2 shows the distribution of pretest scores for each condition. Through an ANOVA, the hypothesis that pretest score means for each condition are equal cannot be rejected ($F(2, 343)=2.27$; $p=0.11$). Thus, there is no evidence of a difference in the learners' readiness between conditions.

3.2 Analysis of performance test

Table 3 AIC of Null model (0), Method model (1), and Site model (2)

Model	*Number of parameters*	*Maximum likelihood estimators* μ	σ^2	α						*AIC*
(0)	2	3.72	5.11							1545.9
(1)	4	3.84	4.96	.629		-.311		-.318		1539.7
(2)	13	4.59	4.94	.88	-.32	.03	.03	-.24	.16	1555.9
				-.21	-.09	.21	.02	-.37	-.09	

(n = 345)

To examine an individual learner's performance, we calculated relative gains, which is defined as the posttest score minus the pretest score. Figure 3 shows the distribution of relative gains in each condition. There was a significant difference among the means in relative gains ($F(2, 342)=5.12$; $p=0.006$). However, it should be discussed which factor - learning method or site - is more likely to account for the data beforehand. Consequently, Akaike Information Criterion (AIC) (Akaike 1974) values of the following three models are compared as shown in Table 3, where AIC represents how well a stochastic model fits data, taking the number of parameters used in the model into account.

Null model (0): All the data are samples from $N(\mu_0, \sigma_0^2)$.
Method model (1): For each condition ($i=1...3$), the data are samples from $N(\mu_0+\alpha_i, \sigma_0^2)$, where $\Sigma\alpha_i=0$.
Site model (2): For each site ($j=1...12$), the data are samples from $N(\mu_0+\alpha_j, \sigma_0^2)$, where $\Sigma\alpha_j=0$.

An AIC value of the ANOVA model is given by the following formula (Suzuki 1995), where σ^2, n, and c is maximum likelihood estimator of the variance, the number of samples, and the number of parameters used in the model, respectively.

As shown in Table 3, the models have the following relationship based on their AIC values.

Site model (1) < Null model (0) < Method model (2)

As a result, it is confirmed that the learning method factor influenced the learner's performance, while the site factor was not significant.

From the result, we concluded that the learning method factor was significant. Therefore, it is essential to identify the differences in methods. Table 4 shows the results of multiple comparisons and the mean of relative gains for each condition. As shown, LIVE is more effective than the others, while there is very little difference between HDTV and NTSC.

Table 4 Multiple comparison tests between conditions

	LIVE	*HDTV*	*Mean of relative gain*
LIVE			4.466
HDTV	.029*		3.525
NTSC	.028*	1.000	3.519

Turkey's HSD multiple comparison *: $p<0.05$

In the precedent study by Iimori et al. (Iimori et al. 1993), as mentioned earlier, subject groups who watched a video program depending much for explanation did not show any differences in memory and understanding between HDTV and NTSC. From our result that the difference in quality of visual information was not influential, the lecture in this experiment was considered to depend basically for lecturer's verbal explanation as well, even though many visual aids, such as document camera and computer screen, were used. This result implies that the lecture-like style of instructional method used in the experiment, although it is generally used in distance education, cannot take full advantage of high definition of HDTV in terms of the learning performance.

3.3 Analysis of subjective evaluation

First of all, we tried to categorize the items according to the tendencies of their response patterns. By applying factor analysis to the HDTV and NTSC data, we extracted eleven factors whose eigenvalues were larger than 1.0. Items in the questionnaire were categorized according to the factor loading after vari-max rotation. Figure 4 shows the items grouped by horizontal lines according to the factors and the means of responses for each condition.

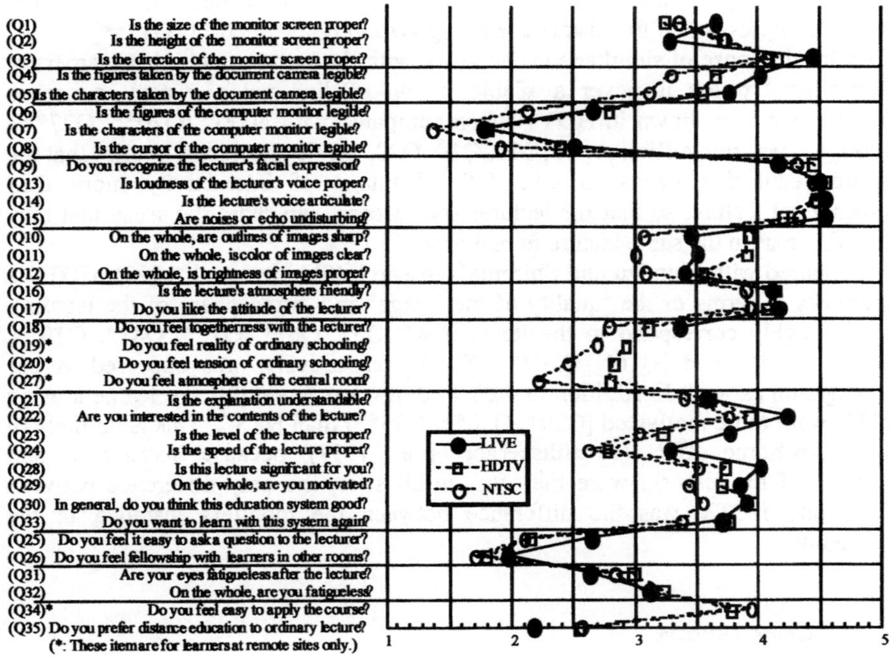

Figure 4 Results of the questionnaire. (The original questions were in Japanese.)

In general, as shown in Figure 4, there was no problem with audio [Q13, Q14, Q15], and video images were sufficient for seeing the lecturer's face [Q9] and fair for reading documents [Q4, Q5]. However, the legibility of the computer monitor screen was poor in all conditions [Q6, Q7, Q8]. Overall, there was a favorable impression of the lecture [Q21, Q22, Q23, Q28, Q29] except for its speed [Q24]. The lecturer was friendly [Q16, Q17], but putting a question to the lecturer was not very easy [Q25]. The learners did not feel any belongingness with other learners [Q26], and learners in remote sites did not feel as if they were actually at the central room [Q18, Q19, Q20, Q27]. The learners said that this educational system is good [Q30], and that they may learn by this system again [Q33], but prefer a live lecture to distance learning [Q35].

The items that showed a significant difference between HDTV and NTSC are as follows.

Q4*, Q5*, Q6**, Q7**, Q8**, Q10**, Q11**, Q12**, Q16*, Q20**, Q27**, Q29*, Q30**, Q33** (**:$p<0.01$, *:$p<0.05$)

This means that HDTV is significantly better than NTSC in viewing documents [Q4*, Q5*] and monitor screens [Q6**, Q7**, Q8**], although the image of the computer screen is not entirely satisfactory [Q6, Q7, Q8]. On the whole, HDTV's superiority in the quality of the images was appreciated [Q10**, Q11**, Q12**].

Moreover, the atmosphere of the lecture was friendlier [Q16*] and more realistic [Q20**, Q27**] in HDTV. HDTV learners were more motivated and had a more favorable impression of the distance learning system [Q29*, Q30**, Q33**].

As for the sense of simultaneous presence with the lecturer and other learners at other sites - which is never available by an off-line video system, a certain improvement was shown in HDTV when compared with NTSC [Q20**, Q27**], although it was not sufficient yet [Q18, Q19, Q20, Q27]. This result implies that the distance education needs to take full advantage of interactivity more than conventional lecture, so that the lecturer and learners can share the sense that they are taking part in the same lecture in real time.

Compared with Shimizu and Shiroma's research (Shimizu et al. 1990), HDTV's superiority in terms of the 'quality of the image' and 'atmosphere of the lecture', which roughly correspond to the items [Q4*, Q5*, Q6**, Q7**, Q8**, Q10**, Q11**, Q12**] and [Q16*, Q20**, Q27**] respectively, was observed in our investigation as well. In addition to their findings, we found that the learners using HDTV were more motivated [Q29*, Q30**, Q33**] than NTSC. This is unlikely to be a Hawthorne effect (Roethlisberger et al. 1939), because instructions and activities of the learners were the same in all sites; the only difference between NTSC and HDTV was the difference between the monitors installed in the classrooms.

4. Conclusions

The same lecture was given live (face to face) and over distance learning systems, one using HDTV and the other using NTSC. A pretest, posttest, and questionnaire were conducted to examine the differences between them.

As far as learner's performance is concerned, the LIVE condition was significantly better than remote conditions, and very little difference was found between HDTV and NTSC.

From the learner's subjective evaluation, we found that even HDTV was not legible enough to display a high-resolution image of a computer screen. The size of characters on the monitor seems to be more dominant than the resolution of the screen, so using a device to enlarge a part of the monitor screen is desirable. On the whole, however, learners recognized that HDTV was apparently better in image quality than NTSC. Consequently, the reality of the lecture was increased, and, moreover, learners were more motivated with HDTV than with NTSC.

A problem in our experiment would be a period of learning. Considering actual use of distance education, three hours may not be long enough. At present, we have contrary views in terms of effects of a longer learning period; one is that learner's positive impressions toward HDTV take positive effects to their performance, and the other is that HDTV's superiority in impressions declines after a long experience. Thus, a longer version of the experiment remains as a part of future works. Another remaining work is about a style of education. This result implies that the conventional lecture cannot take full advantage of high definition of HDTV. It is plausible that there is a more suitable style for distance education than a lecture, so exploration for a better style is needed.

5. Acknowledgments

This investigation was commissioned by the Hi-Vision Promotion Association Incorporated and performed in cooperation with Japan Hi-Vision Corporation and NTT. The authors would like to thank Dr. Masahiko Kurata and Mr. Hiroyuki Naito of NEC Corp. for their helpful advice, Mr. Hideyuki Suzuki of NEC Corp. for his help in processing the data, and Mr. Fujio Abe of NEC Corp. for his contribution to the lecture design.

6. References

Akaike, H (1974) A new look at the statistical model identification, IEEE Trans. Autom. Contr., AC-19 716-723

Iimori A et al.(1991) The use of hi-vision in education, The NHK Monthly Report on Broadcast Research, **41** 10 14-27

Iimori A et al.(1993) Use of hi-vision TV in school broadcasts: from the results of a comparative survey with conventional TV, regarding effectiveness in education, The NHK Monthly Report on Broadcast Research, **43** 6 28-39

Roethlisberger, F J and Dickson, W J (1939) Management and the worker, Cambridge, Mass.: Harvard University Press

Shimizu, Y and Maesako, T (1986) Evaluation of TV-lecture connecting two campuses by optical fiber cable, Trans. IEICE, J69-A 10 1181-1189

Shimizu, Y and Shiroma, S (1989) Evaluation of distance education between two campuses by HDTV, IEICE Technical Report, ET89-37 63-70

Shimizu, Y and Shiroma, S (1990) Evaluation of HDTV closed circuit system for distance education, J. ITE Japan, **44** 12. 1717-1722

Shimizu Y et al (1995) Evaluation of a HDTV distance lecture transmitted by satellite, in Proc. the 11th Conf. on Educational Technology, E23 41-42

Shiratori T (1988) A two-way distance education system using advanced creative education: NESPAC, NEC Tech. Jour., **41** 10 139-146

Suzuki G (1995) Jouhouryou-kijun niyoru toukei kaiseki nyumon, Kodansha Scientific, Tokyo

Tanaka, M (1993) A trial on distance education and training through the PARTNERS network, IEICE Trans. Fundamental, E76-A 7 1195-1198

Yamasawa K et al (1991) Tele-education by using the cooperating system of the Shinshu University video and data network and INS-net64, IEICE Technical Report, ET91-78 23-30

Hiroshi Kato joined NEC Corporation in 1983. From 1989 to 1990, he was a visiting researcher at CSLI at Stanford University. He is currently a principal researcher at the C&C Media Research Laboratories of NEC Corporation and visiting associate professor at Saitama University. His research interests are in the area of situated cognition and computer support for collaborative learning.

Mitsushige Iwamoto joined NEC Corporation in 1974. He has been a sales engineer and currently a system-engineering manager at the Kyushu System Center, C&C Systems Market Development Division of NEC Corporation.

Hideki Asahi joined NEC Corporation and has been engaged in educating operations of personal computers and its application programs. He is currently with C&C System Education Division of NEC Corporation.

7. WHY INFORMATION ETHICS EDUCATION FAILS

Tatsumi Takeo,
Harada Yasunari,
tatsumi@mn.waseda.ac.jp,
harada@mn.waseda.ac.jp
Waseda University Media Network Center,
1-104, Totsuka-cho, Shinjuku-ku, Tokyo,
Japan, 03-3203-4141

ABSTRACT

So-called 'information ethics education' at Japanese universities falls far short of expectation. This is partly because we do not have clear enough idea what to cover, but also reflects some basic cultural and philosophical confusion. We argue that we need to discuss information risk management rather than trying to formulate what information ethics is. Instructors equipped with all the necessary background expertise are severely lacking, and that creates a bootstrapping problem for teacher education. We propose simulated network emergency exercises for familiarizing future teachers with potential risks of the Internet.

Keywords

Higher Education, Teacher Education, Educational Management, Case studies, Culture, Electronic Mail(E-Mail), Literacy

1. Introduction

In this article, we discuss three reasons why information ethics education in Japan is still something to be worked out and for several years to come it will remain a complete failure. First, this term is a misnomer and its contents are poorly defined at best. Second, higher education is not the right place to teach basic rules of human interaction while elementary and intermediate schools are not well prepared for the kind of computer literacy education that are required to prepare the generation to live in the next millennia. Third, there are very few professors, teachers and instructors equipped with all the necessary background expertise to handle the course materials required. We go on to propose several strategies for a successful course and curriculum design for what is broadly, and perhaps wrongly, covered by this term. First, we need to provide the students with a precise understanding of the underlying ethical principles and detailed technical knowledge of the information society we are going to spend the rest of our lives. Second, we then need to consider how to bring together researchers and educators in various related fields to discuss and formulate what should be taught in this subject matter in elementary, intermediate and higher levels of formal education. Third, we must consider how to provide teachers at appropriate levels with necessary background knowledge.

2. Why Information Ethics Education Fails At University

Despite the widening awareness that ethics is an integral part of information literacy education, few educational institutions in Japan can be said to be quite successful in implementing such education. There is little consensus, if any, as to what the actual contents should be of the information ethics education. Very few teachers engaged in information/computer/multimedia literacy education is equipped with all the necessary background information such as technical details of the digital networks, its socio-cultural and economic implications and its legal ramifications. (Tatsumi, et. al. 1996; Harada, 1996)

2.1 A case study

Novice network users cause a wide variety of confusions and troubles. Most computer primer courses at the university level today incorporate some kind of information ethics instruction. This section will summarize the findings by Yokoyama et. al. (1998) on how students at Tokyo Gakugei Daigaku viewed various related issues.

Table 1 Facts on differences at information ethics education

	good		bad	
Question	*before*	*after*	*before*	*after*
1. make passwords out of telephone numbers	31%	0%	69%	100%
2. share an account with others	67%	26%	33%	74%

	OK		not OK	
Question	*before*	*after*	*before*	*after*
3. duplicate magazine photographs	92%	97%	8%	3%
4. use images from TV program	67%	86%	33%	14%
5. use photographs of celebrity	46%	91%	54%	9%

Table 1 suggests that the course material had good effects on how students control and guard their own passwords. Questions 1 and 2 shows that most of the students have a good understanding in the need for authentication and the potential risk of tampering by crackers.

While students say, in answers to question 1, that they wouldn't use copyrighted programs without authorization, in answers to questions 3, 4 and 5, it is shown that most students tend to be carefree and careless concerning copyright and privacy. It seems that the students tend to think that materials that have been broadcast or published can be freely reused. Such tendency may be rooted in the technical ease with which digital material can be duplicated.

The basic ethical principle of the Internet is to respects the rights and property of other network users. What constitutes inalienable human rights on the Internet or how to define property in the digital world is yet to be resolved. And this case study shows that teaching students technical or legal issues does not suffice to change how they behave.

2.2 *Why information ethics education is an issue now*

With the advent of WWW, the Internet population showed an unprecedented explosion, and universities in Japan are responding to the students' demand by adding more and more Internet-accessible machines. Here at Waseda University, with something like 50,000 students and 1,500 full-time faculty members, we have more than 6,000 Internet-connected personal computers and workstations, at least half of which are available for students in general. User accounts for Internet mail/netnews usage, originally issued upon request basis for a handful of users, now exceeds 48,000, almost every member of the entire university will have such an account. Needless to say, this is not a situation unique to particular universities in Japan, nor is it limited to this country or that.

This catastrophic growth of network users in Japanese universities resulted in various confusions in the network usage, and administrators and faculty members are becoming more and more aware that education in `information ethics' is at least as important as, and probably more important than, guidance and instructions in the use of hardware and software of computer networks.

2.3 Connotation of the term `ethics'

According to the on-line version of the Webster's dictionary, the term ethics means something like the following:

1: the discipline dealing with what is good and bad and with moral duty and obligation, 2a: a set of moral principles or values, 2b: a theory or system of moral values, 2c: the principles of conduct governing an individual or a group

When we talk about `Ethics', Japanese people in general feel we are discussing either highly moral standards that are completely unrelated to our daily life or historical discussions of philosophers who have argued for various ideas decades, centuries or millennia ago that are unrelated to our modern present-day life. One particular problem in the Japanese intermediate education is that philosophy and ethics are taught as a rote memory practice of various sequences of trivial historical events such as which philosopher in the European history wrote which pieces of work at what year rather than as reading and discussing these writings in relation to the students' everyday life.

There is an additional confusion in the discussion since the Japanese language counterpart of the English word `ethics' does not clearly distinguish between ethical principle and ethical judgments. For instance, when discussing information ethics, knowledgeable and intelligent people respond differently and argue among themselves in unreasonable terms regarding whether information ethics is different from our daily ethics. All we have to do to avoid unnecessary terminological bickering is to be careful not to confuse ethical principles and ethical judgments. Judgments on particular action, such as sending a file of a particular size over a particular network configuration, may change when available resources change. It may have been regarded offensive to send an e-mail message of 500kb at some time, but it may become OK in the near future to send an e-mail message with attached 10MB images. Ethical principles that pertain, not to send a file that would disrupt your server, the intervening networks, and your recipients' machine, which in turn is an application of the Golden Rule, however, does not change. In this respect, we may say that the ethical principles of information society is, or should be, no different from the rest of the world and history, but the ethical judgments of particular actions must take into consideration various social and technical aspects of the particular system that the action takes place in.

Another source for potential confusion in the discussion is that information ethics used to refer to professional code of conduct for Information Technology experts, while what we are considering here is more of a matter for every consumer of `information product, hardware, software or contents'. For instance, when discussing copyright protection in computer courses, all we had to do was to stress that software products in general are copyrighted, and piracy may result in civil liability and criminal prosecution. In the world of WWW, where every private person can publish whatever she/he intends, we need to stress that almost anything that can be distributed on-line are copyrighted, and an act of uploading a file that contains materials that you did not make for yourself in its entirety may be considered to constitute an act of copyright infringement. Thus, what we discuss here in this note is more of consumer education rather than professional education.

2.4 *What people expect of information ethics education*

Despite the forgoing discussion, what people expect of information ethics education is everything that does not fall under hardware or software instruction. Computer centers do not want the students to bring in food or drinks and smoking is not allowed. Machines should be logged off or shut down before switching off for security and maintenance reasons. Waste printouts should not be left over around the printers. Pagers and mobile telephones should be shut off during class or inside a terminal room. E-mail messages should contain signatures not exceeding certain lines. Transfers of files exceeding certain sizes should be refrained from during the daytime. All these good manners and etiquette are regarded as matters to be taught by the computing center or in the computer literacy education, and through lack of a better place, they tend to be placed under the category of information ethics. But are they?

If you use a toilet, you are supposed to flush before leaving. Good citizens are not supposed to litter and environment-conscious consumers are supposed to recycle. These are again applications of the Golden Rule, but most people would never dream of including them as part of formal university education. If you go to a movie theater or a concert hall, you will be asked not to bring in food or drinks and refrain from smoking, and in recent years, they ask the audience to switch off the pagers and mobile telephones. These are matters of house policies and common decency.

If you use a foul language, your parents used to scold you in various ways depending on the culture. Here we may have a slightly different situation from our old worldly existence, since our communication was limited among people existing in physical proximity, so that more often than not, agents participating in a conversation or those overhearing them shared a greater part of their common sense. On the digital network, such presupposition cannot hold. People participating in the global network should always be aware that what he takes as common sense may be heresay to some others. What he considers foul may be neat to some others.

This may suggest that we have a real new agenda for the information ethics, but the guiding principle behind the ethical judgment is again the Golden Rule. (The on-line version of the Webster's dictionary has that Golden Rule is `a rule of ethical conduct referring to Mt 7:12 and Lk 6:31 and stating that one should do to others as he would have others do to him.') What is new is the understanding that the world today is connected in a different way than the world before the Internet, or the pagers and mobile telephones, or for that matter, telephone and telegraphs. Digital networks brought the worlds together in virtual proximity, so that anyone engaged in network communication must bear in mind that he is participating in a cross-cultural global communication.

2.5 Who can teach such subject matters?

Very often, computer literacy education in Japanese universities today is conducted by people in the computer science departments or related fields. With limited exceptions, such people are not equipped with the kind of understanding necessary to teach information ethics. As a result, those actually engaged in computer literacy education, or for expert computer science education for that matter, are quite reluctant to cover matters relating to rules, regulations, etiquette and ethics during their instructions.

Given that citizens/consumers of the information network society is just emerging, that those learning to use computers and networks as daily clerical and communications media are just graduating from universities, that these young generations will form the founding ancestors of the networked world tomorrow, situation today is critically serious in this matter.

On the other hand, experts on ethical study in Japan tend to prefer philological, historical and philosophical discussions the relevance of which is not immediately understandable to the common students. Experts in legal study are minutely segmented, and those working on copyright issues may prefer not to discuss trade mark or patent litigation.

3. Three Ingredients Of Information Risk Management

3.1 What should be covered by information ethics education

Ethical judgments on particular action depend on the precise understanding of social and technical aspect of that action. And the implication of such actions change depending on the technical infrastructure of the environment such as network bandwidth, hardware and software configuration, rules and regulations, user contracts and so on. Therefore understanding of such subject matter is the prerequisite for adequate judgments. A course on information ethics must contain:

- discussion of historical and contemporary ethical ideas
- ethical codes of various professions
- social and technical analysis of the present day world
- information risk management
- discussions of rules, regulations, laws and conventions
- discussions of e-mail manners and etiquette
- how human rights have been neglected

With the introduction of such a course in elementary and middle education, we expect that students' lives will become safer, sounder and more efficient. The 3 Rs of E-Mail(Diane, 1996) is a good candidate textbook for such a course at the college level. We have to offer students how to deal with information risks that we encounter in this digitally networked society of today, where freedom with responsibility and fairness and equal opportunity are the key ingredients.

3.2 Ethical principles of the present world

A civilized person in the global communications network today should be aware of his responsibility, should be fair and should be law-abiding as a consumer of information resources. The global communications network brings together parties in different countries, different regions, different seasons and different time zones, where language, culture, religion, economic conditions and common sense are world apart.

Formal education conducted by national or standardized schools more often than not emphasized giving a standardized package of knowledge to children, so that adults can participate in the local community with the shared common sense. The degree with which standardization and diversity are enforced or allowed may differ from country to country or from time to time, but the whole point of literacy education is to enable people to communication with each other in an efficient way. A new challenge that we face today is how to teach children to communicate with people who are brought up in a different ethno-cultural, socio-technological and econo-legal background.

3.3 Science and technology behind information networks

Understanding protocols of TCP/IP helps us to understand how e-mail sent while the mail exchanger server is down does not fail and so does not return immediately. If you want to avoid `Information Risk', it would be better for you to understand mathematical logic and programming, processing speed of computers, memory storage, transfer of packets, character codes, protocols and formats. Also the standards of industrial products are necessary for cooperative exchange in world-wide communication. Among them we note: International and industrial standards such as keyboard layouts, standards of paper sizes, and the contribution and significance of national standards such as JIS and international standards such as ISO.

3.4 Legal issues: rules and regulations

Rules and regulations that we make, know, need and obey are consequences of applications of principles to technology and standards. Therefore, if some principle differ at different parts of the world or in different social systems, rules, and regulations differ accordingly. For example, in a strict communist society, people do not posses private property. If some technology or standard will change in future, these rules and regulations will change too.

4. Bootstrapping Problem

4.1 Educating future teachers

Given the diversity and the expertise required for teachers of this kind of subject matter, we see how difficult it would be to implement such ideas immediately. On the other hand, the explosive growth of network users that we see demonstrates that we cannot wait for a generation until such information risk management courses are taught at the elementary or intermediate schools. Therefore, we must seek a way to bring up teachers who are ready to handle such subject matter, on the one hand, and re-educate present teachers to equip them with necessary prerequisites.

In ordinary elementary schools and high schools, only limited numbers of computer or network literate teachers are available. National and local government and school boards are trying to instruct teachers unfamiliar with computers how to handle word processing software, e-mail handler, and WWW browsers. Although such guidance is necessary, what is really needed is that teachers become aware of various potential risks of computer and network usage. Letting the participants into simulated emergency situations is a good way to familiarize them to the important issues of information risk management.

4.2 Emergency exercises

Although not all automobile drivers are trained to cope with emergency situations, dealing with simulated emergency situations is an integral part of an airplane pilot training. Similarly, although it may not be necessary for all students to be exposed to simulated network emergency, such exposure is an integral part of teachers engaged in education in a networked environment. As examples of such exercises, we can list something like the following.

- excessive traffic or mail loss caused by machine failure
- illegal entry from outside
- violation of copyright and libel/defamation on WWW by students
- publication of outside obscene material via WWW by students

- unwanted disclosure of personal information
- leaking sensitive information by colleagues
- Internet money game or SPAM
- false reports from outside parties of students' misconduct

5. Conclusion

In this article, we have discussed why information ethics fails at universities and elsewhere in the school system and have proposed new designed plan to educate or re-educate teachers who will engage in education of literacy.

It has been shown that the subject of information ethics education at universities or K-12 schools must include principles of the Internet-Society, technology, national and international standards, regulations, rules and laws and ethics. So, we have called the contents of this subject matter information risk management.

In education of information risk management to future school teachers, we proposed that the programs include emergency exercises. In dealing with these emergency exercises, future school teachers will realize potential risks of the Internet at their schools and will lean how to control and manage these risks.

6. References

Hartman, Diane B. and Nantz, Karen S. (1996) The 3 Rs of E-Mail: Risks, Rights and Responsibilities. Crisp Publications.

Harada, Yasunari (1996) The Internet and Communication Meltdown: How can Information Ethics Education becomes feasible, panel session at the second meeting on Information Literacy Education, *Annual Report of Meiji University Information Science Center*.

Tatsumi, Takeo, Kakehi, Katsuhiko, and Harada, Yasunari (1996) WWW server for everyone: how it was constructed and how it failed, *Bulletin of Centre for Informatics*, 20, 33-40. Centre for Informatics, Waseda University.

Yokoyama, Setsuo, et. al. (1998) A study on authentication and security for using the Internet for educational purposes (in Japanese). Research report for Japanese Ministries of Education grant 086-80224, Tokyo Gakugei Daigaku.

7. Biography

Tatsumi, Takeo: Research assistant at `Advanced Research Institute for Science and Engineering, Waseda University' and Research fellow at `Media Network Center, Waseda University.' Fields of study: Automated theorem proving, partial evaluation, and information ethics education.

Harada, Yasunari: Associate Dean at Media Network Center, Waseda University. Also Professor at School of Law, Graduate School of Education, and Institute of Language Teaching, Waseda University. Fields of study: cognitive science, formal semantics and pragmatics, computational linguistics.

8. TRENDS IN INTERNET-BASED ELECTRONIC COMMERCE: RESULTS OF AN INITIAL SURVEY

R.I. Ferguson, P. Cranner, D. Grey, S. Kerridge, A. Slade, J.B. Thompson and A. Williams
Centre for Electronic Commerce, University of Sunderland, St.Peter's Campus, Sunderland, SR6 0DD, ian.ferguson@sunderland.ac.uk, Tel: 0191 5152754, Fax: 0191 515 2781

ABSTRACT

Early results from a survey of organisations undertaking electronic commerce (EC) on the Internet are presented. The survey aimed to establish what hardware and software environments are currently in use, whether bespoke software is being used or whether off the shelf packages to support EC have matured sufficiently to gain acceptance in this market.

Keywords
Business/Commerce, Database, Hypermedia, Internet

1. Current state of Electronic Commerce

1.1 Reasons for surveying

The explosion in popularity of all things Internet flavoured has tempted many commercial organisations to dip their toes into the waters of electronic commerce (Adam, 96). In the rush to gain a foothold in cyberspace, many websites have been hastily created with scant regards for the disciplines of software engineering. As part of Tradepoint (Kerridge, 97), an ongoing European funded project at the Centre for Electronic Commerce at the University of Sunderland, the authors wished to establish the degree of "maturity" of current web-based trading systems. Two measures of this maturity might be the proportion of systems that utilised bespoke software to those that used off-the shelf solutions and the proportion of systems using a structured (database based) back-end to those using a less structured flat file approach(Kalakota, 97). A survey was thus undertaken.

2. Methodology

2.1 Initial Survey vs Complex Survey

The survey was performed in two stages. Firstly an initial survey of 4 questions was sent via email to the webmasters of 70 randomly selected websites using catalogue based systems to sell products and/or services. Those that replied to the initial questionnaire were invited to submit further details of their operation via a web-based form. This paper describes the results of the initial email-based survey.

2.2 Selection of companies -

The Centre for Electronic Commerce maintains a directory of organisations engaged in electronic commerce (Ferguson, 97b). From that list a random selection of 70 organisations was made. Each website was inspected to find the email address of the person responsible for creating/maintaining that site. The questions described in the following section were than emailed to that person.

2.3 Questions

The questions were designed to ascertain the extent to which electronic commerce has become established on the Web. Indications of this should be the emergence of standard means of implementing e-commerce systems. The survey aimed to find whether *ad hoc* implementations were the norm or whether more structured means were in common use. The questions were as follows:-

Catalogue - Bespoke vs Off-the-shelf

"Is the catalogue system you use: a) custom made for your site or b) a proprietary piece of software? (If so which one?)"

It was hypothesised that the emergence of propriety (off-the-shelf) software to support electronic commerce would indicate that a certain level of maturity had been reached by Internet-based EC.

Database Usage

Does your catalogue system use a database? a) Yes. (If so, which one?) or b) No.

The authors suspected that in the rush to enter the field of Internet-based EC (and given an initial shortage of expertise in Web-based programming techniques) many EC systems have been "hacked together" rather than properly engineered. The use of a structured data representation underlying the implementation would indicate that some measure of design had gone into a given system.

Hardware/Operating system -

What hardware/software does your catalogue system use?

a) UNIX based workstation, b) MS-Windows NT, c) MS-Windows 95, d) MS-Windows 3.X or e) Macintosh

In its initial phases of development, the Web was almost entirely based upon UNIX technology(Berners-Lee, 92). As it popularity has increased, a move towards PC technology has taken place on the client side. For the server-side however, UNIX technology has remained popular. UNIX is however perceived (wrongly or rightly) as being a more complex system than PC based operating systems (Net.Genesis, 96) and thus a potential barrier to the spread of EC. The authors wished to ascertain whether this "folk-wisdom" on the usability of UNIX had any effect on the spread of EC.

Geographical Location Whereabouts are you based?a) USA, b) Europe or c) other.

Although the Web was initially a European development (Berners-Lee, 92), the first area in which it has spread into home use (rather than academic) is the USA. The authors wished to investigate whether the provision of EC services in Europe lagged behind the US, and if so, by how much?

3. Results

3.1 Response rate

Of the 70 emails sent out, 31 responses were received within a 2 week interval. The original data for the survey can be found on-line at the CEC website (Ferguson, 97a).

3.2 Catalogue - Bespoke vs Off-the-shelf

The answers to question 1 are shown in Figure 1

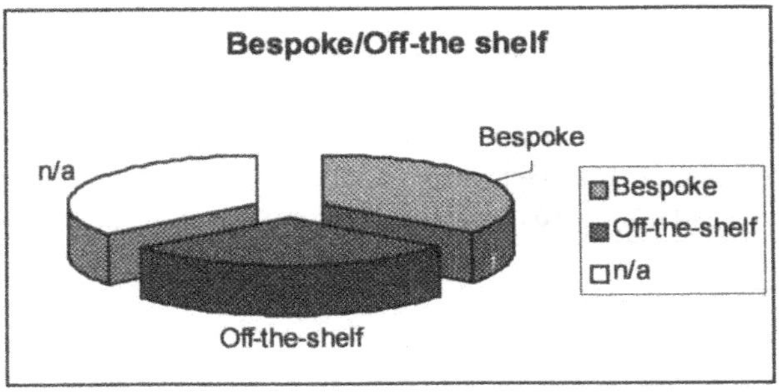

Bespoke 11
Off-the-shelf 9
No-answer or answer not applicable 11

Figure 1 - Bespoke vs. Off-the-shelf systems

3.3 Database Usage

The answers to question 2 are shown in Figure 2

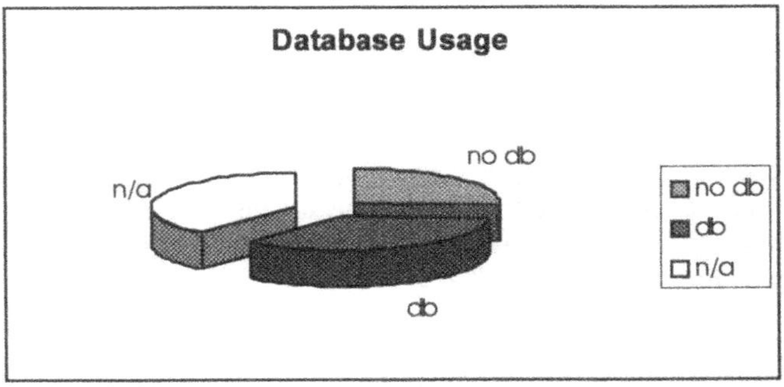

Database 11
No database 8
No-answer or answer not applicable 12

Figure 2 - Database vs. no database System

For the systems that did use a database, the breakdown is shown in Figure 3.

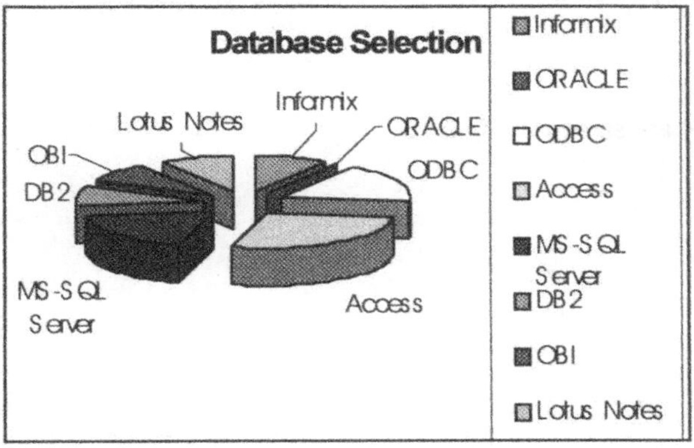

Informix	1
ODBC	2
MS Access	3
MS SQL Server	2
IBM DB2	1
OBI	1
Lotus Notes	1

Figure 3 - Database selection

3.4 Hosting Platform

The answers to question 3 are shown in Figure 4

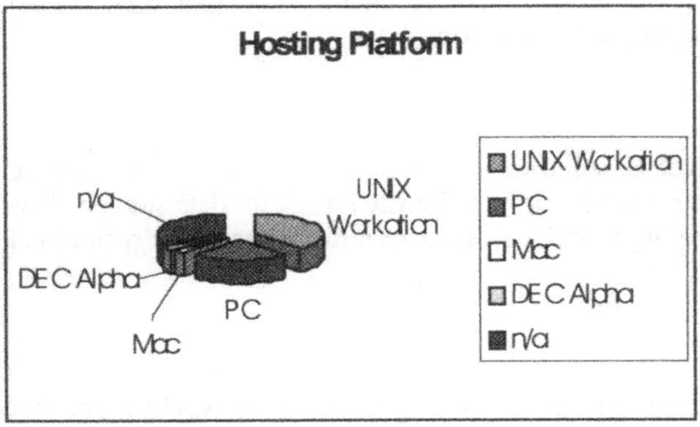

Unix	12
Win	7
Dec Alpha	1
Macintosh	1
NA	10

Figure 4 - Hosting Platforms

Development Platforms Of the 12 respondents who used UNIX , 3 indicated that the system had been developed under Windows and then moved onto a UNIX host.

3.5 Location

The answers to question 4 are shown in Figure 5

Figure 5 - Location

4. Conclusions

4.1 Response rate

The response rate of approximately 50% is in the experience of the authors unusually high, particularly when compare to other surveys carried out at Sunderland in the field of information systems (Hardy, 94). Given the small sample size of the survey however, the results must be treated with a certain amount of caution.

4.2 Catalogue - Bespoke vs Off-the-shelf

Around half of the Web-based catalogue systems built use bespoke software. This suggests that Electronic Commerce is still in its infancy and that off-the-shelf software to support it has not yet reached maturity.

4.3 Database Usage

Only around half of the Web-based catalogue systems built use an underlying structured databases with the remainder using a flat file format for data storage. This implies that software engineering techniques have been discarded in the rush to get EC systems onto the Internet.

4.4 Hosting Platform

UNIX is still the most popular system for hosting websites. It would seem that website administrators prefer flexibility offered by UNIX. It is noteworthy that these are commercial systems using what was once seen as an operating systems purely for academics. This trend may also indicate the relative merits of server software supported by the various operating systems. Since the initial development of the web was UNIX based, the server software developed under UNIX has had some 3-4 years longer in which to evolve into a mature stable product. The number of respondents developing under Win95/NT and hosting on UNIX may indicate a lack of suitable UNIX based development tools.

4.5 Location

Uptake of Web-based Electronic Commerce seems to be equal on both side of the Atlantic. This is surprising given the larger domestic user base in the US. This seems to indicate that European organisations are being quicker on the uptake of EC. This result is somewhat counter intuitive and needs further investigation before the position can be definitively stated.

5. References

Adam, N.R. & Yesha, Y, (Eds), *"Electronic Commerce: Current Research Issues and Applications"*, Springer-Verlag, 1996

T.J. Berners-Lee, R. Cailliau, J-F Groff, B. Pollermann, "*World-Wide Web: The Information Universe*", in "Electronic Networking: Research, Applications and Policy", Vol. 2 No 1, pp. 52-58 Spring 1992, Meckler Publishing, Westport, CT, USA.

Ferguson, R.I., Cranner, P., Grey, D, and Williams, A."*A Survey of Web-based Catalogues: Original data*", http://cec.sunderland.ac.uk/surveys/survey1/originaldata.html

Ferguson, R.I., Cranner, P., Grey, D, and Williams, A."*A directory of Electronic Commerce Websites*", http://cec.sunderland.ac.uk/Cec_website/links.html

Hardy C., Thompson, B. & Edwards, H.M., "A *Survey of current method usage for software development in the UK*", BCS Conference on Information Systems Methodologies, Edinburgh, 1994

Kalakota, R. & Whinston, A., "*Frontiers of Electronic Commerce*", Addison-Wesley, 1997

Kerridge, S. "*Tradepoint User Requirements Document*", Unpublished Internal report of the Tradepoint Project, CEC, University of Sunderland, 1997

Net.Genesis Corporation, "*Build a World Wide Web Commerce Server*", Wiley, 1996

6. Biography

Ian Ferguson is a Senior Lecturer in Computing. With a background in Software Engineering, he has published in the fields of CASE and MetaCASE before becoming interested in the WWW in 1992. Responsible for running one of the first WWW servers in the UK, he has gone on to publish on interfacing databases to the WWW and Internet based software repositories.

9. TOWARDS A STANDARD MONITORING SYSTEM FOR COMPUTER SCIENCE STUDENT PROJECTS

R. K. Mazhindu-Shumba
G. T. Hapanyengwi
Computer Science Department, University of Zimbabwe, MP 167, Harare, Zimbabwe

ABSTRACT

This paper describes two types of Computer Science projects that students get involved with. It then proposes a monitoring system for projects. The proposed system has been developed and used in the Department of Computer Science at the University of Zimbabwe. The monitoring system involves (a) an effective reporting structure, namely end of task reports and fortnightly reports, (b) three oral presentations, (c) a final system demonstration. The monitoring system has been used for the past three years and has been found to be very effective.

Keywords

Computing, Assessment, Information Technology, Software Engineering

1. Introduction

The Department of Computer Science at the University of Zimbabwe offers structured Computer Science undergraduate courses to students in the Faculties of Commerce, Engineering, and Science. Among the courses offered from second year level to fourth year level is a Project. A Project is a major Computer Science course in which students are expected to develop and demonstrate both powers of initiative independent thought and a professional standard in report submission. A Project addresses real world problems using Computer Science skills at the student's disposal. Projects are either hardware projects or software projects.

In this paper we describe the two major types of projects undertaken by students, the developer-solicited project and supervisor-assisted project, and then propose a monitoring system[1] for the projects. The proposed monitoring system has been developed and implemented/used in the Computer Science Department of the University of Zimbabwe by computer science project supervisors. A supervisor is an academic member of staff to whom the developer is answerable. Our experience of using the system has shown that it is a very effective monitoring system which when properly implemented benefits both the student and the supervisor.

2. Background To Projects

Student projects are of two types: student-solicited and supervisor-assigned. Student-solicited projects result from either a vacation-attachment or project initiated by a client. We shall refer to these as vacation-oriented and client-oriented projects respectively.

A vacation-oriented project might be part of a more comprehensive project. In such a case a student has to understand the more comprehensive project. The comprehensive project becomes part of the environment of the project. The problems related to the vacation-oriented projects are that either the student is tempted to implement what has already been implemented or the student may feel that scaling down of an already developed system might constitute a project. In such a case, students are advised to seek clarification from a more experienced fellow-student or a prospective supervisor. These two should help in ascertaining what should pass as a sufficient project.

Client-oriented projects solve specific problems, which are not necessarily related to other aspects of the day to day function of the client's business. Depending on the calibre of the client, it might be up to the student to extract a manageable subset of the problem at hand.

Student-solicited projects usually end up with two supervisors; the internal supervisor who is an academic member of staff and the co-supervisor from the client organisation who is responsible for the project. It is the student's responsibility to work hand in hand with both supervisors.

[1] This monitoring system is specific to software projects.

Supervisor-solicited projects are based on problem areas, which are workable within the given time and resource limits. The student normally relies on the supervisor's experiences in determining the resources. However, the student still needs to determine appropriateness of the project with respect to her abilities and her interests.

3. Team Projects

Projects may be done individually or in teams. Teams are usually made up of students enrolled in the same programme. The need for teams could be due to the size of the project or to the diverse skills required for a given project. Our experiences of supervising projects show that properly coordinated teams tend to produce better quality projects. This, we feel, is attributed to the sharing of ideas among the team members. In fact team projects allay student fears. Students doing a project for the first time (second year level students) are not sure of what is expected of them. The fact that the students are expected to produce a software system is, on its own, scary to most second year students. From experience, students are more comfortable the time they learn that a project is a team project. Although teamwork helps make students more comfortable, there are a number of issues to be considered by students in choosing a team project:

- Choice of the team members
- rapport within the team
- accountability of the team members
- Reporting structure and authority within the team.

4. The 1997 Practical Projects In Computer Science Department

1997 saw a proliferation of projects of which about 60% were supervisor-assigned and about 40% were student-solicited. Of the 60% supervisor-assigned projects, 20% were hardware projects and the rest were software projects. Software projects require that students go through the whole software development process.

A software development process may be viewed as comprising requirements analysis and definition, system design, program design, program implementation, unit testing, integration testing, system testing, system delivery and maintenance. The requirements describe what is required of the system. Once the requirements are defined, a system design is created to meet the specified requirements. The system design shows the user what the system will look like from the user's perspective. The user then reviews the design. When approved, the overall system design is used to generate the designs of the individual programs involved. When programs have been written, they are tested as individual pieces of code (unit testing) before they can be linked together. An integration test is then done. The final testing phase, called system testing, involves a test of the whole system to make sure that the functions and interactions specified initially have been implemented properly. At last, the final product is delivered. Software projects require students to design and implement software systems.

Some of the projects done during the 1997 academic year include; A Pharmaceutical Monitoring System, A Tourist Market Research Tool, Computer-Aided Educational Tools for Primary and Secondary Schools, A Car Hire System, Help Desk Automation System for the Computer Centre, A Till Reconciliation System, and A Project Recording and Consultancy Tracking System. We shall briefly describe two of the projects.

One of the Computer-Aided Education tools developed is the "Indigenous People and their Life Style System". Besides producing a map of Zimbabwe showing the geographical distribution of tribes, the system allows for the viewing of the following: the languages, the crafts, sacred places and taboos, beliefs associated with the tribes, the staple foods and the agricultural activities for the respective tribes. The main benefit of such a system is that it allows for quick and easy access to information about lifestyles and the indigenous people. Such information is invaluable in teaching and preservation of History. Since the system gives the proportion of each tribe relative to the whole Zimbabwean population, this gives policy makers a good planning platform. For example, the proportional distribution of languages gives an insight to the amount of literature to be produced.

A Business Studies Department lecturer solicited the development of a Tourist Market Research Analysis tool. The developed system addresses one problem facing many disciplines today, that is the fragmentation of information. Tourist information is so fragmented that it cannot be used for any specific purposes. The Tourist Market Research Analysis tool captures and stores data pertaining to tourists visiting Zimbabwe. The data stored include; the profile of the tourist, tourist products (places of interest), gaps with respect to products being offered (improvements to present tourist offers by the Zimbabwe Market), food and beverages, accommodation, transport used, entertainment, and curio (types of curio bought and the price). The data is then analysed for example by country to show the number of tourist that visit Zimbabwe from a given country, their sex, expenditure pattern and average income. Narrative reports graphs and tables are then given to present the results.

5. A Proposed Monitoring System

As mentioned in Section 3 of this paper, the main tasks of a software Practical project include problem definition, feasibility study, project planning, requirements analysis, design, implementation, and then finally the testing. These tasks are performed over a period of about seven months. Our experience of supervising projects has shown that students, who work steadily following the proposed monitoring system, tend to produce better quality projects. However, for the other students who strive to do the whole project within a "month" before the submission date, usually stress themselves up and in the end do not perform as well.

We therefore are proposing a number of measures to monitor the progress of the students' projects. The proposed measures have been implemented in the

Department of Computer Science over the past three years and have been found to be very effective. The measures include:

- An effective reporting structure: end of task & fortnightly reports.
- Three oral presentations
- Final system demonstration.

6. An Effective Reporting System

6.1 Fortnightly Reports

The student should maintain fortnightly written reports, in a folder, from the day of commencement of the project. Such a reporting structure assists the student with a systematic and structured record-keeping format. Figure 1 gives the layout of a typical fortnightly report.

*Project Title:*____
*Developing Team:*_____________________________________

1. The Plan for the coming two weeks.
2. Work done in the previous two weeks.
3. Problems faced during the previous two weeks and their solutions.
4. The current status of the project.
5. Any other relevant information.

Figure 1: Fortnightly report for a project

We encourage students to submit both previously corrected documents and current documents for discussion. This assists with keeping track of the progress of the project. It also makes discussions non-repetitive. The reports should also constitute meetings between the supervisor and the student. Reports for discussion should be handed to the supervisor at least forty-eight hours before the scheduled meeting.

6.2 End of Task Reports

As we noted above, students are expected to perform certain tasks. We expect that at the end of each task, a progress report be produced. In all, each student should produce the following reports:

- An initial project document.
- A specification document.
- Feasibility/scope and objective report.
- IEEE SPMP report
- Analysis report.

- Design report.
- System assessment report.

Within two weeks of the start of the project, we expect an initial project report. At this juncture the student ascertains a few points with regards to the choice of the project and the development team. Figure 2 is a sample of the report structure for the initial project document.

*Project Title:*____
Developing Team: _____________________________________

1. Brief Summary of the problem
2. Non functional requirements
   Any materials and resources needed to understand the fuzzy aspects of the problem
3. Summary of adequacy of the project
   3.1. Challenging aspects of the project
   3.2. Progress control mechanisms

Figure 2: Initial project document

The second report that the students have to produce is the requirements specification report. This report specifies the system requirements in a more formal structure. A typical structure is given in Figure 3. On average this report is produced a month after the start of the project.

After performing the requirements and specifications the student has a clearer picture of what the project entails. The student should then perform a critical analysis of herself with respect to the task at hand. This analysis is to determine whether:

- There are aspects for which the student is not adequately prepared. In this case the student has to work on acquiring the relevant skills.
- The whole project is too much to handle in which case whether there is need for expanding the developing team or whether it is prudent to abandon the project all together.
- The whole project is not as comprehensive in which case there is a need to expand the requirements or trim down the size of the team.

*Project Title:*____
*Developing Team:*_______________________________________

1. Introduction
   1.1. Need for the new system
   1.2. Brief description of how the system fits into the business
2. Functional Requirements
   2.1. Description of services provided to the user
3. Boundary of the System
   3.1. Description of the environment
4. Non-functional Requirements
   4.1. Relevant Costing
   4.2. Hardware and software requirements
   4.3. Manpower requirements
5. System Evolution
   5.1. Assumptions on which the system is based
   5.2. Anticipated changes due to hardware evolution
   5.3. Anticipated changes due to software evolution
   5.4. Anticipated change in user needs
6. Prototyping report
   6.1. Goals for prototyping
   6.2. Functions prototyped
   6.3. Prototyping results
7. Glossary

Figure 3: Specification Document

Upon completion of the Specification Report, we expect the student to demonstrate the developed prototype system. This helps the supervisor to confirm the student's progress.

At this stage of project development the student should have a firm direction as to what needs to be implemented. To reaffirm their understanding the first oral presentation should be given. This presentation should give a clear and concise summary of the project, highlight the cost and the benefits, and present the results and recommendations of the feasibility study.

At the end of the feasibility study, a report has to be produced. A typical structure of the report is given in Figure 4.

Though planning is an ongoing process, it is at this stage that a project planning report is compiled. Figure 5 is an example of a typical project planning report. The report is adopted from the IEEE-SPMP.

*Project Title:*________________________________
*Developing Team:*____________________________

1. Executive summary: A clear and brief summary of the feasibility study:
    1.1. key sources of information
    1.2. alternative solutions considered
    1.3. highlights of the costs and the benefits
    1.4. results and recommendations from the study
2. Appendix:
    2.1. Charts
    2.2. Graphs
    2.3. Interview lists
    2.4. Selected interview summaries
    2.5. Memos and notes
    2.6. References

Figure 4: Feasibility/Scope and Objective Report

*Project Title:*________________________________
*Developing Team:*____________________________

1. Introduction
    1.1. Project overview
    1.2. Project deliverables
    1.3. Reference materials
    1.4. Definitions and acronyms
2. Project Organisation
    2.1. Project responsibilities.
3. Managerial process
    3.1. Management objectives and priorities
    3.2. Risk management
    3.3. Monitoring and Controlling mechanisms
    3.4. Staffing plan
4. Technical process
    4.1. Methods, Tools and Techniques
    4.2. Software documentation
    4.3. Project support functions
5. Work Packages, Schedules and Budget
    5.1. Work packages
    5.2. Dependencies
    5.3. Resource requirements
    5.4. Budget and resource allocation
    5.5. Schedule

Figure 5: IEEE SPMP Report

At the end of the analysis stage, an analysis report is produced. The contents of the analysis report are as illustrated in Figure 6.

*Project Title:*______________________________________
*Developing Team:*__________________________________
1. Presentation of a model[2] for the whole system.
2. Relevant data dictionary
3. Presentation of process logic using one of the tools

Figure 6: Analysis report

The system's analysis and design at this stage needs external assessment. Such assessment can be achieved through an oral presentation. The presentation should be targeted at a diverse audience to include the developer's peers, the user (if the user is competent to evaluate a project at this level), the supervisors, and other informed outsiders. This oral presentation should include the following aspects:

- A brief description of the requirements definition and specification of the project
- The analysis results: justification for choice of analysis tools
- Summary of the project plan
- The design: System Relationship Diagram (SRD), and structure chart
- Problems encountered

*Project Title:*______________________________________
*Developing Team:*__________________________________
1. Design of sub-units
1.1. Algorithm for each sub-unit
1.2. An SRD for the sub-units
1.3. Structure chart for the sub-units
1.4. Flowcharts for any complex logic
1.5. An assessment of quality of the algorithm
2. Design of user interface
2.1. Forms
2.2. Menus
2.3. Reports
2.4. An assessment of quality of user interface

Figure 7: Design report

[2] A **model** can be presented using either a **DFD** or an **ERD** or a combination.

At the end of the systems design stage a design report is produced. The contents of the design report are as illustrated in Figure 7. This report can also be used in the oral presentation.

At the end of the implementation stage a system assessment report has to be produced. In this report an outline of the various parameters of assessment is made. Figure 8 outlines the structure of the system assessment report. What have to be brought out by this report are the strengths and the weaknesses of the system. Thus, in assessing any one of the aspects it should be clear as to how well the system handles that specific aspect.

*Project Title:*______________________________
*Developing Team:*___________________________

1. Adequacy
2. Portability
3. Reusability
4. Adaptability
5. Environment chosen.

Figure 8: System assessment Report

The final demonstration is a one-time affair. Interim demonstrations can be arranged any time. The developer should not only use the supervisor as the tester of the system. In fact, as part of the developer test plan, the developer should have a panel of people whose job is to test the system. It is always easier to rectify an error, which is discovered earlier in the development process.

Unfortunately it is not always possible or advisable to get the user involved in testing an unfinished product. The developer, however, has to simulate the needs of the user as closely as possible. A very productive thing to do is to have one of the developer's classmates play the devil's advocate every so often. The developer might be amazed as to how much help a fellow student might give.

6.3 The electronic report folder

In an institution with an Intranet and a computer network, communication between the supervisor and the project team can be significantly enhanced. A project folder is created for each of the projects. Each folder is accessible through a password known to the supervisor and the development team. The folder is located in the workspace of the developing team.

The structure and organization of the folder is akin that of the paper folder. Correction of a report is maintained by keeping a version of the given report. The supervisor and the project team are each allocated a different color or type font to use. In this way, distinguishing the various contributions is straightforward. Drawbacks with such a system include documents needing intensive correction and limited typing capabilities on part of the supervisor.

7. Conclusion

This paper has explained two types of projects undertaken by Computer Science students: supervisor-solicited and student-solicited projects. Student-solicited projects can either be vacation-oriented or client-oriented. Regardless of the type of project, a student has to fully understand the subject area for any chosen project. In some cases, it might be necessary that the student carry out relevant research in order to acquire the pertinent knowledge.

The tasks for a given software project include problem definition, requirements analysis, feasibility study, project planning, requirements analysis, design, implementation, and testing. Our experiences of supervising projects has shown that there is need for a monitoring system. We have therefore proposed a number of measures that may be put in place to monitor the performance of students. The measures include an effective reporting structure: fortnightly reports and end of task reports, three oral presentations and a final system demonstration.

The standardisation of the monitoring system is an on-going exercise. We feel that this can be extended to the grading of the project. There is actually some work in the Department of Computer Science on the standardisation of the grading system for Computer Science projects.

8. References

Schach Stephen, R. (1993) *Software Engineering*, Second Edition. Irwin.

Britton, C. and Doake, J. (1993) *Software System Development*. The McGraw-Hill International Series.

Somerville I. (1995) *Software Engineering*, Fifth Edition. Addison Wesley.

9. Biography

Gilford Tapera Hapanyengwi is the Director of Computer Center at the University of Zimbabwe. He holds a PhD and MS degree in Computer Science from Vanderbilt University in the United States of America and a BSc degree in Computer Science and Mathematics from the University of Zimbabwe. Gilford's research interests are in Knowledge Discovery in Database Systems, Geographical Information Systems, Software Engineering, and Computer Education.

Rose Kudzai Mazhindu-Shumba is the Chairperson of the Computer Science Department at the University of Zimbabwe. She holds a PhD in Computer Science from Birmingham University in England, a M.Sc. in Computer Science from University of Manchester in England, and a Bachelor's degree in Computer Science and Business Studies from the University of Zimbabwe. Rose's research interests are in Software Engineering, Object Oriented Systems, Operating Systems, Programming Languages, and Computer Education.

10. EDUCATIONAL MULTIMEDIA IN A NETWORK CENTRIC SOCIETY: REQUIREMENTS, ENABLERS AND NEGATIVE ASPECTS.

K.D. Levin
Tel Aviv College of Management
7 Rabin Blvd, Rishon Lezion, Israel,
Phone: 972-3-9634267, Fax: 972-3-9634210
email: dlevin@colman.ac.il

ABSTRACT

The purpose of the paper is to identify the basic requirements for a network centric education and learning and to discuss the technological developments that enable the applications of educational multimedia over the network. Some of these applications will be reviewed as well as the problems ("balkanization", inequality and economical cost) associated with the positive and the negative impact of the network centric society.

Keywords
Distance Learning, Home Learning, Multimedia, Videoconferencing

1. Introduction

As education and learning moves beyond the recall of facts and into the area of creativity, problem solving, analysis and evaluation, learners require inter personal communication in order to question, challenge and discuss (Bates 1994). With the explosive growth in Internet connections worldwide, networked communication has the potential to shrink geographic distances and facilitate information exchange among people of various backgrounds.

There are positive and negative outcomes to these developments. Information and communication technology can link geographically separated people and help them locate interesting or compatible resources. Although these attributes have the potential to bridge gaps and unite communities, they also have the potential to fragment interaction and divide groups by screening out less preferred contact.

In section 2 we will identify the basic requirements for a network centric education and learning. In section 3 we will discuss the technological developments that enable the applications of educational multimedia over the network. In section 4 we will review some of these applications. The negative impacts of "balkanization" (Alstyne and Brynjolfsson 1997), inequality and economical extranalities will be discussed in section 5. Section 6 concludes the paper by identifying problems for further research.

2. Basic Requirements

Regardless of the model of pedagogy that one works with, interaction between instructor and student and among students is central to the process. Traditional distance learning programs have most often replicated the teacher lecture model. These environments primarily utilize one-way transmission of video signals, with limited student feedback (via telephone calls). Interaction between the teacher and students is limited and interaction between students at different sites is non existent.

The network centric educational context will need to encompass the following:

- Support for individual work, interacting with learning material that may be available locally or remotely.
- Support for collaborative work both locally and at different remote sites, either asynchronously or synchronously, and most likely in a multimedia form.
- Support for a student role guided by an instructor.
- Support for an instructor role supervising and guiding the students.

The Interactive Multimedia Distance Learning (Wilson and Mosher 1994) is a good model for the "virtual classroom" (prototype by Rensselar and AT&T) that combines rich communications' capabilities of 2 way, real time, video and data sharing among students and teacher.

In traditional classrooms, instructors use text, graphs, animation, videos, sounds or live demonstrations to present curriculum content to students. They create exercises for students to work in a shared space (the blackboard), and they can write comments on student's work. Students are taking notes and can work on exercises locally on their desktop as well as on the shared blackboard. They can collaborate with other students and may alert the teacher that they would like to ask a question. The instructor is the leader of the class and may pass control to students in order to present their work or to ask questions. However, only the instructor may pass control and can take it away from the students. The basic features of the traditional classroom should be supported in a network environment in order to maintain a class structure. These features require:

- One workstation configured to be the leader. The leader can pass the focus to a participating workstation.
- Interconnected workstations configured to follow the actions of the leader.
- Events sharing mode were text, graphics, video or audio is presented to the workstations. When the focus is passed from the leader to the student's workstation, the students control the flow of shared events and everyone may see or hear the student's presentation.
- Each workstation can work independently.
- Hands raising were the students send a message to the instructor's workstation, letting the instructor know that they have a question. The instructor may choose to acknowledge the question or to respond to it at a more convenient time. When the instructor answers the student the focus may be passed to the student's workstation so others can view the discussion in an event sharing mode.
- Instructor pointer were the instructor can move a pointer around the students screen to emphasize important points in the information display.

In this environment, the instructor may use the lecture mode when appropriate, or to interact with the students performing work on their workstations. Students may share their work with other students and can engage in multiple discussions were control of the session is passed back and forth from instructor to student.

3. Technological Enablers.

Multimedia in education is developing fast due to the convergence of different media (text, data, graphics, video, audio) into a common digital platform. However, while stand-alone applications of multimedia will continue to be important in education, a much more significant development will be the application of high speed multimedia networks for educational purposes.

Software, hardware and content providers are struggling to provide standardized multimedia solutions, but the co-existence of numerous media standards and the rapid proliferation of these technologies presents problems. In an effort to resolve these conflicts, Netscape Communications', Progressive Networks and 40 other companies agreed on a proposed standard communications protocol for the real-time delivery of multimedia information over the Internet. The Real Time Streaming Protocol (RTSP) addresses issues such as fidelity, packet loss, latency and reliability. PC technology is beginning to impact the entertainment, education and communications' industries as companies begin to leverage the performance and features.

The convergence of multimedia capable computers, user friendly environments and relatively fast transmission technologies have led to an acceptable on-line experience for the average consumer. The Internet experience today has been largely constrained by limited bandwidth. There are times when getting information over the web justifies the humorous reference to the WWW as the "World Wide Wait".

An indication of this converging of computers, cmunications, content, and consumer electronics is a new standard being considered by the World Wide Web consortium called "Synchronized Multimedia Integration Language," that offers to enhance both the old (television) and the new (Web). SMIL enables authors to bring television-like content to the Web, avoiding the limitations of traditional television and significantly lowering the bandwidth requirements for transmitting this type of content over the Internet (details at http://www.w3.org/Press/SMIL).

As the Internet access marketplace continues to mature, telephone carriers, cable companies and others are racing to evaluate and deploy high bandwidth technologies in homes and in businesses.

Even with a vast increase in the bandwidth of the Internet, optical media will be able to deliver a significantly better multimedia experience for the future. Educational multimedia applications should integrate both technologies. They should be delivered on the Internet while high quality multimedia experience will be delivered on optical media, augmenting and enhancing the on line (Internet) version of the product.

What is emerging is a highly connected network providing access to sources, tools and information across disciplinary, institutional, and national and international boundaries. It will soon be difficult to imagine a course not on the Web. However, the challenge is to deal with the technologies at hand, which are quickly outdated, while not being overwhelmed by the new and exciting opportunities available and promised.

4. Network Centric Educational Applications

The Web-based education market is showing continuous growth in terms of the number of programs, the number of venues and the number of certified people. Lotus and Microsoft are playing a leading role in using the Web as a medium for the delivery of training material. Web-based training makes bad instruction impossible because such factors as poor instructors or class room logistics cannot affect the training. However, inspiring lecturers are absent in Web training, even though students can ask questions and receive answers over the Web.

The Interactive Distance Education Alliance (IDEA) proposal is a distance learning solution that was presented to several large companies, including Intel and TRW. The study determined that there was a high demand for distance programs in business and engineering, and focused on interactive teleconferencing and Web-based delivery. The study showed that faculty could adapt to the electronic classroom model quickly, given appropriate technical support. The IDEA proposal was presented to several companies, with two firms, Intel and TRW, agreeing to fund initial study projects beginning in January 1996..

The Global Information Network in Education (GINIE), became operational in early 1996. GINIE, funded by UNESCO and the US Agency for International Development, serves as a multi-channel information network to collect, analyze and disseminate information of use to policy-makers, educators, government and agency officials and local communities. The network also provides education information to nations in crisis, such as Bosnia-Herzegovina, the People's Republic of China, and others.

Pennsylvania's Education Network (PEN) is not just for Pennsylvanians any more. The network's Digital Object Repository (DOR) will store curriculum frameworks and components in a variety of multimedia data types, including video, audio and images. PEN-DOR is a Technology Testbed Project funded in part by Pennsylvania's Link-to-Learn program. Its purpose is to provide Pennsylvania schools, libraries, and communities with virtually unlimited access to the information available on global networks. Its purpose is to provide multimedia education materials to the Keystone State's teachers and students over the World Wide Web. The system, which can expand to meet growing needs, will be integrated into the Global Information Network in Education (GINIE) and eventually will be accessible to students and educators worldwide via the Web.

Colleges and universities throughout the US are increasing their on-line-based course offerings, allowing working students to receive the benefits of a secondary education from the convenience of their home. Many students physically unable to attend colleges because of work-duty or geographic locations are thus able to earn business degrees they ordinarily would not receive. Duke University, UCLA and UC Berkeley each offers diverse business curricula through their on-line services, and students can easily form study groups with fellow classmates through on-line chat rooms and contact instructors via E-mail.

Thanks to the Internet, credentials from UCLA are just a mouse click away from evening classes at your local community college. You can take courses at your own convenience and have the worldwide library of the Web at your fingertips for instant research. The cost for taking on-line courses is comparable with physically attending class, but without transportation, accommodations, and other sundry costs. More important, in response to the mushrooming number of small businesses, universities today are offering a variety of entrepreneurship cybercourses. Here's a sample of on-line business courses offered by major universities.

- Duke University's Fuqua School of Business's Global Executive MBA offers access to Fuqua's MBA program via the Internet (www.fuqua. duke.edu).

- The University of California Los Angeles recently opened up its extension classes to the Internet through a partnership with The Home Education Network (www.then.com).

- Florida-based Open University offers a truly virtual campus with a series of business classes available exclusively on the Internet (www.openu.com).
- New York City's New School for Social Research provides on-line education through its Distance Instruction for Adult Learning program (www.dialnsa.edu).

The U.S. Government, with assistance of public and private organizations, steadily implements policy in cooperation with the former USSR, in the areas of education, business, economics and culture. California State University, Los Angeles is reaching out to build more academic bridges in the world. Their Center for Newly Independent States Studies (CNISS) contributes to the strategic goals of building and securing educational, business and cultural links between the U.S. and NIS countries.

Other initiatives at the international arena include the followings: Australia - Technical and Further Education institutes will provide 30 percent of their education programs over the Internet. Japan - Nippon Telegraph and Telephone Corp. New videoconferencing system "Konet Plan," is intended to bring Japanese school teachers and students together using both videoconferencing and the Internet. Canada - Stentor, an alliance of Canadian telephone companies, is financing a 10 year initiative, called Beacon, that will bring broadband, multimedia services to 80% of all home and businesses in Canada by the year 2004.

5. The Negative Aspects

Over the last several decades, there has been a decline in both civic engagements and in the norms, trust and features of social life needed to achieve social objectives. Since 1965, the amount of time Americans spend in local clubs is down by one half. Attendance at town meetings is down 39%. The number of people working for political parties dropped 56%..

The general argument is fairly simple Internet users can seek out interactions with like-minded individuals who have similar values, and thus become less likely to interact with people whose values differ from their own. If IT provides a lubricant that allows for contact that is more focused than contacts available locally, then, local heterogeneity can give way to virtual homogeneity as communities coalesce across geographic boundaries.

With increased connectivity and bandwidth an emerging global village represents one possible outcome from a range of possibilities. It is also possible that improving communication's access through emerging technology will fragment society and introduce balkanization of preferences (Alstyne and Brynjolfsson 1997), social, intellectual and economic affiliations, analogous to geographic regions. Just as separation in physical space can divide geographic groups, separation in virtual space, or "cyberbalkanization" can divide special interest groups. Several virtual communities based on identity derived from racial origin [NetNoir—http://www.netnoir.com/index.html], geographical location [Blacks-burg Electronic Village—http://www.bev.net] and social issues [Public Electronic Network—

http://pen.ci.santa-monica.ca.us], have appeared in recent years. These virtual communities, serve to satisfy the needs of the users based on commonalties. They can be broadly categorized as communities of relationship, communities of interest, communities of transaction, and communities of fantasy (Armstrong and Hagel 1996).

At some point, almost everything needed for teaching and learning will be provided on the Internet: textbooks, encyclopedias, magazines, newspapers, library books, multimedia software, research databases, photos, videos, and more. Most of it is not free. Valuable and substantive educational resources cannot be researched, developed, tested, and disseminated without cost. It takes a great deal of effort to develop valuable material. That effort must be compensated in order to continue. It can cost as much as $1 million to produce an educational CD-ROM, and even more to publish a textbook. The sooner we all recognize the fallacy of free education on the Internet, the sooner publishers and developers will be willing to take the risk of embracing the Internet for delivering quality instruction.

The result of a recently completed RAND study on the distribution of information and communication capabilities across the US populace indicates that since 1989 (and even before), gaps in access to computers and networks have increased significantly over time as a function of income. The gap between the information rich and the information poor can widen with virtual communities (Alstyne and Brynjolfsson 1995) and there should be no illusions that a greater sense of community will inexorably result. The small computer finally gained classroom acceptance, though, largely due to parent lobbying and aggressive advertising by manufacturers. While many believe today that computers, unlike radio and TV, may qualitatively change education, there is a growing apprehension that classroom IT has widened the gap between the have and have-not.

Operation Social Development (OSD) was established by a coalition of Israeli high technology industry leaders in cooperation with Israeli government. The ground breaking project, A Computer for Every Child, supplies disadvantages children from all backgrounds with state of the art home computers, top quality educational software, access to the Internet and comprehensive user instruction. Even more powerful than placing computers in schools - where too little time and too few facilities limit usage - A Computer for Every Child gives disadvantaged youth direct, unlimited access to their own PC.

Critical to the success of the project is the 60 hours of required instruction in computer hardware and software. Topics include use of the Internet, electronic mail, access to databases and programs which aid in the research and presentation of school papers and projects. After successfully completing the training course, the children receive the full package of educational programs on CD-ROM's. All programs are approved by the Israeli Ministry of Education and are used by most Israeli schools.

6. Conclusions

Electronic communications have become increasingly important to the conduct of higher education. The new digital technologies are changing the way instruction is delivered. In this paper we identified the basic requirements for a network centric education and learning and discussed the technological developments that enable the applications of educational multimedia over the network. There are positive and negative outcomes to these developments. Information and communication technology can link geographically separated people and help them locate interesting or compatible resources. Although these attributes have the potential to bridge gaps and unite communities, they also have the potential to fragment interaction and divide groups by screening out less preferred contact.

The following summarizes some of the issues discussed in this paper:

- We are breaking with the "credit for contact" model and considering alternatives to lecture as a delivery mode. Students are not place-bound or time-constrained.
- Students are developing new skills to access, organize and synthesize information received via the Internet.
- Teachers need incentives to incorporate technology into their educational programs. They must see benefits to their own teaching and to their students' learning.
- A new role for the teacher has been identified, one of facilitator and coach, thus establishing a new relationship between teacher and learner.

What is emerging is a highly connected network providing access to resources, tools and information across disciplinary, institutional, and national and international boundaries. It will soon be difficult to imagine a course not on the Web. Yet in spite of those major advances in networking technology, there are important applications that faculty and students can not pursue. Learning networks should promote acquisition and knowledge building to enrich locally available resources. However, the challenge is to deal with the technologies at hand, which are quickly outdated, while not being overwhelmed by the new and exciting opportunities available and promised.

Further work needs to be done to study the pedagogical, economical and sociological implications of network centric education. Some of these issues are:

- What kinds of class activities are best performed locally on individual work station and what activities are best performed through interactions over the network.
- How to assure the privacy of the student and the confidentiality of data?
- How to provide sufficient compensation to providers of classroom activities? How to finance this compensation?
- How can we guarantee that humans, not computers, are still identified as the instructor?

7. References

Alstyne, M. and Brynjolfsson, E. (1995) "Communication Networks and the Rise of an Information Elite — Do Computers Help the Rich get Richer?" Proceedings of the Sixteenth International Conference on Information Systems, 1995, pp. 93-96.

Alstyne, M. and Brynjolfsson, E. (1997) "Electronic Communities: Global Villages or Cyber Balkanization?", Proceedings of the Seventeenth International Conference on Information Systems, 1997, pp. 373-379.

Armstrong, A., and Hagel III, J. (1996) "The Real Value of On-line Communities," Harvard Business Review (74:3), May-June 1996, pp. 134-141.

Bates. A.W. (1994) "Educational Multi-Media in a Networked Society", Proceedings of ED-MEDIA 94, pp. 3-8.

Jordan, E. and Hewett, W.G., (1997) "Discussion Group: Teaching and learning using the WWW", The Place of Information Technology in Management and Business Education, pp. 219-230, Chapman and Hall, 1997.

Wilson,J.M. and Mosher,D.N., (1994) "Interactive multimedia Distance Learning (IMDL) The Prototype of the Virtual Classroom", Proceedings of ED-MEDIA 94, pp.563-570.

8. Biography

K. Dan Levin is currently a senior lecturer at the College of Management. He was a senior Lecturer and the head of the information system program at the faculty of Industrial Engineering & Management, Technion, the Israeli Institute of Technology and an associate professor of decision sciences at the Wharton School, University of Pennsylvania. He has over 30 years of experience in the high technologies sector. Specialization in the political, technological and market forces operating at the intersection of computers, communications and image processing.

11. THE APPLICATION OF THE INTERNET AND INTRANETS IN BUSINESS

M.A.Murray, S. Kerridge, A. Slade, D. Grey, I. Fergusson, J.B. Thompson.

ABSTRACT

The Internet and its corporately owned counterpart, intranets, continue to prove fertile in spawning a wide variety of business applications. The superimposability of Internet/ intranet based solutions onto the needs of business is explored in this review, and asserted as a pivotal reason for this phenomenon. In terms of business utility the splicing of IT/IS and telecommunications that comprise networks has proven ever more useful in recent years making this technology strategically significant and demanding strategic management. The significance of generic categories of application is addressed with examples provided for illustration. These categories include communication, publishing and enterprise support. Problems of security are discussed and ways of circumventing these problems considered. Finally a summary is given in which is the importance of these networks to business is reasserted.

Keywords:
Electronic Commerce, Electronic Procurement, Internet, Intranet.

1. Introduction

The history of the Internet from its inception as a US military project to its ubiquitous presence in the 1990's is well documented (Comer, 1994), yet given its proliferation in terms of the numbers of providers and users involved its scale is difficult to quantify accurately. The spread of corporately owned intranets has been every bit as prolific. Intranets have led to a re-evaluation of organisational processes to see where they can be used to cut costs and advance competitive advantage.

The open TCP/IP (Transmission Control Protocol / Internet Protocol) suite has allowed wide proliferation of the Internet/intranets. Diverse computer resources often cause discontinuity, in the form, for example, of users having to switch between systems to achieve their aims. The traversability promoted by unifying TCP/IP protocols is essential not only to the Internet but also large corporate intranets which often consist of diverse computer systems. Open protocols deployed on intranets can prove a more cost-effective method of intra-organisational networking than proprietary systems, (the alternative) which often lead to organisations being 'locked' to one vendor and limit that organisation's options to scale-up. Related to this, the formation of *extranets* (essentially an intranet connected to an external body) is more cost-effective via an Internet link rather than a point-to-point connection hired by the organisation. Cost-reduction is emphasised by Segal (Segal, 1996) as being instrumental in the Internet's adoption in recent years by so many users.

To begin with section 2 will explore the Internet/intranet paradigm. This will be considered in terms of its proliferation, it paradigmatic fit and its strategic fit in subsections 2.1,2.2 and 2.3 respectively. The business applications will be considered along with the security problems involved.

2. Exploration Into The Internet/Intranets

2.1 Proliferation

Figure 1 shows how Internet use has increased in recent years. The Internet has moved from being a specialist domain to being commonplace in a much wider arena.

A reflection of its popularity in Britain is the UK Prime Minister's (Tony Blair) promise to have every school in Britain connected as soon as possible, which is to be achieved by a partnership between government and telecommunications companies. To accompany this rise in popularity, there has been a rapid increase in the number of companies with intranet installations. Figure 2 shows that the sales of servers for intranets have over taken that for the Internet, which is consistent with Netscape's claim that 80% of their revenue now comes from servers bound for corporate intranets. Shamoon (Shamoon, 1996) predicts that intranet popularity will increase further once the model assimilates all the functionality of groupware.

Figure 1 Growth of Internet (Stobart,1995)

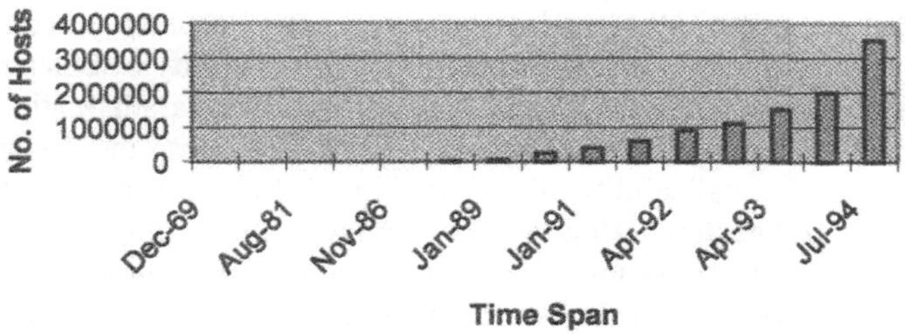

Figure 2 Server Software Unit sales (Carr,1997)

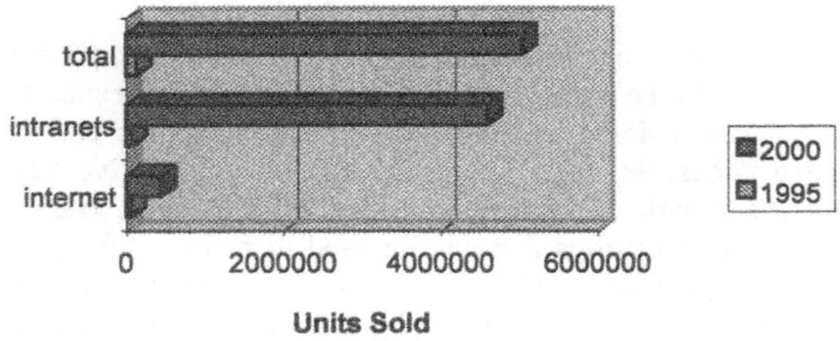

2.2 Paradigmatic Fit

This section looks at the Internet/intranet model as a useful tool in commerce.

The fusion of connectivity and ease of use that typifies today's Internet and intranets represents the further improvement of networking. It has emerged that intranets, in particular, provide versatility that can be applied effectively in many situations; Ward (1996) asserts that intranets represent the first time technology has mapped directly onto business needs both in terms of utility and cost. A small intranet can be established on an existing network simply by installing:-

- A TCP/IP router.
- A web server and browsers.
- An HTML editor

In IT/IS terms none of these items is particularly expensive. The software elements can often be acquired free of charge from the large vendors. It can be accepted a priority that this will be highly attractive to IT managers looking for solutions within the constraints of tight budgets.

Once an intranet is established, open standards ensure that it can be easily expanded throughout an organisation and if necessary can be used to connect geographically separated sites; basically the versatility and scalability of this model ensures that a suitable topology can be found . It is asserted that paradigmatic 'fit' of these networks or the superimposability of related solutions and business architecture advanced by the malleability of the paradigm, is the chief factor in their popularity. Business architecture (Hogbin & Thomas, 1994) comprising data models and processes of an organisation, can be as dynamic and as multifarious as the organisations themselves. Adaptability of any system is of the essence, so clearly a system that uses open standards has advantage over proprietary systems, particularly once that system has gained wide acceptance the way TCP/IP protocols have. Further, TCP/IP support in many operating systems allows users to work in their preferred (native) environments, negating the need for extensive retraining.

2.3 Strategic Fit

By virtue of the wide scope of business applications they enable, consideration of these networks is elevated to the strategic level. The strategic significance of IT/IS, long recognised by writers (McFarlan,1984; Porter, 1985) requires that IT/IS be strategically managed if business is to fully exploit it for competitive advantage. Without getting into the minutia of the various models of IT strategy, many involve identifying development trajectories that can be used to make useful predictions regarding IT investment (Robson, 1997). Generally the strategic management of IT/IS is complicated by the mutable nature of the underlying technology which makes strategic management difficult. In such an environment traditional accounting methods for appraising investments such a ROI or NPV are not always suitable for IT investments because of the difficulties in quantifying the benefits of IT (Walsham, 1993).

3. Applying The Technology In Business

Much of the utility of intranets comes from their ability to disseminate information rapidly throughout an organisation. Organisations have been involved in the acquisition and the distribution of information for centuries. This dissemination, of information (the lifeblood of most organisations) has been speeded up by the technologies of the Information Society and is now being catalysed by Internet / intranets. The first organisations to utilise the technology did so in mission-critical areas; The American video company Home Box Office (HBO) used an intranet to distribute its promotional materials to its many salespeople, effecting an improvement on distributing the same materials as hard copy. There are numerous other examples in the literature (Shepherdson, 1997) of how this technology is being deployed in mission-critical areas.

Three areas of application will be considered here:-

- Publishing Documentation
- Communication
- Enterprise Support

3.1 Publishing Documentation.

Often an organisation's first venture into this technology will be a publishing project -often just a telephone directory. Affordable storage media such as large hard disks and writable CD ROMs ensure that even small intranets make perfectly adequate repositories of all types of content. The London Underground Corporation in the UK recently published a huge 13 volume safety manual on an intranet as part of a pilot scheme to assess the viability of a corporate intranet. This scheme relied on the willingness of the of users to pull information from the intranet as opposed to having it 'pushed' as hard copy. The scheme was reported a success (Ward, 1996). Ultimately the bulk of an organisation's documentation can be moved onto an intranet and a 'workflow' system be introduced (Vasali, 1997). Workflow systems are an attempt at computerised storage, manipulation and management of documentation that facilitate monitoring of products and resources as well aiding accountancy tasks such as invoicing and undertaking audit trails. The efficacy of documentation publishing on the Internet / intranets is furthered by HTML links and search engines that allow complex searches to be made to enable the locating of specific information. Naturally some materials are more suitable to network publishing than others; likely candidates include, materials that can completely substitute the printed page, materials that are frequently updated and materials such as reference works that can take good advantage of hypertext links (PTWEB, 1996).

Though the publication of materials on the Internet is limited by confidentiality of much corporate material, there still is good scope for certain types of publication.

The infinite storage capacities of the Internet make it perfect for storing huge catalogues that can be used in Electronic Commerce, allowing consumers to assess products online. Problems regarding on-line payments have not been completely resolved, yet governments across the globe, including those in the EU and the USA, are sponsoring initiatives to encourage the use of e-commerce - recognising its significance in modern economies. The attraction to producers of having their products displayed in virtual outlets on the Internet is immediately apparent when the number of potential browsers is considered. Anderson (1997) informs us that there is a great deal more business to business e-commerce than consumer e-commerce, with electronic procurement and tendering becoming widespread.

As well as representing a new departure in terms of speed and distribution capability,electronic publishing is important because of the amount of materials it saves. The potential for saving paper copy is massive. Take, for instance the case of a large organisation issuing an Invitation to Tender. Rather than send huge volumes out to each interested party the company can publish the Invitation on the Internet and tender can be made electronically.

Advanced transmission methods such as UDP and TCP multicasting (Dyson et al 1997) and improvements in modems and ISDN have ensured that publishing is not restricted to static content. Animation, audio and video can now be added to static content and accessed by any user with a browser with the required capability.

3.2 Communication tools

Communication at all levels is enhanced by Internet/intranets. Inter departmental communication is enhanced by the intranets while communication between subsidiaries is enhanced by linking their respective intranets. In this context these networks represent a continuation of the marriage between telecommunications and IT that has led to such a radical increase in the availability of information (Forrester, 1985) over the last few decades.

The most obvious way in which these networks aid communication is via e-mail and newsgroups, both of which benefit from the robustness of the TCP/IP suite. Newsgroups help people who would not normally meet to communicate and discuss/exchange ideas, while e-mail permits instant communication with anyone connected to the Internet with an e-mail account. Each of these tools is now taken for granted yet their importance as an enabler of communication should not be understated.

Increasing bandwidth also permits the use of video conferencing which uses various Electronic Meeting Systems (EMS) to allow real-time conferencing across networks. An extensive survey by Pollard (1996) revealed that many large organisations including IBM, American Express and the Royal Bank of Canada are now deploying EMS and that moreover it is becoming more extensively used. The survey found that managers saw advantages in EMS including efficient use of time, the promotion of organisational flexibility, and the creation of greater scope for collaborative working. Given improvements in transmission and the wider acceptance by the business community of Internet technology, there is no reason why this technology should not become more prevalent.

To deny the significance of the Internet/intranets to communication is difficult - even after discounting the enthusiasm reflected in companies rushing to install intranets and in literature replete with panegyrics and superlatives. The use of the Internet has led to the term 'Global Village' being used to describe a world community of users constantly in communication with each other. Intranets allow the formation of corporate villages in which communication in the organisation is enhanced. Further many management writers (Burnes, 1997; Mullins, 1996) expound the importance of communication in organisations especially at times of change.

3.3 Enterprise Support

Enterprise support is (of necessity) a broad category encompassing many forms of organisational behaviour. This section could be broken down into subsections on phenomena such as electronic commerce, electronic procurement and banking, but given the taxonomical uncertainties inherent in these nascent fields, and the scope of this paper, the broader category will suffice.

Any process involving transmission of information can benefit from networking. Existing applications can benefit by being integrated with the intuitive browser interfaces and by having their use extended across operating platforms. Additionally the diversity of Internet/intranet compatible applications is increasing; intranet compatible databases alone include Oracle, Sybase and DB2, while ODBC (Open Database Connectivity) conformance ensures that many other systems can share data across networks. Products such as JAVA, ActiveX and Livewire have been produced by the big players viz., Sun, Microsoft and Netscape respectively to provide a broader range of application programs that will function across these networks.

As well as a diversity of applications produced for this paradigm users are beginning to find new ways of applying the paradigm itself to enhance their business processes. James (1996) provides a good example of this. James relates the case of the American telecommunications giant AT&T who used an intranet to reduce the number of their customer support line from 23 to 1. Having 23 lines was seen as wasteful of both employee time and customer time, with customers often having to be passed from one person to another until their problem was solved. An intranet was introduced to allow telephonists to share information pertaining to many different problem areas. The intranet used a standard web browser for finding information and this required little retraining of employees. The scheme's success was down to the user's willingness to pull information from the intranet and share it with other users.

A second example, this time of the Internet being utilised concerns the field of corporate intelligence (Vine, 1997). Now that many organisations regularly publish materials on the Internet to achieve a corporate presence, there is now a great deal of information available for the perusal of interested competitors. The Internet provides the perfect platform for this type of intelligence activity, with millions of users constantly depositing and retrieving information it is debatably the biggest database in the world, with search engines boasting in-built Artificial Intelligence information on the most obscure subjects in readily accessed. Such practices naturally raise questions of confidentiality and morality.

James (1996) argues that intranets as well as being useful in functional areas of business but that they have the potential to revolutionise business organisation. He cites the use of intranets in the process of Business Reengineering, a process involving the reorganising of business with a view to improving efficiency. Many reengineering programs failed because of the lack of organisation-wide cohesion. The introduction of organisational intranets can counter this by improving communications and processing the huge volumes of data generated in this process. Of course, as well as re-engineering intranets can be usefully deployed in other management strategies e.g. TQM

4. Potential Security Problems Engendered By The Internet/Intranets

When confidential materials are deposited on networks organisations must accept as corporate responsibility their security. There is a fine balance between allowing legitimate users access to conduct their business freely while at the same time stopping intruders. Internal threats can be inadvertent as well as malicious and include:-

- hardware threats such as theft or tampering
- Accidental deletion and theft of software, bugs and by viruses
- threats to sensitive data

Any organisation that is reliant on IS/IT, particularly in the form of networks which involve a good deal of shared data, must see to it that back-ups are routine and that disaster recovery is planned and regularly rehearsed. A system known as RAID (Redundant Array of Inexpensive Disks), whereby several small hard disks are used to store data as opposed to one large one, has been used to minimise the impact of disk failure.

Many systems have emerged to protect intranets with links to external networks, i.e. extranets, from external threat. 'Firewalls' are configurations of software and hardware that act as selective barriers monitoring use and denying access when necessary. For business on the Internet the primary method used in encryption.

It has to be emphasised that an intranet without a link to an external network is no more of a security risk than any type of corporate network. The choice of whether or not to conduct business on an intranet or an extranet (depending on how they're configured) will always be more secure; indeed the difference in scale between intranets and the Internet renders intranet security problems much more tractable.

Apropos of the Internet, its very public nature and size are cause for security concern. Several issues cause difficulties:-

- lack of ownership
- legislation cannot keep up with technological change
- human nature being what it is security will always be a problem on a public network.

What all this boils down to, is that security should be one of the first considerations of any company doing business on the Internet.

5. Summary

The Internet and intranets are widely used by business for a wide variety of applications including processes that involve communication, publishing and enterprise support. Examples from Sunderland University are the Elpro and Supplypoint systems.

Elpro (Electronic Procurement for Europe) handles electronically the whole public procurement lifecycle. European procurement legislation requires public authorities to publish tenders above a certain value so that companies in all member states can bid for the work. Elpro handles the process from the initial Invitation to Tender, and PIN notices, through to contract award. Access is provided through the system to published public procurement information such as is currently available in such formats as Tenders Electronic Daily.

The Supplypoint project addresses the need of SMEs to match skills bases and form virtual companies to big for large contracts. SMEs participating in the system require the inclusion of a range of administrative services in the available skills base. These services include project management of large construction programmes, and also accounting and legal services dealing with the formation of virtual companies and the submission of bids. Supplypoint acts as a forum for SMEs to match skills, and locate partners with whom to bid for large contracts, and also incorporate the required range of administrative services into a virtual company. Supplypoint will link to the Elpro system, so that virtual companies can submit bids directly through the European procurement process.

The reason for the applicability of these networks is largely versatility which allows a huge rage of topologies and scale-up options. Behind this versatility lies the robust TCP/IP suite. As these technologies are widely adopted related security issues have to be addressed and resolved. Security threats have been shown to be both internal and external and can be inadvertent and malicious. Given the scope of security concerns, any organisation employing these networks must make sure security is reviewed and an appropriate security policy instigated.

6. References

Anderson, C. (1997) In Search of the Perfect Market, *The Economist* 14/9/97

Comer, S (1994) *Internetworking with TCP/IP*: Prentice Hall

Dyson, P, Coleman, P and Gilbert, L (1997) *Intranets: Plan and Build an Effective Inranet*, Alameda: Sybex.

Forester T. (1989) *The Information Technology Revolution*. Oxford: Basil Blackwell

Hogbin, G. and Thomas, D.V. (1994) *Investing in Information Technology*, Maindenhead: McGraw-Hill

James, G. (1996) *Intranets Rescue Reengineering* httm://www.datamation.com/Plugin/issues/1996/dec/12bpr.html Accessed 20 February 1997

McFarlan, F.W. (1984) "Information Technology Changes The Way You Compete", *Harvard Business Review*, May - June, pp. 98-103

Netscape (1997) Intranets Redefine Corporate Information Systems.
http://home.netscape.com/comprod/at_work/white_paper/indepth.html
Accessed 15/07/97

PBTWEB (1996) Intranet Criteria.
http://www.pbtweb.com/pbtweb/intranet.htm
Accessed 15/07/97

Pollard, C.E. (1996) Electronic Meeting Systems: *Journal of Systems Management* May/June pp 22-28

Porter, M.E. (1985) "How Information Gives You Competitive Advantage", *Harvard Business Review*, July - August, pp. 149-160.

Robson, W. (1997) *Strategic Management and Information Systems* (2nd Ed.) London: Pitman Publishing

Segal,B(1996) *A Short History of Internet Protocols at CERN*
http://wwwcn.cern.ch/pdp/ns/ben/TCPHIST.html
Accessed 10 December 1997

Shamoon, D.N. Intranets Boost IS Buudgets, *Datamation*, Nov, 1996, pp 68-71.

Shepherdson, L (1997) The Mission Critical Browser.
http://www.simware.com/whitepapers/salvo/
Accessed 30/07/97

Stobart, S. (1995) *Introduction to the Internet,* Sunderland University Publication.

Vine, D (1997) ISPY : Gathering Business Intelligence. *Internet World* March

Visali S (1997) Information a la carte *Information Age* October pp 14-16

Walsham, G. (1993*) Interpreting Information Systems in Organisations*, Chichester: Wiley

Ward, A. (1996) *Intranet,* Information Age. December 1996, pp 42 -53.

12. A CASE BASE REASONING SYSTEM ON THE INTERNET FOR KNOWLEDGE SHARING / REUSING ON INFORMATION TECHNOLOGY EDUCATION

Toshio Okamoto & Masaki Nakagawa
Graduated School of Information Systems,
University of Electro-Communications
1-5-1 Chofugaoka, Chofu, Tokyo, 182-8585,
Japan,
okamoto@ai.is.uec.ac.jp

ABSTRACT

We are building a database (DB) which covers actual cases of Information Technology Education (ITE), together with a management system based on Cased Based Reasoning (CBR), accessible to the public through the Internet. Teachers can input their experience of ITE into the system, or check among past cases, similar to their present application. By using this system, teachers from any educational environment can share a common knowledge of ITE practice.

Keywords
Teacher Education, Information Technology, Internet

1. Foreword

Education in information and networking society has brought about a new type of teaching which has not enough history to refer to and apply yet. Existing cases are unknown to the public, and there seems to be no market to exchange ideas and information on such experiments, hidden as teachers' private experiences. It is required to create a place where private knowledge may be shared by a wider group of teachers through ITE for a global refining and quality improvement. Our aim with this research is to construct a Case-Based System for Information Technology taught at high schools nationwide and put it on the Internet. A great number of teachers could access it at and use this system anytime and in anyplace.

The core of the awareness/literacy is expressed by the following four pillars each aiming at the increase of actual advancement of application of ability for operating/utilizing information by computers.

(1) Judgement, Decision, Organizing and Processing of information, Creation of new Information and Raising of ability for transmitting the information.
(2) Understanding of features and structure of information society, its influence on people.
(3) Recognition of the importance of information, Responsibility for information.
(4) Rudiments of information science, Understanding of characteristics of information tools, Mastering basic techniques to handle information.

Primary, secondary and high schools have been allocated their own curriculum to achieve, according to their level of students, in terms of these rationales and goals. It is called "Cross Curriculum." However, it is noteworthy that such subject items of Informatics are taken as a "the rest of our job" and that computer study is hard to handle in math or science class and what is worse, is that "Informatics based thinking/viewpoints" and "system science based thinking/viewpoints" are not

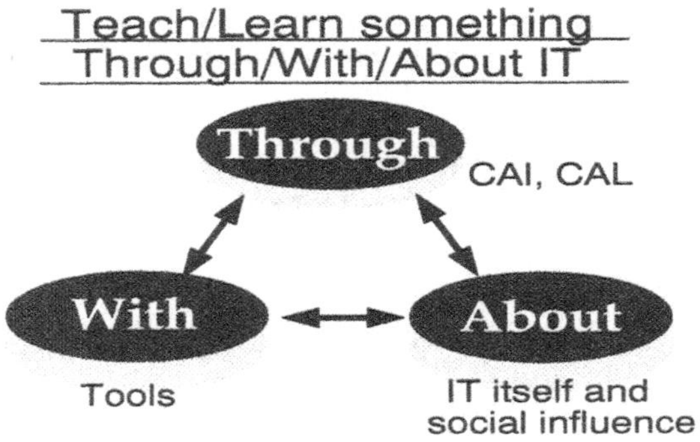

Figure 1 The integrated framework of IT-education

applied in school subjects in the course of study at school (Okamoto 1997). Of course, there are several tasks about how we treat it as either independent subject curriculum or cross curriculum. Figure 1 shows this feature. Here, "about-education" stands for teaching/learning something about information technology/science itself. "With-education" stands for utilisation of information tech-nology as tools for problem solving, communication and so on.

"Through-education" stands for teaching/learning system like CAI and CAL.

2. Study Purpose

The users of our system will be teachers who are actually contributing to ITE and others. The system enables us to build a DB for actual practices of ITE and accepts searching and registration of cases. For ITE contributors reference to past similar cases will help to improve their teaching methods. For the rest the system will offer past good and bad examples, as guiding points for their future research.

By the way, what is motivation of this study? In Japan, Ministry of Education is going to introduce the new curriculum about ITE. Especially, in high school level, we decided officially to introduce the new subject related to IT as

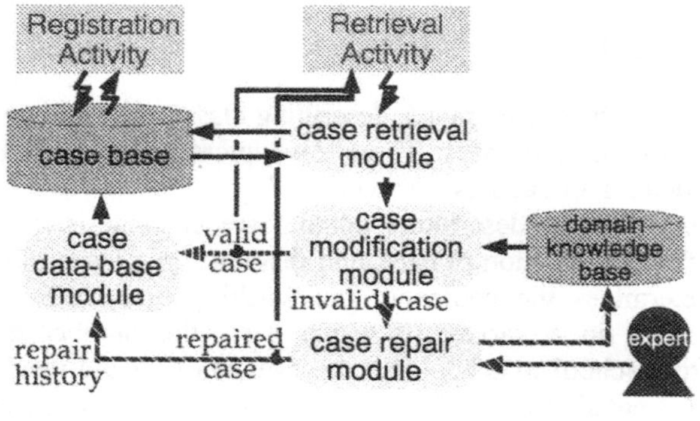

Figure 2 A typical example of CBR

independent/separate one. This subject will become compulsory. So far we have much experience about ITE in existing subjects such as math, science and music/art etc. as tools from primary school level to high school level. Pupils have learned something much for problem solving, communicating as self-expression and so on by using computers, Internet, multimedia and so on.

However, we have not accumulated teachers' teaching experience of it systematically so far. So we try to develop the case based reasoning system about teaching experience of ITE, we can share the knowledge about teaching practices, then can re-use those knowledge by putting this system in Internet environment.

3. Case-Based Reasoning

To construct the above system we use CBR theory of knowledge processing and technology. CBR consists of a set of problem solving architectures leading to a solution, while using past cases of success and failure, similar to a given problem (see Figure 2) (Matsubara 1992). An exhaustive search through the case base takes a lot of time, so CBR reduces the tracking space by applying filtering criteria directly to an index file, so our system can be implemented on middle range computers. When the result matches the problem, it becomes the solution. Still the result can be far-fetched, thus the need of adjustment using appropriate domain knowledge within the case repair module. If this solves the problem, it is added to the DB as a successful case (Kobayashi 1992) (Hammond 1990).

4. Representation of Cases and Retrieval

The Case Based System is developed using an interactive WWW interface so that teachers and common users far from each other have access to the same system. It doesn't require specific browsers, and offers search and registration service at anytime and in anyplace. Users' information is processed systematically by the CGI. Cases are kept as HTML files. For efficiency, an index file keeps profile descriptors of the cases and is used in actual searching.

4.1 Case Base (CB)

The CB has two kinds of files: CB frames describing class cases, and an index file, with specific descriptors of the cases. Three descriptors create each HTML file frame: the profile, contents and address descriptor.

Profile descriptors : Those descriptors contain the characteristic elements of actual class cases. The combination of class and thematic type leads to a variety of output data and determines the choice of the teaching procedure. In a class computers can be used in a variety of ways. Also, the number of available computers varies from school to school. So the evaluation of the results of using computers in a class is not simple. Table 1 shows the slots of profile descriptors and their possible values (range facets). When actual cases are searched, these values are referred to, and the DB contents are compared to the search tags.

Resultant achievement descriptors : Those descriptors stand for the details about the teaching method/evaluated result of each case. Table 2 shows the examples of slot and value of the resultant achievement for a case. At the end of each class session, achievement of classroom teaching is evaluated by a teacher under his reflective feeling. The points of evaluation for learning behavior are as follows: a) planing/design aspect, b) production/execution aspect, c) evaluation aspect, d) reporting/presentation aspect and so on. The points of evaluation for learners'

Table 1 Profile descriptors : Range and Facet-values

Slot Names:	Range of Facet-Values:
1) Teaching subject	Math, Science, Social study, Language, Music, Art etc
2) Learning content (topic/goal)	Simulation, Algorithm, Modeling, Communication skill, Network society etc
3) Relationship between this topic and IT education	Relativity value between teaching contents and IT (0-10)
4) Teaching time of spending this topic	X hours within the total Y hours
5) Compulsory / Selective	C or S
6) Grade	High school X grade
7) Class size	5 – 50 Pupils
8) No. of engaging teachers	1 – 3
9) Teaching style	Teacher centered – Learner centered
10) Learning form	Lecturing, Individual learning, Group learning, Exercise/Practice, Experiment/Lab. work, Discovery learning, Guided discovery, Exploring learning, Productive learning, Collaborative learning etc
11) Relative time of computer usage a class-teaching	X %
12) The kind of IT-media (hardware) used in a class	PC, VTR, Projector, Internet, Scanner, Multimedia device, CAM etc
13) The kind of software used in a class	Word-processor, Spreadsheet, Database, Drawing tool, Web-tools, CAD, CASE, Simulator etc
14) No. of using computers	0 – 50 terminals

achievement are as follows: a) cognitive aspect, b) motional aspect, c) psycho-motor aspect, d) interest/motivation aspect, e) attitude aspect and so on. Additionally, following slots are provided: list of products by learners, the degree of self-evaluation of teaching, improved points in the teaching, the degree of preparation loading of teaching. Those slots/values become a kind of solution of which users(teachers) ask this system.

Address descriptors : Those mean the environmental information of each teaching class: school name, where the teaching has been carried out, teacher's name(s), class name(s), class tag and students' grade, eventually school URL.

Slot Names:	Range of Facet-Values:
1) Teaching strategy	Fill in freely
2) Teaching tactics	Fill in freely
3) Used materials	Fill in freely
4) Evaluation stance for learning behavior	Investigation/Analysis aspect: Planing/Design aspect: Production/Execution aspect: Evaluation aspect: Reporting/Presentation aspect: The others aspect: Fill in freely for each sub-slot
5) Evaluation method / tools	Fill in freely
6) Achievement of learners	Cognitive aspect: Emotional aspect: Psycho-motor aspect: Interest/Motivation aspect: Attitude aspect: Fill in freely for each sub-slot
7) Products by learners	Enumerate pupils' products concretely
8) Self-evaluation of teaching	0 – 100 with comments
9) Improved points	Fill in freely
10) Preparation loading of teaching	0 – 100 with comments

Table 2 Resultant achievement descriptors : Range and Facet-values

4.2 Case Search

The case search module draws search patterns from the information clients have given (keywords from the key descriptor's value column and search formats). Search formats, class genre and class contents determine the values of the appropriate slot. The system searches for cases matching them in the index file, inputs these cases into a similarity function and draws as satisfactory cases as possible.

Then a user can take a more adequate case by similarity function from the case base. Some slots in profile descriptors have numerical values. Of course, a user would input the numerical value which he requires for some slots. So the system tries to compute the N-dimensional vector space distance of the corresponding slots-values between a user's asking case and every case in the case base, then the system chooses the case with the most neighboring distance computed by this similarity function.

5. Learning

The main system's training consists in the roles and functions of the case modification, the case diagnosis and the case repair modules.

5.1 Case Modification

In case searching, the most similar case, according to the user's search conditions, is gathered. The profile descriptor of the searched case and the user input search conditions are rarely in perfect concordance, so cases are tuned by the modification mechanism. During tuning, the system gives some alternative values so the user can modify the case easily (Figure 3). Our system is used as a tool for teachers so the system allows the teacher to decide the value of the modified slot.

5.2 Case Diagnosis

The case diagnosis mechanism (Figure 4) is testing the validity of the case which was modified and using the domain knowledge base of relations between the slots or the slots' value. If the result is valid, the case and the modification information (modified slots and values) are passed to the case repair module. If not, the reason of invalidity is shown to the user, and a new modify process starts. If the system has knowledge of suitable values for the slots, it shows some alternative values. By using domain knowledge, our system evades failures which generally happen in the case repair process. Users modify the searched case by changing slot values. Based on these changes the system calls the predicates and the slots which need diagnosis are determined and checked. The system creates diagnosis conditions based on the domain knowledge for each slot. If all conditions are fulfilled, the modified case is evaluated as valid, else, the system uses the CB to check these conditions and shows two information to the user: the reason why the case is invalid and alternative values for the slots which were evaluated as false.

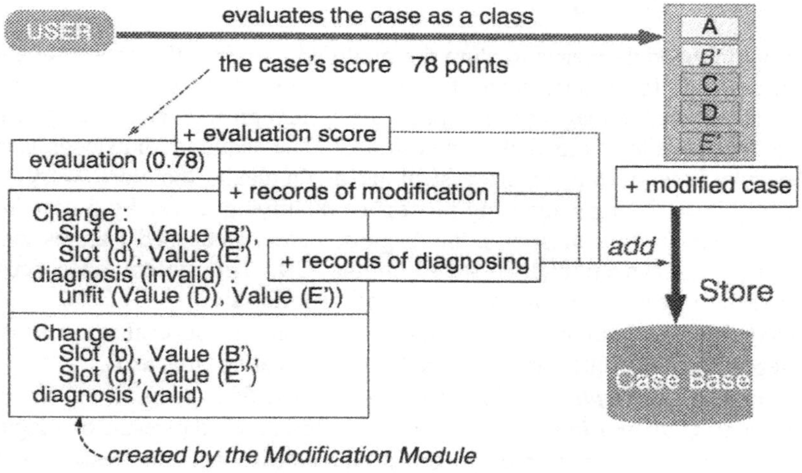

Figure 3 An example of modification

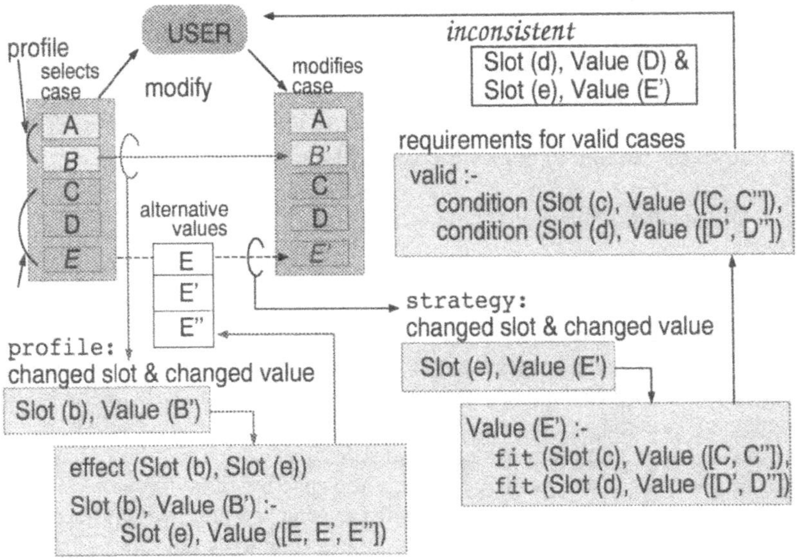

Figure 4 An example of diagnose

5.3 Case Repairing

The repairing module means to store the modified case into the case base and the system can look for a more adequate case efficiently, adding/utilizing the revised information related to diagnosed result. So the system grows incrementally with the function of so-called "knowledge acquisition." The acquired knowledge is stored in the rule base of the expert system as a simulator, therefore works more effectively in retrieving/diagnosing process of modifying a case by a user in later session. After the case diagnosis, the diagnosed case is attached features with the case repair mechanism and is stored in the CB. The system adds repairing information to a case repair information frame, as follows:

- *records of evaluation* : Two types of information: the evaluation score (an integer from 0 to 100) and the reason for the evaluation (free text).
- *records of modification* : Modified slots and modified values.
- *records of diagnosing* : Three types of information: the result of diagnosing (proper/improper), a pointer to the searched case and the reason why the modified case is invalid (only for invalid cases).

These information are used for case search, case modification and case diagnose (Fig.3, Fig.4). Suitable cases are searched in consideration of the records of evaluation (evaluation score). The user can refer to evaluation comments given by other users. If the searched case has been referred before and has an evaluation score, the system records the average of the scores to a slot which expresses the quality of the case. The system supports the user's case modification process with the records of modification and the records of diagnosing. The records of diagnosing are used to diagnose a modified case efficiently. During case search, the system looks for the case input by the user (we call this case the original case). If nothing matching is found, the system searches the modified CB, based on the original case and the case modification information frame.

6. Evaluation and Discussion

As the system requires from users to specify the desired relative value between the input case and the actual teaching subjects stored in the DB, a precise assessment is achieved. Also, as desired patterns have to appear in the teaching contents, a more flexible search than simple keyword matching is allowed.

The system has now been actually implemented, can accept case registration and provides the search function. We had some experiments at three different remote sites (Tokyo, Tottori and Naruto) to examine its reliability. At present, we have 157 cases in the system and tested around 70 searching trials. The ratio of appropriate hitting was 71 including case modification. However, we can conclude that this kind of ratio is dependent on the content quality (validity) and grain size of case explaining by a case registrar (teacher).

7. References

Okamoto T *et al.* (1997) The Practice and Current Situation of IT-Education in Primary /Secondary School Education , *J. of IPSJ*, **38**, **7**, 594-9.

Kobayashi S. (1992) Present and Future of CBR, *J. of JSAI*, **7**, **4**, 559-65.

Matsubara H. (1992) CBR as a Mechanism for Reason and Learning, *J. of JSAI*, 7,**4**,567-75.

Hammond K.J. (1990) Case-based Planning : a framework for planning from experience, *Cognitive Science*, **14**, 385-443.

8. Biography

He took his Dr. of Engineering from Tokyo Institute of Technology. Presently, He is a Professor in the Graduate School of Information Systems, University of Electro-Communications, engaging in AI, ITE, CAI research. He is a vice president of the Japanese Society of Information and System in Education and a member of the Board of the Japanese Society of Educational Technology, a.s.o. and has a lot of important official functions for promoting the field of computers and education in Japan.

13. THE KNOWLEDGE-NAVIGATION SYSTEM IN HYPERSPACE WITH NEURAL NETWORKS

Mizue Kayama & Toshio Okamoto
Graduate School of Information Systems,
University of Electro-Communications
1-5-1 Chofugaoka, Chofu, Tokyo, 182-8585,
Japan,
{kayama, okamoto}@ai.is.uec.ac.jp

ABSTRACT

We propose a mechanism for the knowledge navigation based on the sub-symbolic approach to decide the appropriate navigation strategy. A neural network (NN) was used as a navigation strategy decision module in that system. In exploring hyperspace (HS), users often tend to be in undesirable states (e.g. "get lost" a.s.o). To improve these undesirable redundancies, we have constructed a sophisticated hypermedia system which can identify the user's needs a.s.o, and give some appropriate advice to the user in his/her exploring learning process.

Keywords
Hypermedia, Artificial Intelligence, Flexible Learning, Knowledge Based

1. Introduction

Hypermedia is a tool for user-driven access to information. It provides an effective learning environment, where users can acquire knowledge by exploring the HS in his/her own way. But, often there appears the phenomenon of redundant information access. To improve these undesirable effects on users, many researches have been working to construct sophisticated hypermedia systems which can identify the user's interests, preferences and needs and give some appropriate advice to the user in his/her exploring learning process. In this paper, we propose a user model that represents exploring activities in HS and a mechanism based on a sub-symbolic approach, to decide appropriate navigation strategies. This paper also shows the training procedure of the NN and its result.

Adaptive hypermedia is a flexible system which infers the learning goal of the current learning state, by using the exploring history, the structural characteristics of the hypermedia a.s.o. As a result of its inference, this system changes its own performance to adapt to the user. The methods for adaptation are two types. One is the content-level adaptation (adaptive presentation). This method changes the contents of the node which the user will refer in next step. The other one is the link-level adaptation (adaptive navigation support). This method changes the links in the current node. The ELM-ART (Brusilovsky, 1996), which is an Intelligent tutoring system, is one of the most famous adaptive presentation systems. Its adaptation was realized based on a specific domain knowledge with a symbolic approach. So, the generality of the adaptation mechanism and the flexibility of the functional extension of this system are not high. The Adaptive HyperMan (Mathe et al., 1996) is one of the most famous adaptive navigation support systems. This system is an example of interactive adaptive hypermedia. The exploring characteristics of each user are acquired through conversation with him/her. This system is useful for a situation in which a frequent interaction between the system and the user is needed.

We have developed an adaptive educational hypermedia system based on the sub-symbolic approach. In cases of educational use, usually, as the exploring aim of students is usually fixed by a teacher in advance, frequent interactions with the system may be obstacles for the free exploring learning of a student.

2. Hyperspace Structure

2.1 *Student exploring states*

In this research, our purposes in giving guidance to the students for navigation towards their learning goal is *to support the smooth progress of the exploring study*. As a result of the observation of the exploring behavior of students and after interviewing them, undesirable cases, which are likely to happen during the learning process, are classified as follows : blind in HS, lost in HS and redundant or suboptimal references in HS. *Blind in HS* are the students who do not know how to follow the links to go to the target nodes. The target nodes are not read before. The students can not infer the relation between the current node and the target nodes. *Lost in HS* are the students who do not know the relative position of the current node and referred nodes. *Redundant or suboptimal references in HS* are taken by students who follow a longer path than necessary to go to the target nodes or to achieve their learning goals. Two types of data are needed, to distinguish between the students who are in the undesirable learning states we described above, and the

Table 1: The indicators of the exploring activities and their computation ways

1.	validity of the reference (VR)	combination value of the importance of the already read nodes and the degree of relation between referred link and current node
2.	exploring stability (ES)	variance of the reading (reference) time of all referred nodes
3.	rate of understanding (RU)	mean value of the frequency of the reference of all referred nodes
4.	rate of glanced nodes (RGN)	ratio of nodes only glanced at, to thoroughly referred nodes
5.	rate of surface understood topics (RSUT)	ratio of topics, whose number of referred nodes is less than the ideal ratio of referenced nodes, to all topics
6.	rate of favorite topic (RFT)	ratio of the nodes in the topic, which has the maximal number of referred nodes, to all referred nodes

Table 2: The knowledge navigation strategies

1.	understanding the outline schema (UOS)	content-level adaptation	displays the hypermedia structure of the current teaching material
2.	magnification of the exploring concept (MEC)	link-level adaptation	recommends a node which has a link with the highest degree of relation to the current node
3.	focusing on the exploring concept (FEC)	link-level adaptation	recommends the unread nodes in the topic which has the maximal number of referred nodes
4.	changing of the exploring concept (CEC)	link-level adaptation	recommends the unread nodes in the topic which has the minimal number of referred nodes
5.	recognition of the exploring history (REH)	content-level adaptation	displays the explored nodes in order
6.	retreat (R)	link-level adaptation	recommends a node which has the greatest number of links among already referred nodes

other students. They are physical information on the exploring activity (e.g. reference time, number of referred nodes a.s.o), and semantic information on the exploring activity (e.g. degree of importance of the referred node, degree of relation between two nodes a.s.o).

From these information, from the behavioral features of students in undesirable states and from the structural model of the HS, we defined 6 indicators which represent the exploring activities in HS (Kayama et al., 1997). The labels and meanings of each indicator are shown in Tab.1. The needs of the students who are in undesirable states are considered to determine the strategies, which will support their smooth progress during the exploring study. The structure model of the teaching material and the methods of presentation of the needed information are also considered, in order to develop the 6 knowledge navigation strategies. The labels and functional details of these strategies are shown in Tab.2. Our system makes its adaptation by using both methods, the link-level adaptation and the content-level adaptation. To the first type of adaptation belong UOS and REH, to the other type MEC, FEC and CEC. The adaptability of our system is increased by including both types of adaptation.

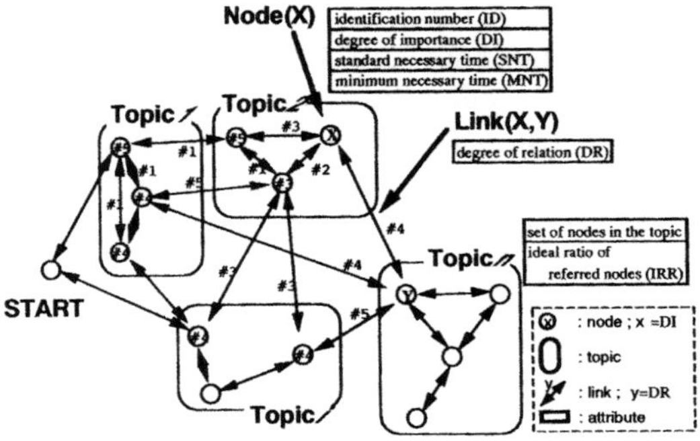

Figure 1: The partial structure model of Hyperspace

2.2 *The structure model*

Fig.1 represents the structure model of the HS. A topic has two attributes : the set of nodes which are included in it, and the ideal ratio of referred nodes (IRR). A node has four attributes: identification number (ID), degree of importance (DI), and the standard and minimum necessary time for reading (SNT, MNT). DI is defined as the degree of contribution towards the achievement of the current learning goal. Its values are integers from 0 to 5. A link has only one attribute, the degree of relation (DR) between two nodes. DR is defined as the strength of the relation between the contents of linked nodes. Its values are integers from 1 to 5. This value is used to evaluate the efficiency of referring that link between the nodes.

Our knowledge navigation system supports an educational hypermedia system with all of the attributes mentioned above. So, the teacher who wants to use our navigation system needs to arrange his/her hypermedia which is used as a teaching material. There are no limitations or rules to set concrete values for each attribute. Using those attributes of items of the HS, we describe the formulas of each of the indicators mentioned above (kayama at al. 1997).

3. System Configuration

The prototype navigation system is working and the selected theme for the teaching material is "The positioning at tennis (for doubles)". Our system has five modules and two databases and is shown in Fig.2. The system interferes only when the user wants to be guided in determining his/her next exploring activity. Our system is implemented for educational use, so we do not attempt to interfere in the students' learning. Only direct navigation requests from the students can trigger the interference of our navigation system.

Each exploring state (ID and reference time) of a student is recorded by the exploring data recording module as a piece of the history exploring database. When a student requests navigation guiding from the system, the exploring activity evaluation module develops the model of the current state of the student. This model is expressed by the six indicators which were mentioned above. The student model is handed over to the next module, the navigation strategy decision module, which contains a NN as an inference engine. Only one navigation strategy is selected by the navigation strategy decision module from the output of the NN. The definite content of the navigation guidance information is created in the definite

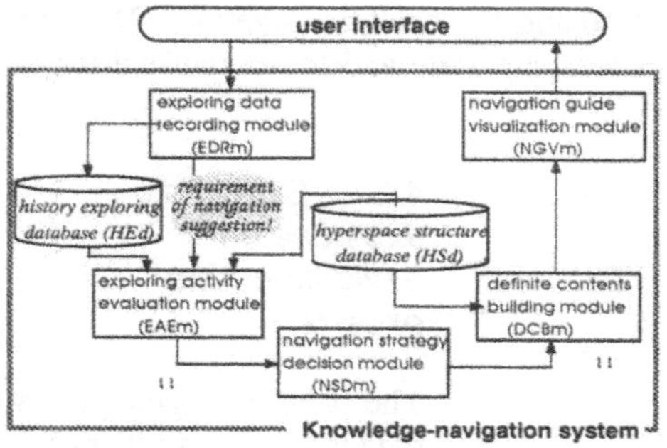

Figure 2: The structure of the navigation system

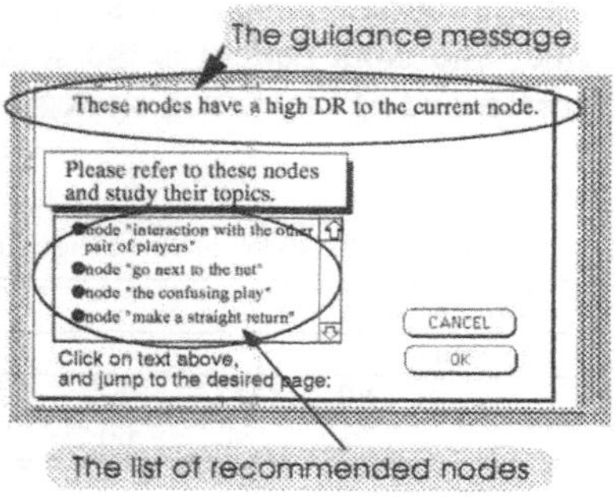

Figure 3 : An example of the navigation

contents building module by using the strategy determined by the NN engine and the knowledge of the HS attributes from the HS structure database. Then, the results of the processing are shown to the student by the navigation guide visualization module as the current navigation guidance information. Fig.3 shows an example of navigation guidance information (the guidance message and recommended nodes).

4. Navigation Strategy Decision Module

4.1 *The algorithm and input data of the neural network*

In this research, a sub-symbolic approach is taken to develop the navigation strategy decision module. To infer the appropriate navigation strategy, the expertise on knowledge navigation is learned by a supervised NN. This expertise is formed by the pair {learning state of the student; adapted strategy, which should help him/her find the right exploring path}. By using this sub-symbolic approach of inference with the NN, it is possible for the system developer to improve the flexibility and the generality of the mechanism of the navigation strategy decision processes. In the case of using a symbolic approach, like a production system for implementation of a navigation strategy decision module, expertise is represented as production rules. When the items of the condition part in those rules are changed, it is needed to re-arrange the expertise. The more the number of the exploring indicators or the values of the indicators increase, the more difficult it is to express the rules, because of the explosion of the possible combinations between exploring states, which are expressed by the exploring state indicators, and the navigation strategies. It is hard to represent the production rules which cover the whole domain world. On other hand, in case of using a sub-symbolic approach, the extraction of the expertise is equivalent to the collecting of the training data for the NN. The training phase of the NN means the arrangement of the expertise. These embedded processes make the task of experts and system developers easier. It is thought in knowledge navigation systems that the load of extracting and arranging expertise is reduced The NN which is used in our system is a supervised multi-layer feed-forward model. The engine learned pairs consisting of possible student states in exploring learning and the appropriate navigation strategies, by using the back-propagation (BP) learning rule. The input pattern is the student's learning state and the output pattern is the corresponding navigation strategy.

4.2 Extracting expertise on navigation from experts

Table 3: The extracted navigation knowledge

redundant 390						
necessary 339						
	UOS	MEC	FEC	CEC	REH	R
	9	81	60	90	18	81

The pairs of learning state and navigation strategy are prepared from the results of experiments whose subjects are experts in some educational fields. In preparation for this experiment, experts are given the explanation of the means and the ways of calculation of each exploring indicator, and the ways of navigation for each navigation strategy. Experts' understanding of the indicators and navigation strategies is confirmed by researchers. According to the questionnaire method, the sets of learning states are gathered from experts. The experts are required to answer in pairs of learning state and suitable navigation strategy. Also, the experts attach to each learning state grades for the indicators. During this process, learning states which are not needed to express a certain strategy are allowed to be included in the experts' answer. By arranging the results of this experience, all learning states are classified. The results look as in Tab.3. The learning states extracted are the ones computed by selecting the answer of the majority from the collected results. The rest of the data are classified as being "redundant" states for the navigation. Subjects are 5 teachers who all have already used the hypermedia system for their teaching. The pairs of data are teachers' expertise on navigation. This knowledge is independent of the teaching domain. The extracted knowledge is used as training patterns for the NN. The way of extracting the navigation knowledge from teachers is closely related to the navigation strategy decision module performance. The learning result of the NN determines the validity of our navigation system. The functional distinction area of the NN which is trained by supervised learning is approximately defined by the boundary lines between the sets of training data with the same output patterns. Therefore, an efficient NN training needs patterns which have an even (normal) distribution of the input data. In this experiment, 3 categories ("high", "middle" and "low") are used to represent the score of each indicator and there are 729 (= $6_{indicators}^{3\ categories}$) learning state patterns in total.

Table 4: The fine tuning parameters of the network

parameter	value
number of units in the hidden layer	16
learning rate	0.3
momentum	0.5

4.3 The neural network structure

The NN in the navigation strategy decision module has 3 layers. The input layer has 12 units. One indicator is assigned two units so that 3 categories of evaluation can be expressed. The output layer has 7 units. These represent the 6 navigation strategies and the "redundant" output. The number of the hidden layer units are determined by successive training simulations. The final number of neurons in this layer is the number which assures the highest performance. Moreover, other parameters are needed to be tuned in order to achieve a better efficiency of the NN. These NN parameters are the learning rate and the momentum. The fine tuning parameters are shown in Tab.4. All of the navigation knowledge is learned by the NN. It means that this trained NN can decide upon an unique appropriate navigation strategy for each exploring state at the rate of 100 %. When the navigation strategies are changed or the relation between the learning state and the appropriate navigation strategy is changed, the system developer has only to retrain the NN. The training of the NN has to be done before replacing the old NN engine with the new one.

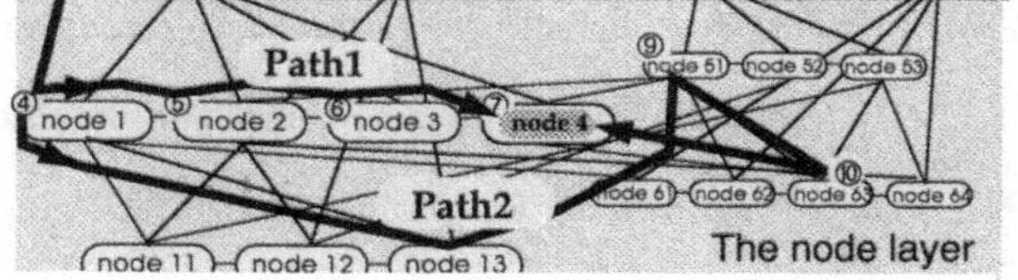

Figure 4: The structure teaching material and exploring paths of students

5. Example of the user model

An investigation was made on several real users to evaluate the appropriateness of the student model. The real users were graduate and undergraduate students who have played tennis for a few years. The students have used this navigation system to confirm their knowledge of the positioning at doubles play. To evaluate the appropriateness of the student model in our system, we have been recording data about users' exploring activities and about the navigation guidance information for 14 days. Data we recorded are as follows : the student's exploring state when he/she requests the system to give a navigation guidance, the name of the navigation strategy applied for the user, the shown navigation guidance (guidance message and recommended nodes or topics), the node IDs which are accessed in the next step and the reason for having demanded navigation guidance. 25 users have used the navigation system during this experiment. Navigation guidance was requested in total for 154 times. The mean time of learning with our system was of 37 minutes per student.

Appropriateness of the student model in the navigation system : Paths in Fig.4 show the actual paths of students' exploring. The nodes with the circled numbers express the nodes searched by the students. The students who follow Path1 are searching for the contents of a specific topic intensively. The students who follow Path2 are searching for items relevant to each node one after another. We describe the results of the evaluation of the exploring activities of our system.

Path2 (1-2-3-4-8-9-10-7) : The navigation guidance was demanded when the user could not find any more nodes related with his/her learning goal. As a result of referring the nodes which were of related contents one after another, the RSUT has become high and RFT has become low. The low value of the VR is due to the low importance of the accessed nodes. The navigation strategy which was applied to this student is the FEC. The shown navigation message was "You have referred nodes on many topics. How about learning more details on a specific topic?". The topics of the accessed nodes were recommended as a next destination to explore.

6. Conclusion

By using our approach, our navigation goal, supporting the smooth progress of the exploring study, is achieved. To realize the other purpose, encouraging students to maintain a positive attitude toward exploring learning, the students' exploring intention has to be added to the user model. As a result of the integration, we expect that the adaptability of our system will increase. This is but one of our future works.

7. References

Brusilovsky, P. (1996). ELM-ART : An intelligent tutoring system on world wide web, Proc. of ITS'96, 261 -- 1269 .

Kayama, M,. and Okamoto, T. (1997). Mechanism for knowledge-navigation in hyper-space with neural networks, SIG-IES-9702, 9 -- 16.

Mathe, N., and Chen, J. (1996). User-centered Indexing for Adaptive Information Access, User Modeling and User-adapted Interaction, 6, 6, 225-261.

8. Biography

Miss Kayama received her Master of Engineering from University of Electro-Communications. Presently, she is a doctoral course student at Prof. Okamoto's Lab. Her main research field is Artificial Intelligent and Education (Intelligent Teaching Environment with Neural Network).

Dr. Okamoto received my Dr. of Engineering from Tokyo Institute of Technology. Presently, he is a Professor in the Information System Laboratory, Univ. of Electro Communications, engaged in AI, ITE, CAI research. He is a member of the Board of CAI Society, of the Japanese Society of Educational Technology, a.s.o. and have a lot of important official functions for promoting the field of computers and education in Japan.

14. THE MANAGEMENT OF WORK FORCE IN NETWORKED ORGANIZATIONAL ENVIRONMENT

Lic.Sc. Jukka Viitanen
Turku School of Economics and Business Administration
Institute of Information Systems Science

ABSTRACT

This presentation focus on describing the management challenges of the work force in turbulent business environments, where corporations rely increasingly on interorgani-zational arrangements. The networked organizational environment has brought along novel requirements for extreme flexibility and openness in directing operations, and consequently, pose novel challenges in managing the human resource pool. These challenges are summarized into two broad categories: promoting cultural integration and ensuring continuous renewal. The integration promotion takes place in core processes for building up the shared social architecture and for realizing the coordinated cooperation. The continuous renewal, in turn, is managed through innovation and entrepreneurial empowerment processes. Based on this examination, we address the questions for the SIS role in supporting the organizational change process and in facilitating the efficient communication in cross-boundary relationships. In the final part, some recommendations are presented for the educational activities and for personnel training in organizations.

1. The Rapid Change in Competitive Environment is Posing New Pressures for Working Conditions in Organizations

This presentation is based on a commonly perceived fact that business environment is changing in ever-increasing pace. Strong forces of chance like escalating customer diversity, blurring of market boundaries, deregulation and technological discontinuities (Cravens et al. 1994; Ilinitch et al. 1996; Prahalad-Hamel 1994) are reshaping the competitive landscape worldwide. As a result most companies are not only undergoing a rapid and radical structural change, but are also experiencing a fundamental shift in the rules of competition and the way the game of competition itself is played. This change process is seen irreversible in redefining the how and where the work is done and how it is organized (Scott Morton 1995). The once clearly defined boundaries of markets and organizations are becoming more intermingled and interorganizational dependencies change gradually the overall working conditions.

This hypercompetitive pressure (Hansen-Bauer-Snow 1996; Ilinitch et al. 1996), under which competitors act boldly and aggressively to disrupt the prevailing status quo, leaves but one choice for managers to radically reshape and redirect their organizations in their ability to counter the external threats and pressures. However, while it is still necessary to maintain some structure in organizing the corporate activities and in building shared visions and values in operations, the managerial equation for managing the work force remains extremely challenging.

Volberda (1997) has stated that in developing the corporate flexibility, we can identify both managerial and organizational design tasks. The flexibility is seen as a function of both the control capacity of the management and the changeability of the organization. It is defined as follows:

Flexibility is the degree to which an organization has a variety of managerial capabilities and the speed at which they can be activated, to improve the controllability of the organization under unexpected disturbance (ibid. 1996,361).

A firm is 'under control' when for each competitive change there is a corresponding managerial capability and firm response. In stable environments flexibility is not a serious strategic option to achieve control, but in hyper-competitive environments the required high responsiveness can be achieved only through an increased flexibility.

The flexibility focus must address to different levels of management action. The *operational flexibility* consists of routine capabilities that are based on present structures or goals of the organization. These routines are used primarily in reactive manner to provide rapid response to changes that are familiar or predictable. Examples are found in variation of production volume, building up the inventories and using temporary work force and multisourcing within the supplier network.

The *structural flexibility* is addressed in creating multifunctional teams and changing managerial roles to facilitate the renewal or transformation of current organizational processes. The external focus is on efficiency and effectiveness of corporate value activities (Porter 1985; Ohmae 1985) by reconfiguring the primary activities with stake holders, and industry wide coordination of activities to maximize the flexibility of the relevant industry value system.

The *strategic flexibility* is related to the goals and competitive moves of the corporation, and must be exercised in situations where management faces unfamiliar changes in environment that have far-reaching consequences for future successful operation. The most effective means are usually some fundamental change/changes in products or processes, application of newest technologies, or creating new product market combinations for competitive control. This most radical type of flexibility is much more qualitative and involves changes in the nature of organizational activities. The creation of new activities in new situations have proved to be important, while in this way the management can commit to an ongoing process of self-renewal and continuous adaptation (Theuerkauf 1991; Hansen-Bauer-Snow 1996). In turbulent environments, this kind of foundation have high tolerance of ambiguity, which is to be promoted by encouraging employees for innovative thinking, entrepreneurship, and self-empowerment, but also maintaining a balanced base in shared values and goals.

As can be seen, the fundamentals for organizing the work force in networked environments differ noticeably from the traditional organizational settings. The requirements for changeability of the organization and flexibility in organizing the work force itself have emerged as the key factors in determining the future operational and strategic success. The organizational renewal and continuous adaptation to incremental changes in business process call for high tolerance for ambiguity and direct management to enforce employees' innovative thinking and self-empowerment. The employees, in turn, should accept both the use of temporary work force and the vague job descriptions, to secure organization's adaptability to change.

2. The Human Resource Management Challenges in Networked Organizations

The networked organizations are highly dependent on their supporting communication infrastructures, while information sharing takes place primarily in connecting physical networks. Thus, the corporate systems architecture is seen as a necessary backbone for interorganizational cooperation. However, it should be noted that this architecture is only a technical enabler in networking process and, as such, remains in a supportive role in explaining the challenges for the actual human resource management.

In networked organizations, the management's attention is focused to the human resource and relationship assets, which are the two key areas for building up the organizational capability (Ross et al. 1996; Manheim 1992). The development of human resource assets is concentrating on motivating and skilling personnel to solve business problems, and aim at developing individual competency on information access and use. The specific IS-related focus is, thus, on boosting IS-related learning and on pooling efficient human resources with SIS (Broadbent et al. 1996). The network must be managed as a combination of both human systems and technology, which evolve in dynamically changing business environments.

While the managerial challenge is to promote integration by providing a basis for shared social architecture and coordination for networked cooperation (Ching et al. 1996; Bartlett-Ghoshal 1993), the management of relationships assets focuses on developing excellence in communication. This focus is closely related to cultural questions both within the given network and in its environment. In this, the connecting infrastructure can support the required high-order stable characteristics of corporate culture, norms etc. by defining the 'degree of belonging' of each individual member through shared understanding of their relative importance and roles in any given network (Hagström 1991). The objective is to create a socially motivating and equal culture for intranetwork collaboration.

To gain collaborative advantages from this collaboration, network members ought to remember at least the following two fundamentals of alliancing and networking (Kanter 1994; Johnston-Lawrence 1988; Lei 1993):

- they cannot be "controlled" by formal systems, but require a dense web of interpersonal connections and internal infrastructures that enhance learning and information sharing, and
- the partners should develop linkages and shared ways in operations so that they can work together smoothly, finally institutionalizing the informal arrangements.

This means that each partner should engage in their shared vision and be ready to invest time and resources in their strategic alliance. They have to behave in an honorable way that justifies and enhances mutual trust, and not to be the first ones to play games at an ally's expense. However, in a network relation the players should be aware of the fact that collaboration is just competition in a different form (Hamel et al. 1989; Jarillo 1988).

The management should emphasize the importance of middle- and lower-level personnel in interfunctional and interorganizational dialogue rather than promoting a rigid top management control and guidance. In this, they should rely heavily on lateral communication instead of vertical dialogue, as well as determine network center as an architecture of communication infrastructure and shared vision, and a protector of knowledge investments in creating organizational capabilities (Hedlund 1994).

In networked organizations, the management focus tend to both narrow and broaden simultaneously. From one point of view, they encourage unbundling and outsourcing of undifferentiated value activities, and from other, expand from maximizing value for an individual corporation to maximizing value for the network as a whole (Hagel III 1996). Accordingly, the human resource management challenges can be summarized into two broad categories: promoting integration and ensuring continuous renewal[3]. The *integration promotion* takes place in core processes for building up the shared social architecture and for realizing the coordinated cooperation. The *continuous renewal*, in turn, is managed through innovation and entrepreneurial empowerment processes.

---

[3] This division is adapted broadly from Bartlett-Ghoshal (1993), Charan (1991) and Kanter (1994).

In building up the shared social architecture, managers must encourage the development of an organization-wide shared vision and personal commitment to jointly determined objectives. This notion emphasizes the need for more sophisticated coordination mechanisms, which can form a portfolio of coordinating processes that are used to cope with formal and informal role assignments as well as institutionalizing the chosen procedures and systems (Lorenzoni et al. 1995; Charan 1991).

The close inter-partner socialization can help individual members to learn, absorb, and internalize the tacit knowledge and skills possessed by their partners (Lei 1997; Culpan 1993). This process must be supported by extensive intranetwork training projects that are managed from the center. This is to promote the emergence of common concepts, terminology and cognitive maps, which it turn, facilitate the creation of commonly perceived internal culture (Jarvenpaa-Ives 1994; Hanssen-Bauer-Snow 1996). Through these commonalities the network can 'walz to the same tune', which encourage joint decision-making, vertical and horizontal planning, and the fusion of competent allies despite their organization cultural differences.

The coordination of cooperation is addressed through synergy management and solutions for communication and information sharing. The overall network structure is syncronized so that individual units work united as a team of organizations and functional synergy potential can be realized.

The synergy management includes mechanisms for identifying the network affinity groups, quantification of the synergy potential and formulation of a clear horizontal strategy for network-wide cooperation (Vitzjak 1994). The network is organized around linked processes, where multiple competencies can be combined to maximize the synergy potential and transaction value both within and across the network boundaries. The technical excellence of individual members can be linked with complementing resources and, then, transferred and leveraged broadly across the entire process (Ostroff-Smith 1992). The cultivation of complementary skills and resources are brought under one united coordination process.

The networked organizations are building their core competence especially on the organizational capabilities and flexibility in international operations (Prahalad-Doz 1989). Therefore, the management focus is on creating positive values, attitude, and behavior towards mutual information sharing, even between competing and collaborating partners. They also aim at developing individual competency related to pooled information use, and leveraging organization's knowledge with public information environment.

Networks must ensure that they maintain their flexibility and responsiveness in turbulent business environment. Consequently, the other broad management challenge is to ensure renewal through continuous innovation, while protecting the accumulated knowhow and organizational capabilities. For this purpose, the networked organizations usually rely on modular structure and changeable process capabilities. How then, the center can promote network's innovative-ness and knowledge transfer?

The management should focus their efforts on to constantly branching out of the new opportunities, to let the network members freely introduce new ideas in pursuing their business objectives (Ciborra 1996; Bartlett-Ghoshal 1993). The center can set up learning races, where partners are given a common goal with a prize for first to achieve the target. Usually this prize in the opportunity to lead off the exploitation of the invented new development, which in turn, may lead to coventuring or internal "intrapreneurship" for future financial benefits (Miles-Snow 1986). The center may act as an innovation market place, where the overall innovation process of the network takes place. In this position, it can both acquire and extend its own competencies as well as promote the network renewal.

The fourt management area is found in empowering the network for entrepreneurial activity. This is promoted by assigning an owner to each individual process and by providing participating members a chance for personal or corporate specific rewards (Ostroff-Smith 1992; Cravens et al. 1994; Jarvenpaa-Ives 1994). This empowerment is, in part, supported with all the above management activities: by creating an appropriate social infrastructure for shared responsibility, promoting investments, and providing the tools for both communication and information sharing. Thus, each member can be equipped for entrepreneurial initiatives. However, since the front line network members decide autonomously how to pursue these opportunities, the final results will emerge only out of free will and in an atmosphere of shared responsibilties. It is also argued, that the assignment process must be realized by protecting simultaneously both personal freedom and privacy.

3. Managerial Action Plan for Enhancing Networking and Improved IS-Related Training for Networked Organizations

In networked environments, communication across organizational borders is the descriptive element of all business activities. For information management (IM), this changed reality means a novel challenge to find common elements across the network as a whole. The IM focus is essentially in gathering, storing and disseminating business information to generate multidimensional knowledge valued by customers or alliancing business partners (Jarvenpaa-Ives 1994; Ghoshal et al. 1994). This knowledge should be available and accessible to any person, who comes in contact with the network, in any form, at any time and in every location. The joint dynamic operations call for flexible architectures with open access to all network information. These demanding requirements create obvious challenges for the interorganizational information management which can be summarized as follows (Jarvenpaa-Ives 1994; Teramoto-Iwasaki 1991):

- building a flexible and efficient information architecture across knowledge nodes located either in headquarters or in subsidiaries,
- creating the values, attitudes, and behaviors of mutual information sharing, even between competing and collaborating partners,
- building applications and databases around network relationships approach
- creating understanding for the mobile and culturally diverse workplace,

- developing individual competency related to transnational information use,
- leveraging and interfacing with public information environment, and
- protecting simultaneously personal freedom and privacy.

As can be seen, these information management challenges combine both organizational and technical IS management within the same frame. It emphasizes the needs for integration and coordination on the global scale especially in human resource and alliancing relationships fields. The technical element, in turn, is seen as an enabler for this interaction.

Several trends in IS/IT industries have supported the emergence of networking. The rapid advancement of the information technology itself, the rise of network computing, and the growth of IS service segments have proved to be providing an alternative to the traditional transaction processing solutions inside and between organizations (Markus 1996). However, the technology development must be balanced with organizational processes to guarantee a possible realization of the IS/IT-related benefits. These notions determine the main challenge for managers in IM function; to create a cohesive organizational climate for future application and architecture development.

In terms of ***integration promotion*** the education and development challenge in IS field is in finding the "right tune" for the formerly separated domains of business and information function. We need to consider the underlying elements of internal network relationships and organizational culture. A technological infrastructure and solutions can be used to connect people and information, but only those organizational settings that favor change sensitive operational logic can adapt flexibly and efficiently to the challenge of turbulent environment. It has also been argued that cultural fit or similarities among participants generally favor the cooperative arrangements (see Ward-Peppard 1996).

In an intraorganizational level the business-IS organizational relationship has always been a troublesome, while the two domains differ remarkably from each other with respect to their cultural basis. This so-called cultural gap is often seen as the main variable to explain the troubled relationship between the IS organization and the rest of the organization (Grindley 1992; Ward-Peppard 1996). In practice, the gap can be seen in difficulties to trust, understand and appreciate the other side.

Information system professionals believe that businessmen are not aware of the opportunities IT offers, that there is no personal gain in understanding business better, and that users cannot be responsible for any part of the IS-related development. Similarly, businessmen feel that IS organization is hardly ever contributing to business performance and success, that technical solutions have rarely any practical use, and that IS-related costs often exceed the achieved benefits. (Ward-Peppard 1996; Neo 1988) Accordingly, management is challenged to create appropriate mechanisms for organization-wide *value management*.

The value management is a mechanism aimed at promoting integration and lowering the communication threshold. Moreover, it helps creating a common language between the integrated parties, thus, fostering the development of shared understanding and trust (Applegate 1994; Hagström 1991). In practice, the senior management may try to bridge the gap through promoting reciprocal education programs and by rotating representatives into rival camps, so that gradually both domains gain knowledge of each other. Similarly, they must communicate their support to these projects, and provide examples of the IT possibilities. The successfulness of these mechanisms depend on combining the management of both 'harder' [structures, systems and processes] and 'softer' [symbols, rituals, routines and metaphors] cultural elements into one shared web (Johnson 1992; Land 1992).

The *technological development*, in turn, focus on creating an open-access interorganizational systems (IOS), where everybody has the freedom to use all information within the network. The network center organizes and manages this infrastructure and builds applications and databases around the shared network relationship approach. The used IOS remain flexible and open in their interfaces across organizational border and, thus, the pressures for change can be adapted in accordance to the external progress and business development.

The IS-education agenda must be extended to cover the newest application development software and internet technologies, so that the IS personnel will gradually learn to master the modern solutions' environment. The on-going training programs support the continuous adaptation process to networking challenge as well as to the interorganizational architecture development (in telecommunications, applications and hardware fields).

The other side in human resource management agenda, *continuous renewal* challenge, calls for *individual skill development* and creating the foundation for organizational learning. This decision-making area deals with creating the required human skills and capability for supporting and shaping the business strategy and the final strategic alignment (Venkatraman et al. 1993; Ross et al. 1996). First, the desired skills and capabilities have to be defined to focus resources on the most promising and critical areas for complementing available or potential IS infrastructure and processes. Second, the efforts should be concentrated on capability development within that defined frame, and finally the mechanisms for continuous adaptation are created (e.g. cross-border transfer of applied technologies).

In this way, the *human resources* are connected to the overall organizational transformation and aligned to the continuos renewal challenge of all networked organizations. When each individual will master the required literacy and tools of both business and IS-domain development, the adaptation takes place more efficiently. Moreover, the individual capabilities play an important role in supporting the aforementioned organizational learning. The common concepts and shared values facilitate a transfer of tacit knowledge across organizational boundaries, and the knowledge and know-how of modern solutions leverage the whole network with other networks.

The *learning races* and *game playing* are common tools in helping organizations to find unique operational solutions for novel situations. The network center may act as an innovation market place, where the overall innovation process of the whole network takes place. The races and games help network members to rise above their routine tasks and observe the turbulent environment as a scene of opportunities, not as a minefield of threats. The game playing opens up new horizons for future operations, and can be used as an educational tool in network development.

4. Conclusions

The networked organizations operate under the pressures and influence of reciprocal interdependence, because they have to adjust their actions to many interacting positions and participants. The IS should support collaborative work, which is much less structured than intraorganizational processes and operations. Therefore, networking parties should actively try to discover elements of deep structures in the interaction situation and incorporate this structure to their evolving use of the information systems.

To manage this change, it should ensure that the organizational climate is right and set up for the upcoming challenges. All the stakeholder groups are to be included to the change process and a more democratic and participative culture should replace the traditional command-control structures. In this way, the ownership of the process itself can be spread throughout the network as well as across the business functions.

In conclusion, we argue that the human resource management agenda in networked organizations has two specific areas of concern. The management should 1) coach the network for creating shared understanding and trust, and 2) train members of organization for working in ambiguous settings. However, this work cannot be done alone in a management level with top-down approach, but should include all levels of organization and all stakeholder groups across the interconnected network. In this way, the collaborating parties may create shared vision of the future, and direct the internal training to the most promising fields.

5. Biography

Mr. Jukka Viitanen is an assistant professor of the Turku School of Economics and Business Administration. He received his Ph.D. in August 1998 from the Institute of Information Systems Science with a topic of Information Management Strategies in the Global Network Organizations. At the moment, he is serving as a director of the Finnish Institute in Japan, in Tokyo, and engage in researching further Japanese business systems and IS utilization.

15. SEVEN YEARS EXPERIENCE AND ANALYSIS ON CORPORATED-WIDE DISTANCE LEARNING FOR ENGINEERS USING SATELLITE COMMUNICATIONS

Kouji Yoshida, Asako Nishio, Hiroshi Hisha, Harumasa Tohda,Tadashi Odaka and Masahiro Kasuga
Institute of Technology,
Mitsubishi Electric Corporation
2-1, Akashia-dai 2-chome,
Sanda-shi, 669-1323 JAPAN
Fax: 81-4-6741-2649
Email:yoshidak@hit.isl.melco.co.jp, asako,hisha,tohda,odaka(@iot.melco.co.jp),kasuga@gad.saib.melco.co.jp

ABSTRACT

At Mitsubishi Electric Corporation, a corporate-wide educational system using satellite communications has been rapidly rein forced since 1990, to meet a wide range of various technical demands to its nation-wide entities including the affiliated ones. It mainly provides 'knowledge-based' courses, in parallel to the 'discussion-based' mid-level and/or advanced ones, long provided at three education centers since 1983. Over the last seven years, in the number of participants the satellite communications system achieved remarkable increase with minimum per-recipient cost.

A series of questionnaires made on the participants shows that, education through effective use of satellite communications is as effective as a center-based one. It has also revealed several distinctive features of the education using satellite communications, i.e. the importance of well-organized and suitable textbooks, and tailored lecturing materials provided by means of visual images such as in-house videos.

In recent years, the system has further adopted bidirectional communications by effectively implementing the fiber-optic corporate VAN. In order to satisfy the day-to-day educational needs in various engineering fields, which include information technology, the company has added providing the intranet and mailing list services.

Keywords
Distance learning, Internet, Networks, Satellites

1. Introduction

The objective of Mitsubishi Electric Corporation is "to contribute to society with excellent technology and creativity." , and to realize this commitment through manufacturing advanced products. Thus, in corporate-wide training and education of engineers , a continual stimuli and integrated efforts are essential. The Institute of Technology has been established in 1990 in order to fulfil such needs.

Mitsubishi Electric's educational system has evolved over several decades and it includes practical and comprehensive in-depth Corporate Engineering Seminars. [1, 2] With the rapid increase in the number of young engineers at our facrories. Research laboratories and branches spread across the nation, the education system using satellite communications with minimum per-recipient cost was the center of its interest in the late 1980s. The distance learning is currently one of the most effective means to provide the engineering knowledge and information in time of needs. [3]

This report describes the overall system using satellite communications and its recent development. It briefly summarizes the results of comparative analysis of the questionnaires given to all the particpants over a period of each year, covering both the seminars using satellite communications, and those using the three education centers. [4] There is an emphasis on the importance of the practical in-depth education in computer-aided engineering (CAE) which is effectively linked by a computer network covering the Institute, research laboratories and the factories. [5] It also establishes a human network, which enables continued comunication between participants and helps mutual upgrading. This can be realized by the latest addition of various services, such as bulletin board and e-mail, through the intranet and mailing list services set up.

2. Outline Of The Education System Using Satellite Communications[3]

2.1 Overall Views and Equipment

There are two satellite communications channels for education. They effectively support digital TV, or moving picture, specific to the aim and purpose of various courses. A still picture, i.e. snapshot from the moving picture, is also provided to help the student's comprehension. Corporate VAN is efficiently used for bidirectional communications between lecturer(s) and students. The students can ask questions by audio, and also answer quizes or questionnaires by selecting the right numbers on their desktop. Furthermore, selected pictures of a receiving room are sent to the studio by the continually upgraded corporate VAN (called MIND) to assist the lecturer.

Since late 1994, the system started linking all the factories, research laboratories and branch offices, and now in 1997, there are 55 receiving sites. Lecturers can select the nearest studio either in the west or in the east of Japan. A typical lecturing scenes is shown in Figure 1.

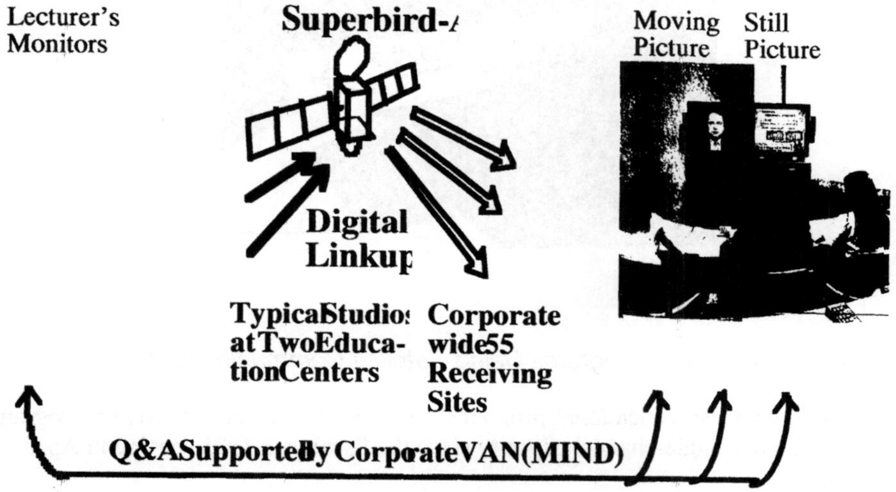

Figure 1. Utilization of satellite communications system with fiber-optic corporate

2.2 *Educational Programs Using Satellite Communications*

The following two educational programs, i.e. work-hours and after-hours program, fully occupied single-channel capacity since the fiscal year 1995 starting in April.

2.2.1 Work-hours Program There are three categories in the work-hours program (figures in 1997):

- 70 basic engineering courses with specialities such as in software engineering,
- 10 introductory engineering courses without specialities,
- 26 engineering-oriented business seminars called MBS'es, e.g. an accounting course, and a proprietary course. Each MBS usually covers a single topic.

The former two courses belong to the Corporate Engineering Seminars.

A basic engineering course consists of five topics, in contrast to an introductory one with two to three topics. According to the students' requirement, the student can attend course; by a unit of one topic, which increases the chance to study. Each topic takes three hours of the day.

Table 1. Typical curriculums of the Seminars using satellite communications (e.g. four couses).

	Mon	Tue	Wed	Thu	Fri
Morning Session (9:15-12:00)	***Java1***	***Java2***	**Inter-net1**	**Inter-net2**	**Inter-net3**
Afternoon Session (13:15-16:15)	***ISO 14001 1***	***ISO 14001 2***	***ISO 14001 3***	*CALS 1*	*CALS 2*

A typical course schedule is shown in Table 1. Lecturers give a short examination on each topic, and the results of those examinations are stored in a database to be used for later personnel development.

2.2.2 After-hours Program At present, twelve new or most popular topics are monthly selected to promote engineers' self-development. Lectures start at 5:30 p.m. on Tuesdays, Wednesdays and Thursdays. Some distinguished guest speakers are twice honored. New topics are constantly added to cover latest development, such as, in mobile communications, proprietary rights in multimedia era, and global warming.

2.2.3 Typical Work-day Schedule and Overall Volume

As stated before, a single-channel capacity is fully occupied. The time schedule and overall volume of engineer education for the fisical year'97 are summarized in Figure 2.

(A good portion of seminars are specific to certain types of computers, thus held separately for system engineers and customers.)

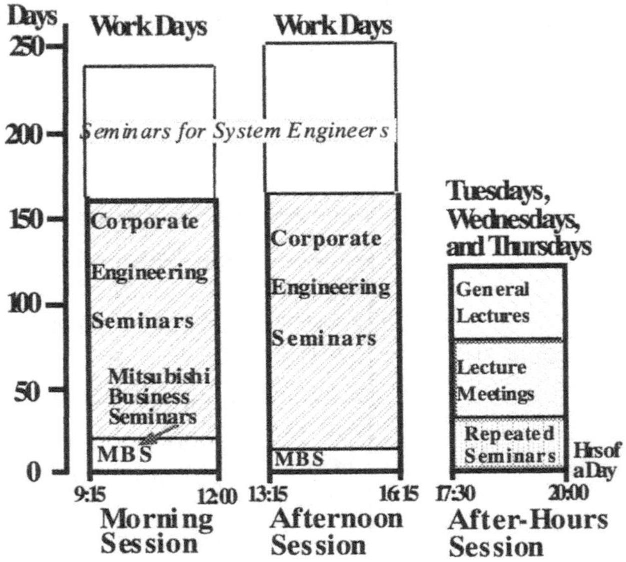

Figure 2. Time schedule and overall volume of the engineer education using satellite communications.

2.3 *Latest Development and Some Results Achieved*

Thus, by carefully selecting suitable topics and using the satellite communications for visual images, such as in-house videos, real models, photos and illustrations, the next two points have been found:

1. The number of attendees or person-courses to the Corporate Engineering Seminars has rapidly increased.

In the fiscal year 1996, the total number to the work-hours courses using the system has increased to about 5,800 person-courses, as this is shown in shadow in Figure 3. On the other hand, the after-hours program achieved 6,500 attendees (not shown in Figure 3). With reference to the number of engineers over some 20,000, about 60% of the engineers receive the benefits of the education using satellite communications in each year. It can be also said that 25% to 35% of the Corporate Engineering Seminars are directly related to information and/or network technology, i.e. proportional to corporate's product share.

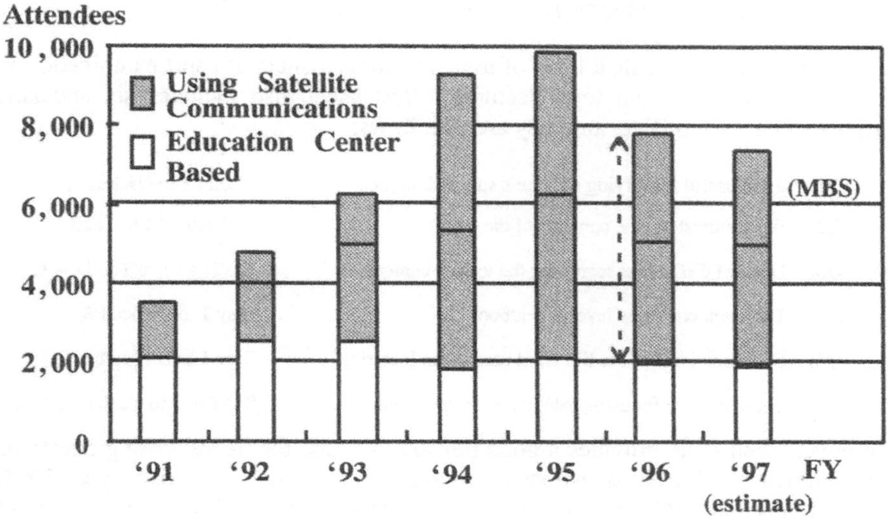

Figure 3. Number of participants of the corporate engineering seminars and engineering-oriented business seminars (MBS)

2. The cost and time spent on travelling to education centers have been reduced and minimized.

It should be noted that there are now participants having access to these education seminars while before they were physically unable to attend due to the distance to education centers.

3. Analysis Of The Education System Using Satellite Communications [4]

A series of questionnaires has been given to the participnants from the start of Corporate Engineering Seminars. A year of records have then been put into comparative analysis and it has revealed the effects of education through a satellite communication in comparison to a center based ones. The reasults are summarised below.

3.1 Standard Questionnaires Used and Analyzed

In order to mainly evaluate a level of understanding, a sheet of short examination is given at the end of each topic lectured. The sheet also includes six standard questions in a scale of five, and they are as follows:

Q1:	How useful in carrying out one's succeeding job	Useful **1** to Useless **5**,
Q2:	Well understood the contents of the topic	Understood **1** to Least **5**,
Q3:	Level of difficulties regarding the topic's contents	Too High **1** to Too Low **5**,
Q4:	Thorough cognition level of textbook	Easy **1** to Difficult **5**,
Q5:	Cognition level of the flip chart used when lecturing	Easy **1** to Difficult **5**, and
Q6:	Topic suitable for using satellite communications	Suitable **1** to Center-based **5**.

Moreover, each sheet provides a good portion of space for freely writing questions and comments. All these questionnaires have well accumulated in fiscal year 1994, to 48 courses or 162 topics, to 12,780 person. In parallel to very similar questionnaires covering the education center-based 90 courses or 1,665 person-courses, a comparative study was carried out upon all the data obtained by above, according to a standard statistical procedure.

3.2 Questionnaires Analysis and Some Distinctive Features Obtained

In order to understand the result easier, the mean of the person-topics sum of each topic is normalized so that the maximum scale-point of each topic calculated becomes a degree of a hundred. Therefore, in case of **Q2** on the degree of understanding, the histogram of the topic frequency is shown in Figure 4.

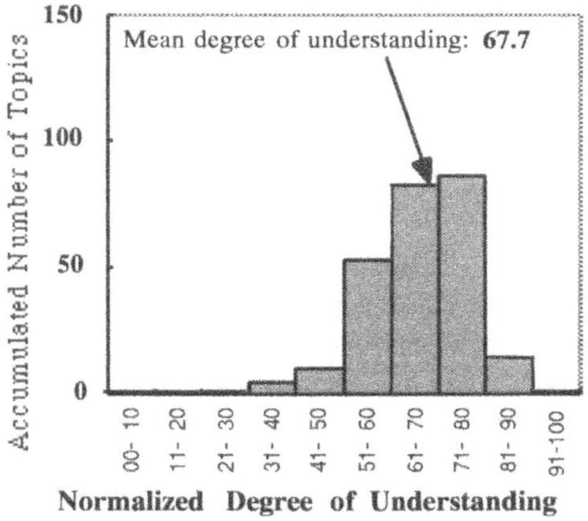

Figure 4. Histogram of 12,780 topics classified around normalized degree of understanding.

It is clear that the best understanding is less at the class of 91 to 100 degree. The mean degree of understanding appears around 67.7. A similar figure is found for the center-based education at around 68.6, which shows that by effectively using the satellite communications, the education is as effective as the center-based one.

Apart from most of the similarities obtained under the comparative study throughout, some distinctive features are also found useful when all the correlation diagrams of which are compared among the six questions **Q1** to **Q6**, two are shown in Figure 5. In case for the textbook evaluation in Figure 5a, relatively strong correlationship exists between the textbook and the degree of understanding (correlation coefficient 0.78). This is less in case of center-based seminars (correlation coefficient 0.24, not shown), although specific textbooks are commonly prepared beforehand as a form of bound lecture notes in four weeks in advance of prior study and preparation for the short examinations given. Similarly, well prepared flip chart is effective on understanding, as this can be seen in Figure 5b. It

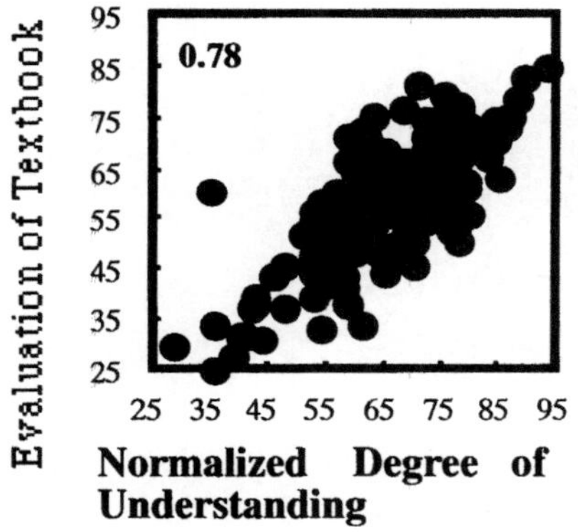

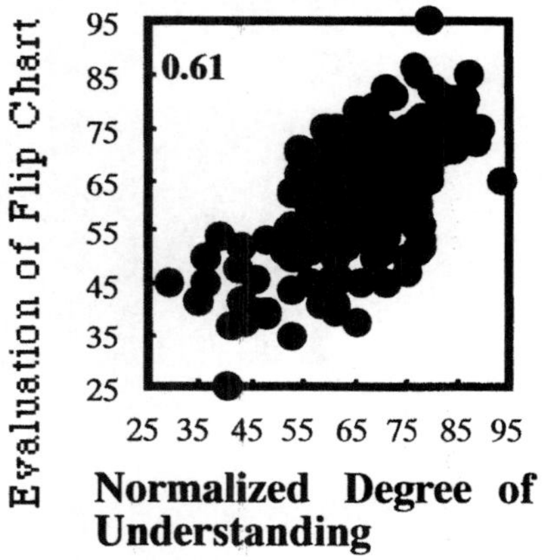

Figure 5. Correlation diagrams for the evaluation of textbook(a) and flip(b) chart with reference to the normalized degree of understanding covering 12,780 topics.

has by now revealed that, owing to the distinctive features of the distance education using satellite communications or alike, the lecturers are strongly advised to prepare well-organized and best-fit textbooks, and tailored lecturing materials provided by means of visual images such as in-house videos, real models, photos and illustrations.

Figure 6. Lecturing scenes with visual images supported by a production team.

To assist lecturers coming to participate from elsewhere within the corporation, a production team is steadily reinforced to create lecturing materials required. Some lecturing scenes are depicted in Figure 6. For example, site location is relatively convenient and strongly effective by showing real things going. With the advent of powerful but low cost personal computers, direct presentation and analytical modeling are getting wide popularity these days. Group lecturing is useful to cover common topics with wider point of views.

Finally, questions and comments are also carefully classified with reference to most to least understood topics. The following features have been found effective by many attendees.

- Practical examples shown by way of videos, and directly from personal computers,
- Before going into the specific details, overall guidance of the relevant topic is given,
- Wordings are properly given before actually used for the profession,
- Story construction is straightforward, and interesting throughout the lecturing, and

- Image information is well knitted and plentiful, but not excessive to follow after.

4. Distance Learning Using Satellite Communications and Various Media Including The Intranet And Mailing List

Since 1983, corporate-wide engineering seminars and workshops have been organized and continually upgraded to cover basic to advanced engineering fields. Satellite communications have been implemented since 1990, to cover nation-wide attendees with minimal per cost, and also to provide basic courses required common to those engineers new to or fresh in the technology. In-house videos and computer desktops are used to describe the basic concept and functions of various products, manufacturing process, evaluation strategy, regulations required, etc. Each of the two studios covers all the current 55 receiving sites including all the office branches.

More advanced and up-to-date courses are annually revised to fit in inter-works requirements, and to exchange the design experiences in the product fields mutually related. Intensive three to five day seminars and workshops are set up based on three education centers to accomplish problem solving tasks of individuals.

A human communications network also provides an important contribution to upgrade those course attendees by means of the e-mail and bulletin board which enable the required consultation on demand among all the participants. With the popularity of the Internet and sufficient proliferation of e-mail especially since 1995, some additional services are rapidly provided to augment the bidirectional features especially found indispensable for distance learning. Staff members of the Institute and people in the network and information technology lead the following activities to service:

- **Intranet server** provides the schedule and brief contents of all the seminars.
- In addition to printed guidebook electronic forms are made available with ease.
- E-mail server accepts **mailing list services** based on the tasks and/or technical fields, thus most of pre-course information is given, and relevant questions followed after.
- Some network related courses provide corresponding **home pages** which enable the attendees ask questions by e-mail and obtain course materials used by the lecturers.

Figure 7. Part of the home page of the Institute of Technology

6. Conclusion

Mitsubishi Electric Corporation, established in 1921 as an electrical machinery manufacturer, has grown to a general electric and electronics manufacturer, expanded a range of products toward systems, and considerably improved its efficiency of the production. Its unique engineer education system has been developed according to the corporate culture, an indispensable role company wide. It is considered that the advancement in the "knowledge creation" is a key factor to continue attaining the prosperity, and to realize a lively society toward the next century.

By using satellite as a main means to provide education to engineers over distance, it has made such education efficient and effective. It has achieved increase in the quantity of education provided at low cost. Additional efforts in the 'visual information' or 'bidirectional communications', provision of well-constructed and suitable textbooks can increase the quality of such educational efficiency.

Education using satellite communications enables simultaneous feeding of the knowledge and information required, but also enhancing the fundamental corporate culture for human resource development. Over seven years, our institute has been active to advance the practicality and effectiveness in engineer education. It stimulates the active learning environments among the engineers. In cooperation with the center-based courses and lately attempting the intranet, "spontaneous education provided upon demand" can be fulfilled by using satellite communications with comprehension.

7. References

1. Gamo, Y., Hisha, H., Yamada, I., and Ohara, Y., **"Continuing Engineering Education System in Mitsubishi Electric Corporation."** In *Proceedings of 5th World Conference on Continuing Engineering Education* (WCCEE), June 2-5 1992, Espoo, Finland. pp. 739-744.
2. Shimada, W., and Hisha, H.: **"Continuing Engineer Education in Mitsubishi Electric Corporation Implementing the 'Active Learning' Strategy Best Fit for the Individuals."** In *Congress Proceedings of World Congress of Engineering Educators and Industry Leaders,* UNESCO '96, July 2-5 1996, UNESCO, Paris, France. Volume II, pp. 35-40
3. Nishio, A., Sakai, K., Koga, K., Shimada, W., and Hisha, H., **"Corporate-Wide Distance Education for Engineers Using Satellite Communications in Mitsubishi Electric Corporation."** In *Proceedings of 2nd Mid-Term AEESEAP International Conference on Engineering Education,* April 23-26, 1996, Makuhari, Chiba, Japan. Paper T6-5 (4p.)
4. Kasuga, M., Nishio, A., Tohda, H., and Odaka, T., **"Analysis of Attendees' Evaluations on Each Type of Education: Education Using Satellite Communications and Center Based Education at Mitsubishi Electric Corporation."** *Journal of Japanese Society for Engineering Education* (JSEE), Vol. 45, No. 3, May 1997. pp. 41-45 Japanese

5. Yoshinaga, K., Hisha, H., and Sakabe, S.: **"Power Engineering Education Utilizing Satellite Communications and Computer Networks."** In *Proceedings of International Conference on Energy Management and Power Delivery* (EMPD) '95, November 21-23, 1995, Singapore. IEEE, 1995 pp. 485-491

8. Biography

Kouji Yoshida recieved the B.Sc.(1972) from Okayama Univ., Japan. He then went on to be a Computer Scientist in the Information Engineerig Works at Mitsubishi Electric Corp, Kamakura Japan. He took part in the development of CAD or CG on the large-sized computer. He is currently a Research and education Scientist in the Institute of Technology. His major research includes Internet/Intranet, distance learning and information gathering on the Internet. He is one of the members of IPSJ, IEICE Japan.

Asako Nishio received B.A.(1991) from Kyoto Univ., Japan, in psychology. since then, she has been engaged in the education of corporate engineers using satellite communications at Mitsubishi Electric's Institute of Technology.

Hiroshi Hisha received B.Sc. (1973) from Hiroshima Univ., Japan, M.Sc. (1975) from UMIST, England, and Ph.D. (1983) from Univ. of Canterbury, NZ, in power systems engineering. He then joined Mitsubishi Electric's Itami Works, to pursue diagnosis application of microelectronics to gas-insulated switchgears. His main interests include the career development of corporate engineers through the Institute of Technology. Members of IPSJ, IEICE Japan and IEEJ.

Harumasa TOHDA received B.Eng.(1974) from Univ. of Tokyo, Japan, inMechanical engineering. He then joined Mitsubishi Electric's Central R&D Lab., to the pursue developpment of practical structural analysis methods to turbo-generators and large ntennas. His main interests include the education of corporate engineers through the Institute of Technology. A member of the Japan Society of Mechanical Engineers.

Tadashi ODAKA received B.Eng.(1966) from Osaka Univ., Japan, in electric engineering, and M.Sc.(1969) in physics from Kobe Univ., Japan, . In 1971, after two years research work in Kobe Univ., he joined Mitsubishi Electric's Central R&D Lab., to pursue materials characterization using electron beams. His main interests include education of the corporate engineers through the Institute of Technology. A member of the Japan Society of Applied Physics.

Masahiro KASUGA received B.Sc.(1992) from Waseda Univ., Tokyo, Japan, in ergonomics. He then joined Mitsubishi Electric's Institute of Technology, to pursue multimedia-based practices in engineering education. His main interests include multimedia service systems and new business development currentl at the Kansai Branch Office.

16. MANAGEMENT SYSTEM FOR TELECOMMUNICATIONS ENGINEER TRAINING

Yasuo Minai
Masayuki Yamauchi
Human Resource Development Center,
Telecommunications Division, Hitachi, Ltd.
216 Totsuka-cho, Totsuka-ku,
Yokohama 244-8567, Japan
e-mail: yasuo_minai@cm.tcd.hitachi.co.jp
masayuki_yamauchi@cm.tcd.hitachi.co.jp

Tsurayuki Kado
Information Systems Group, Hitachi, Ltd.
6-27-18 Minami-Oi, Shinagawa-ku,
Tokyo 140-8572, Japan
e-mail: t-kado@comp.hitachi.co.jp

ABSTRACT

This paper introduces an example of engineer training conducted in a factory where telecommunication systems and related products are developed and manufactured. About 1,400 engineers are being trained. There are seven specialty categories according to the types of duties of the engineers. Guidelines are prepared for these engineering specialty categories to promote well-planned training of engineers. The guidelines are posted on the factory's intranet to invite trainees and to accept their applications.

The training management system stores the individual engineer's training history and future plans in a database based on the trainee's program. A person in charge is assigned to each engineering category to systematically establish new training courses, close obsolete courses, integrate courses, or improve a course's curriculum.

Keywords

Educational management, database, Internet, learning systems, special needs

1. Introduction

The field of telecommunications is in the midst of a great revolution and competition on a global scale due to the rapid development of digitization, as well as borderless and inter-industry competition. It has become more important than ever to provide engineers with training in the basics as well as in the latest technology in the industry to develop, manufacture and sell telecommunications products that satisfy the market needs[1].

This paper introduces the management system for the engineering personnel working in Hitachi's telecommunications factory.

2. Types of Engineers and Training Subjects

The factory the authors are associated with develops and manufactures telecommunications products including central office switching systems and transmission equipment for common carriers, PBXs, multiplexers, and communication terminals for composing corporate networks. Table 1 lists the engineers working in the factory categorized by specialties. Approximately 1,400 of those engineers are taking training.

Customer system engineers (SEs) include the pre-system engineer who proposes a system to meet the customer's requirements that are identified through reviews with the customer, and the post-system engineer who develops and designs the system and its equipment [components]. The actual equipment design engineering requires a hardware design engineer who designs the circuit hardware, a device and packaging engineer who performs physical design engineering, and a software design engineer. A production engineer is needed to put a design into a product. Finally, the quality assurance (QA) engineer is also required to inspect the products and assure their quality in order to place highly reliable products on the market.

The engineer training concerns of the factory are summarized as follows:

1. A single-purpose training course cannot attain all desired results, since the specialties required for individual engineers vary widely.
2. The engineering ability of engineers in the same specialty varies with their experience.
3. It is essential to be able to dynamically cancel old training subjects and establish new training subjects to keep the training courses up-to-date.

Table 1 Engineer Specialties

	Specialty	*Description*
(1)	Customer SE	Pre-SE
(2)	System	Post-SE and equipment design and development
(3)	Hardware	Hardware and circuit design
(4)	Device and packaging	Packaging and construction design
(5)	Software	Software design
(6)	Production engineering	Production engineering
(7)	QA	Inspection and quality assurance

3. Overview of Engineer Training

3.1 Engineer Training Courses and Guideline

Table 2 lists a summary by technical specialties of the engineer training courses the factory currently provides. Course category "A - Common" means a training subject to provide every engineer with basic knowledge and technology indispensable for developing and manufacturing products in the factory. The training subjects also include six other categories, namely, "C - Electronic Circuits," "D - Control and Signal Processing," "E - System Engineering," "H - Telecommunications," "J - Packaging and Construction," and "S - Software."

An experienced engineer at the department manager level is selected as training supervisor. The supervisor and staff establish (or cancel) training course subjects periodically and systematically as detailed in Section 3.3 below.

There are currently sixty mandatory courses, and elective subjects. A course lasts twelve hours on average, although it varies with the subject. A course coordinator is selected for each course. That coordinator determines the details as well as finding the lecturer of the course. That coordinator also decides pass or failure criteria based on attendance and test results. The course coordinator is selected from the experienced engineers in the factory, and the lecturer is usually an engineer also from the factory.

Table 2 Technical Training Course Categories

Category	*Engineering specialty*	*Course*	*Responsible person*
A	Common	Factory rules, cost and VEC, ISO9000/14000, quality/reliability, intellectual property, production processes	X1
C	Electronic circuits	Basics of electronic circuits, analog circuits, logic circuits, LSI design, power supply technology	X2
D	Control and signal processing	Computer architecture, signal processing, voice signal processing, image signal processing	X3
E	SE	System proposal preparation, telecommunication systems, cellular systems	X4
H	Telecommunications	Communication protocols, network configuration and administration, radio communication technology, broadband ISDN, digital transmission, LAN and computer network, RAS design engineering	X5
J	Packaging and construction	Printed circuit board installation, packaging, device evaluation	X6
S	Software	Database, firmware, real-time OS, programming, communication software, software development environment.	X7

As described in Chapter 2, the trainees vary in their specialties and technical levels. Guidelines help trainees select courses based on their technical level. Table 3 lists an example of the courses. The starting class is for technical personnel with one or two year's experience after graduating from college or university; the middle class for experience of three to five years; and the upper class for experience of six or more years. Ai, Ci, Di, ... (i = 1 - n) stand for the courses listed in Table 2, for which different guidelines are provided for each specialty. The time period is set at approximately 80 hours for the starting class, 120 hours for the middle class, and 50 hours for the upper class, approximately 250 hours in total.

The trainees select their own specialty from those listed in Table 1 based on their duties, and register their applications to receive training courses that suit their own levels (starting, middle, or upper) according to the guidelines.

Table 3 Training Course Guidelines (Example)

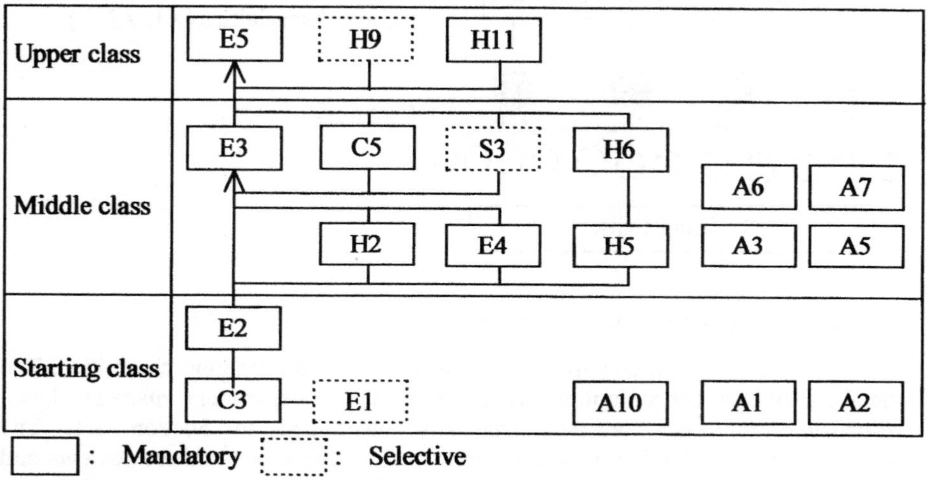

Ai, Ci, Ei, etc. represent course titles.

3.2 *Individual Training History and Training Program*

The individual engineer's training course history is stored in a database. The database includes the individual's data such as personal name, section to which the individual belongs, title or position, and specialty as well as the list of the courses, which shows a training history (the date, pass or failure, passing level) and future training schedule.

3.3 *Technical Training Organization*

Figure 1 shows the organization to promote technical training. One term of technical training is six months, and is planned and promoted on the half-year basis. The training committee is composed of the factory's general manager as committee chair, and department managers. The committee reviews and determines technical training semiannually.

While discussing engineer training in training committee meetings, the factory's general manager asks committee members if the lecturers' or instructors' technical level is acceptable, not to mention the importance of canceling old, or establishing new, training subjects. Although it is a difficult decision to cancel a course – because the lectures are invited from within the company – it is an important matter to be discussed. The committee coordinator asks the training committee members to review the matter.

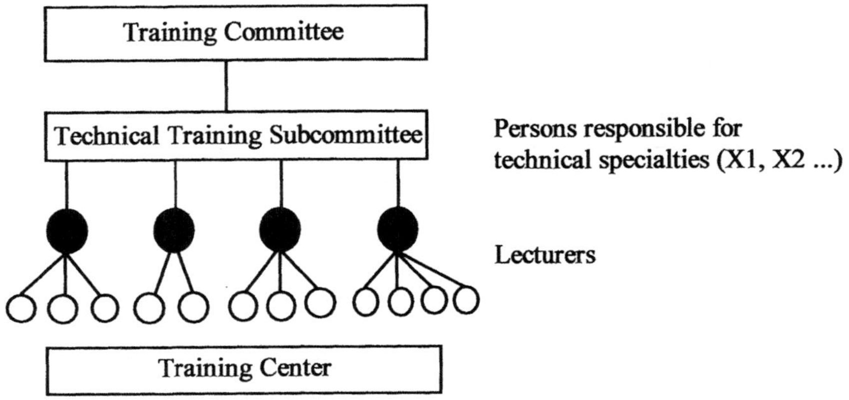

Figure 1 Engineer Training Organization

A technical training subcommittee is organized under the training committee. The members of the subcommittee are persons at the department manager level, responsible for each technical specialty mentioned in Section 3.1. The subcommittee also holds a meeting semiannually. The subcommittee reviews and determines the orientation of all the technical training courses, as well as the integration, cancelation and improvement of courses.

A training center is established as a formal organizational unit with a full-time person in charge to actually manage the engineer training activities.

The engineering training system is improved periodically and systematically to cope with changes and to prevent the training from becoming obsolete.

4. Management System Utilizing the Intranet

The intranet system established at the factory offers a home page for each shop to send out information. The training center provides various items of technical training information. The invitation to the technical training courses and the guidelines for the courses are provided on the intranet. The prospective trainees plan their own training programs and get an overview of the courses. Someone interested can apply for a course and the period from a pull-down list (a menu), then entering the applicant's name, unit, and employee number, and sending the file to the training center. The training center provides a data file for each individual. The data file summarizes the trainee's latest training program plan and history at the time of course application. Discussions are encouraged between the supervisor and the trainee to allow the trainees to acquire the basic technology necessary for performing their work.

Described above are the procedures for applying for a technical course. The courses are provided according to the program plan after the applicants are accepted. The time schedule of the course often changes according to the lecturer's needs. The course program on the training center's home page is useful for schedule changes. The course schedule is modified so that the trainee can check the course schedule beforehand and attend it on revised time.

The home page lists information on other courses to let engineers know about the availability of other training opportunities. An example is the guide to advanced technology lectures, featuring experts inside or outside the company providing engineers with a knowledge of telecommunications and peripheral technologies beyond their daily activities. The home page indicates the dates of such lectures, and outlines the past lectures. The home page also lists the invitations to technical training courses provided by other divisions of the company to enable our own engineers to attend computer-related courses.

5. Conclusion

This paper introduced the technical training provided by the factory, where we develop and manufacture telecommunication systems and equipment. The company's intranet efficiently manages invitations to technical training courses, manages applications, and posts course schedules. The most important matters in engineer training are the contents of the training courses and the establishment of a system to improve the courses to keep up with the technical innovations. The factory selects the coordinators of individual courses and the person responsible for a particular field to manage individual course coordinators to actively establish (or cancel) courses. Also, a technical training subcommittee meets periodically so that the persons responsible can orient and improve the technical training.

The authors expected that engineer training in a factory could be promoted more efficiently and effectively by quantitatively understanding the effects of technical training as well as the effects of establishing new courses, closing existing courses, integrating courses, etc. For this purpose, the authors are searching for a method of measuring quantitatively the effects of training by conducting pre- and post-training tests on the trainees, and applying the test results, that is, the difference before and after the course, to regression analysis[1]. However, no decisive or definite factors have been found so far, leaving the subject for further study.

The authors believe that it is more important to evaluate the training not in its effectiveness but in contribution to the company's activity. Engineer training is one of the activities for developing technical personnel who are able to implement the product development strategy established on the basis of the company's vision and policy. Thus, the extent or degree of engineering training being linked with the product development policy could be used as the evaluation standard.

In the reported training management system, the training results are not subjected to a labor evaluation. The evaluation should be linked with the job, and the technical training should be positioned as a fundamental for success.

6. References

1. Yamamoto, H. et al., "Development and evaluation of computer-mediated education systems for customer engineers," Proceedings of IFIP WG3, 4 1993 205-214, NORTH-HOLLAND

7. Biography

Yasuo Minai joined Hitachi, Ltd. after graduating from the Master of Arts course in Electrical Engineering, Yokohama National University, in 1970, and engaged in research of fiberoptic communications. Then, Minai engaged in equipment and system design engineering of fiberoptic image transmission at Hitachi's division headquarters and factories. He was appointed Manager of Human Resource Development Center, Telecommunications Division, in 1994, and is currently in the same position.

Masayuki Yamauchi joined Hitachi, Ltd. after graduating from the Master of Arts Course in Electrical Engineering, Ibaraki University, in 1974, and engaged in development of electronic switching system software at Totsuka Works. In 1983, Yamauchi was transferred to Human Resource Development Center where he engaged in training customers' engineering personnel on operation and maintenance of electronic switching systems. He then, as Senior Instructor, took responsibility for administration of employee training, and has been doing the same job to date.

Tsurayuki Kado currently holds the unique position of Chief Instructor at Hitachi, Ltd. He graduated from the Department of Science, Gakushuin University in 1964 and immediately started work with Hitachi. Since then, he has worked in the information systems field for thirty-four years. Ten of these years were spent as a designer of hardware and software, twelve as a systems engineer. Since 1986, he has been in charge of education and training. He is a Full Member of IFIP/WG3.4.

17. STUDY PROGRAM FOR NETWORK TECHNOLOGY AND ITS EVALUATION

Hideo Tanaka
Institute of Techhnology Education,
NEC University, Ltd

Yoshiki Noda , Naoki Nakatani
Human Resourse's Development Division,
NEC Corporation

ABSTRACT

This paper introduces the study program for network technology in the NEC in-house education system, specifically a new study program and its evaluation for technical managers, supervisors and senior engineers, etc., in NEC.

1. Introduction

□NEC is ideally positioned to be the leader in multi media, having all three key multimedia technology; semiconductors, computers and communications, and the technological expertise enabling us to provide total multimedia solutions. NEC University (subsidiary corporation of NEC) was established as a total education system (management & technology) for NEC group in 1997.

One of the objectives of ITE (NEC University Institute Technology Education) is to transfer in-house technologies, to spread the most advanced technologies throughout NEC Group employees and to maintain and promote the superiority of the company's technologies. The other is to develop creative human resources.

The results of a recent opinion survey in our company indicate that about 30% of the engineers who responded to the survey, have strong expectations for continuing technological education so that they will be able to grasp the most advanced technology. Therefore, the necessity for an in-house education is strongly endorsed by employees. Especially, the results indicates that many engineers have strong expectations for the education in network integration technology.

2. Objectives and Structures of Study Programs

The needs of technological education have broadly been divided into three categories. One of these is for younger engineers to study, basically and systematically, the technology in the major business fields of the company. Another need is for employees to become leaders in grasping the most advanced technologies in specific fields. Another is to improve rapidly the practical skills directly concerned with the job.

To cope with the above mentioned needs, the ITE has three study program, ITSP (Integrated Technology Study Programs), PTSP(Principle Technology Study Programs), and RTSP(Relevant Technology Study Program).

3. Study program for network technology

1. Study program in PTSP

Themes related with network technology in PTSP are information network, electronic commerce and control engineering for network. The purpose of these study programs, is to deepen student's knowledge of the most advanced network technology, to extend their specialties and also to develop the key people of network technology.

2. Study program in ITSP

ITSP have computer network lectures (computer technology course),network lectures & most advanced specific technology lecture(software technology course),and networking lecture (system technology course)related with network technology. These study programs aimed at saving the knowledge of the basic technology and trends of network technology.

3. Study program in RTSP

The objective of the RTSP is to make rapid improvement in practical knowledge and capability that are directly concerned with the student's job. Courses in RTSP are selected to meet common needs throughout the company. Study programs in network technology have not been available in RTSP.

We planned, the "basic network technology course" as a new network technology study program in RTSP.

4. Practical experience of a study program for basic network technology

There was not a systematic study program with regard to network integration technology and a study program intended for old NEC Group employees, in ITSP, PTSP and RTSP. Therefore, we planned and commenced the systematic study program for basic network technology in RTSP. Moreover, this program intended for research and development managers or supervisors to develop the network integrator and to cultivate the knowledge of network technology. The field of the lecture is the basic field of network technology. The contents of this course are shown as following Table □ . Students take 4 lectures every Wednesday from 9:00 a.m. to 4:30 p.m. at the classroom of ITE , which is located at NEC tamagawa plant.

In each lecture, the stuffs of ITE print out the electronic files which were sent by lecturers, using E-mail and distribute the materials of lecture to every students previously. The curriculum contains wide network technology area from basic theory to network business trends as shown in Fig.1.

For example, communication protocol contains the basic theory of TCP/IP and route control technology etc. Moreover, Network Business Trends contain also the strategies of the charge system of network and so on.

The length of student's service is shown in Fig.2. The average length of service in this course is 14.4 years and longer than that (4 □8 years) of students in ITSP ,PTSP and RTSP.

We evaluated the effect of this course as follows. This course was evaluated by three methods as shown in Table 2.

1. Method 1 was the questionnaire at the end of this course. This method showed total impression for this study program.

2. Method 2 was the questionnaire at the time after each lecture. This method showed each impression for each lecture.

3. Method 3 was the evaluation by examination.

This study program was evaluated by the above three methods. Fig.3 shows the evaluated results using method 1. It was found that almost all students under stood these lectures from Fig.3. Fig.4 shows the evaluated results using method 2. There were a few lectures which almost all students could not under stand from Fig.4. For example, lectures 14 and 22 were not understood. One reason for these results was that these lectures contained numerical formulas and matrix. But, it was found that almost all students could understand other many lectures with the exception of a few lectures. Fig.5 shows the results of examination using method 3. Examination was performed at the end of the course with condition in which students can refer to the text of each lecture. The evaluated scores of examinations spread as shown in Fig. 5.

A few students could not reach the full level of comprehension according to the results of examination. Those evaluated point of a few students were 30□ 40 point as shown in Fig.5. One reason for this results was that these students were not present at the lectures and could not prepare for the examination to be busy with their work. But, the evaluated scores showed that almost all students understood the lectures, because the average value for this examination was 71.9.

Thus, Method 1 was effective for macroscopic evaluation for this course. And Method 2 was effective for detailed evaluation of the each lecture.

Method 3 was effective for actual level check of comprehension.

It was very effective for the total evaluation that this course was evaluated by three methods.

From these evaluations, this basic network technology course contributed to develop network integrators and to save the knowledge of network technology for managers of NEC Group employees.

Table 1 BASIC NETWORK TECHNOLOGY COURSE

NAME OF COURSE	BASIC NETWORK TECHNOLOGY COURSE
PERIOD	3 MONTHS (39 LECTURES + 1 TEST)
STUDY	1 DAY/WEEK 4 LECTURES/DAY 90 MINUTES/1 LECTURE
NUMBER OF STUDENTS	76

Fig. 1.

CURRICULUM OF BASIC NETWORK TECHNOLOGY COURSE

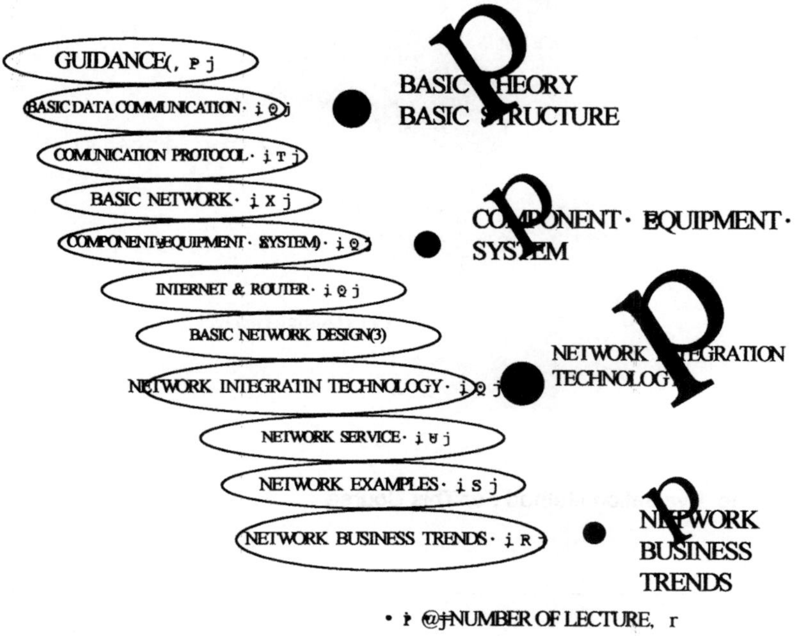

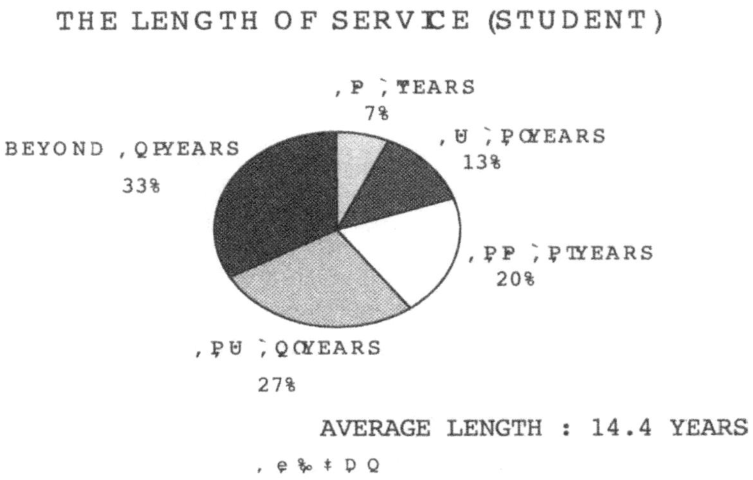

Table 2 The Evaluation Method For This Course

METHOD 1	QUESTIONNAIRE AT THE END OF THE COURSE
METHOD 2	QUESTIONNAIRE AT THE TIME AFTER EACH LECTURE
METHOD 3	COMPREHENSION CHECK BY EXAMINATION AT THE END OF THE COURSE

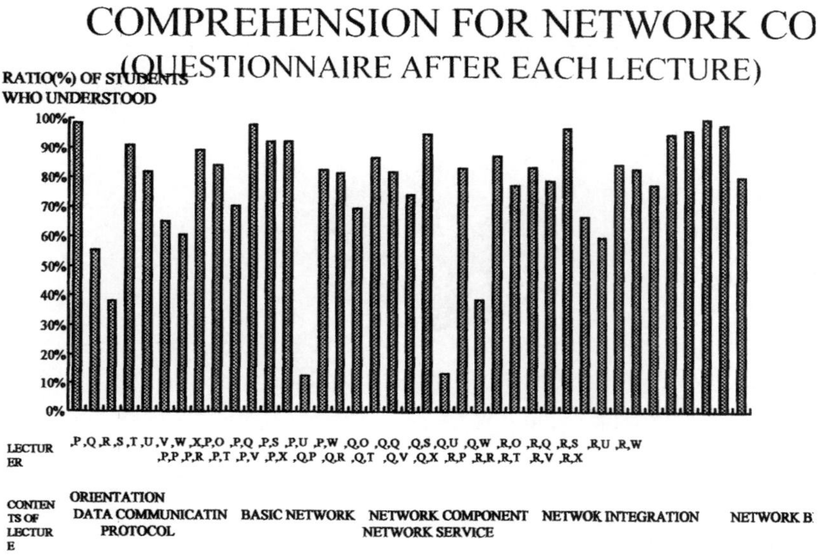
COMPREHENSION FOR NETWORK CO
(QUESTIONNAIRE AFTER EACH LECTURE)
RATIO(%) OF STUDENTS WHO UNDERSTOOD
100%
90%
80%
70%
60%
50%
40%
30%
20%
10%
0%
LECTURER
,P ,Q ,R ,S ,T ,U ,V ,W ,X ,P,O ,P,Q ,P,S ,P,U ,P,W ,Q,O ,Q,Q ,Q,S ,Q,U ,Q,W ,R,O ,R,Q ,R,S ,R,U ,R,W
,P,P ,P,R ,P,T ,P,V ,P,X ,Q,P ,Q,R ,Q,T ,Q,V ,Q,X ,R,P ,R,R ,R,T ,R,V ,R,X
CONTENTS OF LECTURE
ORIENTATION
DATA COMMUNICATIN
PROTOCOL
BASIC NETWORK
NETWORK COMPONENT
NETWORK SERVICE
NETWOK INTEGRATION
NETWORK B

Figure 3.

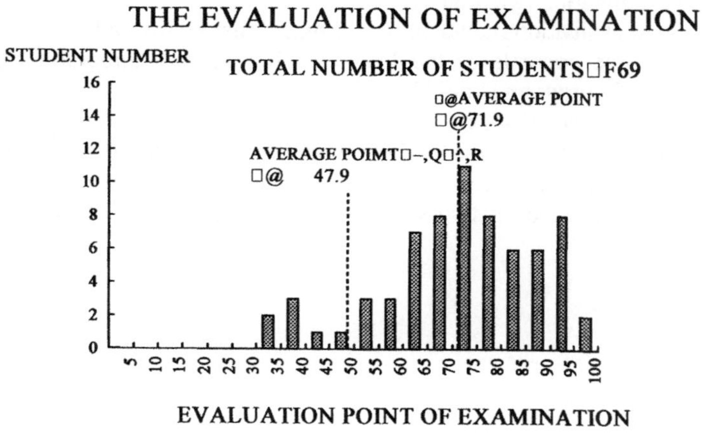
THE EVALUATION OF EXAMINATION
STUDENT NUMBER
TOTAL NUMBER OF STUDENTS□F69
□@AVERAGE POINT
□@71.9
AVERAGE POIMT□–,Q□^,R
□@ 47.9
16
14
12
10
8
6
4
2
0
5 10 15 20 25 30 35 40 45 50 55 60 65 70 75 80 85 90 95 100
EVALUATION POINT OF EXAMINATION

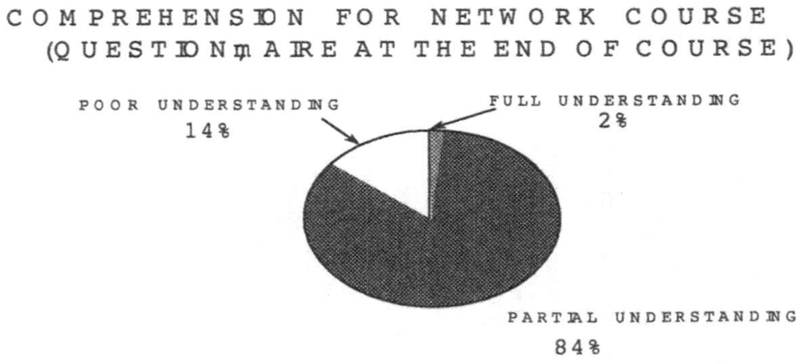

5. Conclusion

We planned and commenced the new network technology course to develop the net work integrator and to cultivate the knowledge of network technology for old NEC group employees. We evaluated this study program by three evaluation me hods.

It was very effective for the evaluation of the study program that these three evaluation methods were applied for this course. This network technology course was evaluated by macroscopic questionnaire (Method 1), partial questionnaire (Method 2) and examination (Method 3).

From these three evaluation methods, we estimated that almost, all students were able to understand the contents of the lectures. It was very important that the evaluation of the study program should be done by the above three methods.

We developed the new network technology course intended for old NEC Group employees and evaluated this course by three methods. As a result, it was found that this study program was very effective for developing the network integrator and cultivating the knowledge of network technology for managers of NEC Group employees.

18. INFORMATION ORGANIZING AND SHARING TECHNIQUE FOR TASK PERFORMANCE AND TRAINING SUPPORT

Hiroyuki Kojima, Takaaki Yamada,
Yoshihiro Mizuno, Toshiyuki Yuasa
Systems Development Laboratory, Hitachi, Ltd.
8-3-45 Nankouhigashi, Suminoeku,
Osaka, 559-8515 Japan
Phone:+81-6-616-1107 Fax:+81-6-6161109
e-mail: kojima@sdl.hitachi.co.jp

ABSTRACT

There is needed a computer system that quickly transfers business procedures, task knowledge that relates to complicated business training or instruction terms under networked databases environment. We describe the human interface for effective retrieval interaction such as a task adaptive electronic manual for filling out a form. For the distributed task information available on the internet or on intranet in the product design field, we propose information organizing and sharing method as a means of getting timely and exact knowledge for a task performance.

Keywords

Higher Education, Human Computer Interface, Information Retrieval, Networks

1. Introduction

Technological innovations and a changing economic structure are forming a society in which knowledge dominates the core part of production capacity and requires workers to optimize their productivity (Nonaka,1995). They are confronted with this requirement as it relates to work using knowledge. Therefore, in every business field, user support technologies are expected to aid and support the activity of workers. Support elements such as advisory, librarian ship, reference, and training function must sufficiently deal with the problems that workers face (Bramer, 1994). In the past, the functions of these elements were put together in the form of a manual. The electronic manual is an OJT (on the job training) oriented performance model that combines increased business performance and business instruction/training (Kojima,1992 Haga,1993 Yamada,1997). It should essentially satisfies the requirements of high understanding of a task procedure, supplying knowledge and know-how at the task execution site, and acting as a task instructor and a task manager.

On the other hand, workers must get timely and exact information for their task performance because this information may frequently change according to rapid progress in economic structures and network technology. So an information transfer method, in this case a dynamic electronic manual, must be able to cope with the above mentioned changes, instead of a typical business manual and execution manner which is systematized and arranged from a long historical standpoint. Basic technology in which workers can change the situation, viewpoint and view angle as well as extract useful parts, change, and add comments to the information is expected. So it must contain an interface that properly presents information for business performance to each person and have information transfer and acquisition mechanism that is oriented toward performance improvement.

In this paper, we first study user interfaces for effective retrieval interaction such as a task adaptive electronic manual for concurrently realizing business performance and training for a solution to the above mentioned problem. Second, we propose the information organizing and sharing method, composed of information watching and gathering, organizing and viewpoint sharing. This conception is adapted to a product design task as an implementation example.

2. Effective Retrieval Interaction For Task Performance Support - Example Of A Task Adaptive Manual For Filling Out A Form-

For insurance contracts, workers must quickly refer to manuals and reply to the queries of insurance agencies and applicants. Employees require a great skill and task knowledge for the retrieval of proper items from a great volume of manual documents. For business performance support, traditionally there is a task manual that provides information and series of procedures for a task execution. To effectively execute a task, it is important to clearly represent the task procedure and to rapidly refer to the necessary manual contents based on task purpose and business procedure.

From the viewpoint of the human-machine interface of a task performance, the following issues must be considered for our task adaptive electronic manual:

1. Structuring and visualization of a task procedure (visual interface),
2. Task ontology (the explicit description of a task concept),
3. Transferring the performance skill of a task item,
4. A connective action for a relative task (the explicit representation of a definite task procedure).

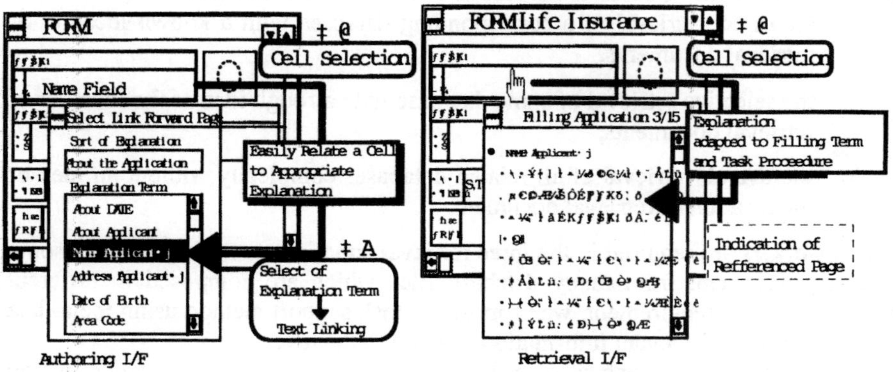

For filling out a form, the following solutions are adopted to deal with these issues:

1. Using an application sheet structure in which each cell requires filling in,
2. A contract task is represented by an item's name in the form,
3. Storing and presenting an application form sample,
4. Automatic presentation of a related item from the contents of another manual.

This manual system for filling in an application form has a retrieval interface tool which enables referral to a suitable explanation in the manual for a task adaptation, and a hyper-link generating interface tool for easy content linking. Figure 1 shows a display example of link authoring and retrieval interface.

3. Information Organizing System For Performance Support Of Products Design Task

As mentioned above, it is effective for retrieval interaction to present an explicit description of a task procedure. In the product design field, design task knowledge, including design know-how or documents, is not always used to arrange or systematize, like manual contents because of production cycle, etc.. On the other hand, in joint products development with a collaborative design process formed in some project style, it is needed to support the gathering and organizing of distributed design information along with a common product design concept, purpose and work progress for related design workers. It is needed to quickly retrieve the design task information adapted from a large number design documents for design specifications, etc..

3.1 Task performance support using an information organizing method

Usually design information is stored in a database, and it is arranged according to each purpose of information creation. The retrieval of design information is divided into the following three cases as the results of a design task analysis:

1. the direct retrieval of a corresponding database with a known location of retrieval documents,
2. the selective retrieval of some database with a rough idea of the location of retrieval documents,
3. the overall retrieval of all related databases completely without an idea of the location of retrieval document.

Design workers are required in the three retrieval situations to rapidly retrieve some necessary document from many database files which are composed in different schemes. For this requirement, we propose the task support method using meta-data which organizes of relevant information adapted to the task.

Figure 2 shows the concept of task performance support system which use an information organizing and sharing method. In this system, the information searcher has selectively gathered material using relevant words defined by a task terminology dictionary. Meta-data describes gathering data which is mutually connected using the task model defined procedures. Meta-data refers to knowledge for the retrieval of design task information. Meta-knowledge, which is composed of the above mentioned task model and related data gathering, is stored in a common database, and results in viewpoint sharing of the internal and external company information.

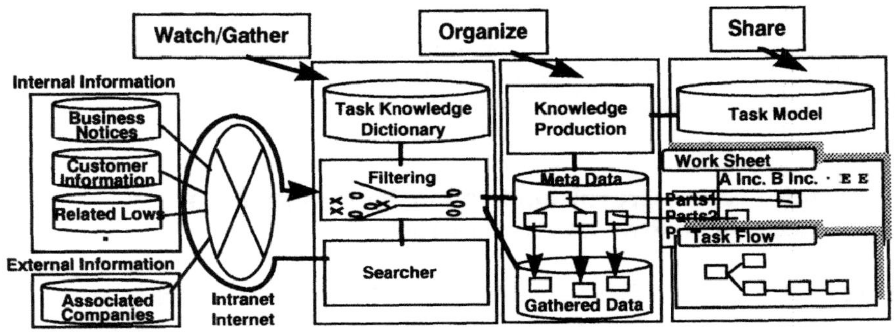

Figure 2. Basic Concept of Information Organizing and Sharing System

3.2 Information organization and retrieval using a task model

In task execution which includes a creating process such as a design task, it is important to present workers with structured information along with a problem solution procedure for a task goal (i.e. task model). This is often needed to retrieve information including documents for parts selection, design memorandums, mail logs, minutes of proceedings, design drawings as well as the relating to this information. However, they usually use normal retrieval tools only. Actually workers must create a retrieval strategy which includes the selection of information sources and keywords in order to obtain useful information for their work. Additionally, the scope of information sources can be so broad that they cannot obtain retrieval results related to their work unless they repeat the retrieval process many times.

In order to solve the above mentioned problem, we use "task modeling" in organizing information for retrieval. The task modeling is based on the concept of "task ontology" (Mizoguchi,1994), and task models are defined and expressed in a form of tree structure or a form of table structure relating to some words of the task item.

A task model is used for an input key of the retrieval process. A piece of meta-knowledge is made by retrieving keywords that are included in the task model, and embedding links that direct the retrieval results into the task model. We developed a prototype system which enables design workers to share contents (such as know-how), create meta-knowledge with a task model and retrieve information related to task items. The information circulation and distribution image using this system is shown in Figure 3.

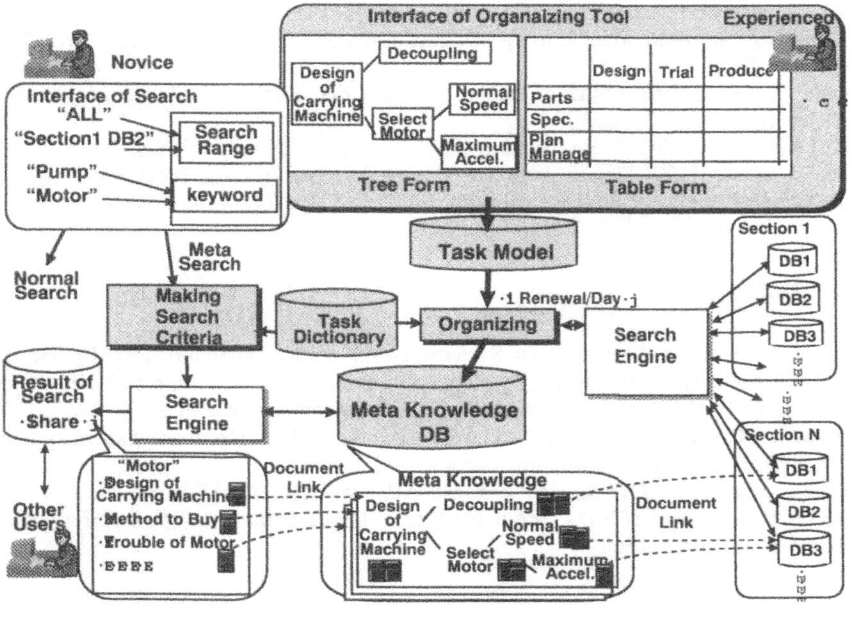

Figure 3. Implementation Image of Information Organizing and Sharing system

4. Conclusion

We have developed an adaptive electronic manual system for filling out a form for an insurance contract. In this system, the form and guidance for the process are related by Hyper-Link. The proposed user interface enable rapid guidance retrieval by indicating a cell of filling form. This retrieval method with explicit task description is much effective for task performance in the same way as typical manual contents.

For distributed design task information, we proposed a method for design task performance support using the information organizing and sharing system. This system has the following functions and is expected to support the design task performance.

1. The experienced designers are able to easily make meta-knowledge for task know-how transferring by using a task model definition interface tool.
2. Beginners are able to obtain organized information in accordance with a task purpose with a few easy operations by retrieving the meta-knowledge created and stored by an experienced user.

5. References

Bramer, W.L. et al., 1994, *Future Work.* The Free Press.

Haga, H. et al., 1993, On the Multimedia Computer Aided Instruction System for Novice Programmers with Exercise Support Facility. IFIP Trans. A Vol.A-35. Kojima, H., 1992, Self-learning Electronic Manual using Multimedia-Basic Concept-. In: IPSJ(Japan), 45th Conf. Proc. B-4.

Mizoguchi, R., 1994, Current State of the Art of Knowledge Sharing and Reuse. In: Jour. of JSAI(Japan), 9(1).

Nonaka, I. et al., 1995, *Knowledge Creating Company.* Oxford University Press.

Yamada, T. et al., 1997, Human Interface Design Methodology for Electronic Manual System and its Application. In: 6th IEEE Int. Conf. on ETFA'97.

6. Biography

H. Kojima is a Senior Researcher of Systems Development Laboratory (S.D.L). He is engaged in the study of business performance and training support system and interactive information retrieval system. He holds a Ph.D. in Computer Application.

T. Yamada is a Researcher of S.D.L. He is engaged in the study of electronic manual system (E. M. System) and community ware system.

Y.Mizuno is Researcher of S.D.L. He is engaged in the development of E.M.System.

T. Yuasa is a Researcher of S.D.L. He is engaged in the development of task performance and training support system.

19. AN EFFICIENT METHOD FOR CREATING MULTIMEDIA COURSEWARE

Yukinori Terahama[†], Hiroyuki Kojima[†] and Hiroh Yamamoto[‡]
[†]Systems Development Laboratory, Hitachi Ltd.,
[‡]Hitachi Electronics Services Co., Ltd.
Kansai Bldg.8-3-45 Nankouhigashi, Suminoe, Osaka, 559 Japan,
Tel:+81-6-616-1108 Fax:+81-6-616-1109
E-mail:{terahama,kojima}@sdl.hitachi.co.jp

ABSTRACT

In recent years, applications in the field of education have been increasing due to pervasive internet technologies. One particular area of study has been on an efficient method for creating courseware, in order to achieve remote education through networking technology. In this paper, we propose a method for creating courseware by the reuse of previous material. We show that the efficiency of the method is about three fold better than that of the conventional method in creating courseware.

Keywords
CAI, Courseware, Efficient method, Network, Multimedia

1. Introduction

Multimedia learning is attractive for use in CAI division support systems which make the most of several media including reflection, shape, sound, and text. Multimedia PCs offer several educational functions in only one PC machine [Fukuhara 91] [Fukuhara 93]. These systems employ frequently internet technologies that have appeared in recent years. In particular, they provide a learning support environment using the WWW(World Wide Web), and are designed to be applied to ITS and authoring environments employing hyper-link [Maruyama 95].

The subject of efficient courseware editing is highlighted to enable various courseware to be offered quickly, in order to achieve remote education at many locations utilizing networking technology. More specifically, in the educational division with one by one renew contents for dizzy progress of technology likely maintenance of PC it takes time to create courseware and to attain the educational objective. For efficient development of courseware, we propose a method that reuses past courseware data to create new high-quality courseware. We compare the new courseware creating method with a conventional one. An experiment was done to verify the educational effect of the proposed method in CAI education. Experiment results show that the efficiency in courseware development is improved about three times compared with the conventional method.

2. Courseware Using A Method Involing Templates

Templates have a structure to allow the reuse of past courseware and material data. In creating new courseware, new courseware structures are made by reusing template courseware. From the reuse of template material data, a display frame is made to improve the making of the courseware.

2.1 *Template refinement of courseware structures*

We created a template frame for a courseware structure that included "Chapter", "Paragraph" and "Term" levels, by reusing already made courseware. A structured courseware template was used to make the new courseware frame. The reused sample of the structured courseware is shown in Figure 1.

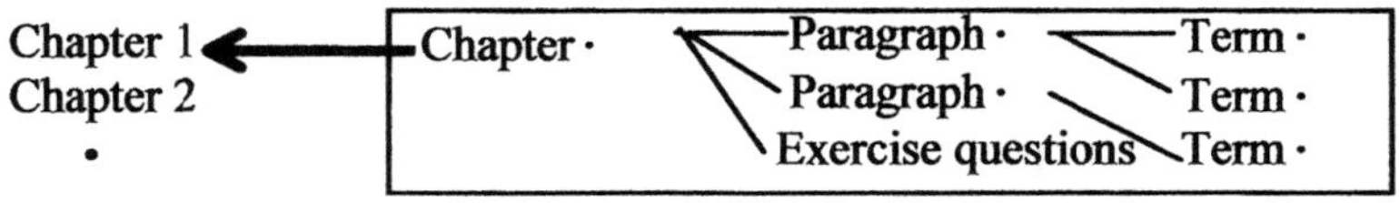

Fig. 1: Reuse of template courseware

Comprehension is simplified if a new courseware structure is made. In the above example, the template can design courseware to satisfy "Chapter", "Paragraph", and "Term", and a related display "Frame".

2.2 Template refinement of courseware material data

A "Frame" applicable to the display of courseware with small changes can be used for efficient design. To achieve this, material data (i.e., existing text and image (movie, picture) data), we search for the courseware necessary for this task in a database, and then we design a new "frame" by redesigning material data.

2.3 Courseware creating function

Figure 2 shows several functional structures to create courseware (like that described in chapter 3.2), and we describe the details of several functions below.

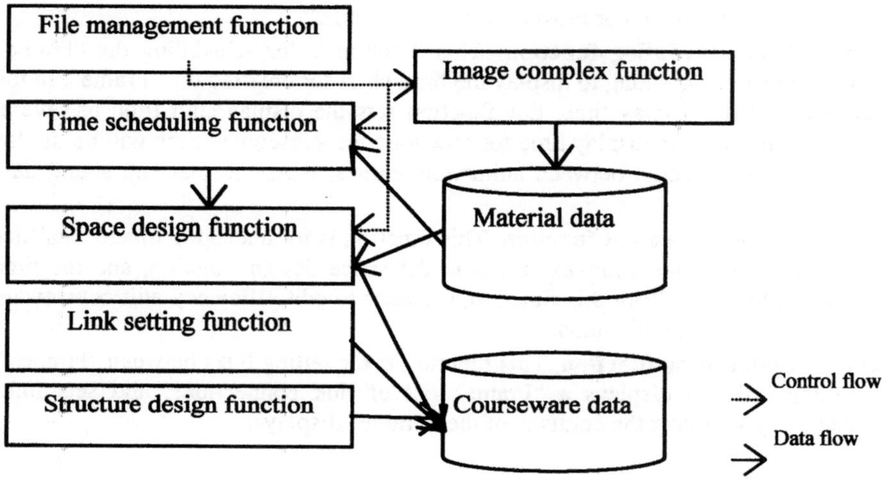

Fig. 2: Structure of courseware creating function

2.3.1 Structure design function This function is for designing the courseware structure in order to satisfy "Chapter", "Paragraph", and "Term". Designing the new courseware structure is handled as the refinement of the parts template the courseware structure. This function involves partial copying, moving and deleting.

2.3.2 Image complex function This function is for creating a new material data by the template refinement of the material data involving the image data. The newly created material data can be reused by performing template refinement again.

2.3.3 Space design function This function is for creating a display location for the material data, i.e., the image data, etc., made by the image complex function on the "frame". With this function, some part of the plural image data set into the same "Frame" can be registered in the courseware database for added efficiency in the making of the . "Frame", and can be reused by being copied or move to another "Frame". The difference between this function and the image complex function is this point of being copied or moved to another "Frame".

2.3.4 Time scheduling function This function is for scheduling the "Frame" display time, i.e., how long to display the time chart for creating the "Frame". In the scheduling of the display time, this function sets the display start time of several "Frames", and sets the display time for how long the subsequent time will be. It also sets the synchronisation between animation frames, where format and sound data are sent.

2.3.5 File management function This function is for managing image data files called from the image complex function, the space design function, and the time scheduling function. With this function,it is easy to edit efficiency edit courseware by copying or moving file units.

2.3.6 Link setting function This function is for setting links between "Frames". In setting links, it displays a "Frame" list of link connections, and sets links efficiency by verifying the contents of the "Frame" displays.

3. Evaluation Of The Courseware Creating Efficiency

We created courseware for an ATM (Automatic Teller Machine) and presumed how long the same task would take in terms of man-hours using the conventional CAI creating method. The proposed method improved the efficiency about three times in comparison with the conventional method.

3.1 Conclusion on the man-hours for creating the ATM courseware

We compared the CAI courseware creating procedure for PC maintenance and that for an ATM, to evaluate the courseware creating man-hours for the ATM. We created courseware under a common scenario, and made the ATM courseware with 30 frames.

Table 1: Conclusion on the man-hours for creating

Steps \ Objective courseware		CAI for PC (140 frames)	CAI for ATM (30 frames)
Text creation		5-man-months	-
All-around design	Scenario creation	22-man-months	8 hours (22 hours)
Detail design	Making of frames	44-man-months	15 hours (44 hours)
Data Creating	Video data creation	9-man-days	1 hour (10.5 hours)
	Graphic data making	10-man-days	9 hours
	Text data making	10-man-days	12.5 hours
Test	Editing, adjustment	15-man-days	22.5 hours

Several working steps were used in creating the text, i.e., all-around design, detailed design, data creating, and test (verification). In Table 1, for the PC courseware involving the typical CAI creating method for text creation, we spent 5-man-months to make the courseware, ATM courseware with the typical CAI creating method because a scenario has already been made. In creating the scenario for the all-around design and creating frame seats in the detailed design, for the CAI making method, we spent 22-man-days and 44-man-days. On the other hand, for the ATM courseware, the all-around design involved 8 hours and the detailed design involved 15 hours. However, the former 8 hours were needed to set an address for analysing already made courseware. Moreover, the letter 15 hours the appropriate new courseware to make, in place of the existing video data.

Therefore, we assumed the presumed value of the creation time, for the all-around design and detailed design of the ATM courseware, to be 22 hours and 44 hours. (a value in brackets in table 1 is a presumed value).

3.2 *Comparison of ATM courseware creation man-hours*

Table 2 shows results comparing the conventional creating method and the CAI courseware creating method (i.e., the proposed method).

In Table 2, we found that this proposed method shortens the time about three-fold compared with the CAI creating method. We analysed the comparison on the working man-hours in several steps as shown in Table 2.

3.2.1 All-around design After we did the all-around design from scratch, we compared with the working man-hours of the CAI courseware using typical image data, about 22 hours were spent. On the other hand, the courseware creation man-hours by the proposed method were about 1/3 the man-hours. We presumed the main factor as the creation efficiency with the improved design method in a top-down manner on the assumption that the courseware was structured by "Chapter", "Paragraph", and "Term".

Table 2: Comparison of courseware with the conventional creating method and the proposed method

Objective courseware Creation steps		Conventional method (30 frames)	Proposed method (30 frames)	Rate of creating man -hour (Usual/Proposed)	Cause, other
All-around design	Scenario making	8 hours (22 hours)	8 hours	(1/2.8)	Structure of "Chapter", "Paragraph", and "Term"
Detailed design	Frame seat making	15 hours (44 hours)	16 hours	(1/2.8)	□Effect of the template of the layout in a frame and several buttons □Difference in the search speed between video and image data □Difference in the ease of correspondence of the display layout (extension and reduction of digital images)
Data creating	Video data Graphic data Text data creation	22.5 hours (32 hours)	15.3 hours	1/1.5 (1/2.1)	□Difference in the ease of management of video and image data (including the digital animations) □Effect of image complex, space design, and time scheduling functions. When the editor needs time to add the sound data, his work becomes more effective.
Test	Editing, adjustment	22.5 hours	5 hours	1/4.5	
Total		89 hours (98.5 hours)	36.3 hours	1/2.5 (1/2.7)	

( ): Calculated value by presumed value

3.2.2 Detailed design Similar to the all-around design, the courseware creation man-hours by the proposed method were about 1/3 the man-hours of the conventional method. We presumed the main factor as the creation efficiency with the improved searching speed from the image database (image data), magnification and reduction were made easier by using the image complex function of this proposed method.

3.2.3 Data creating

3.2.3.1 Creating video data In the CAI courseware assuming typical image data, when we created video, the courseware creation efficiency improved by the proposed method. We presumed the main factor as the improved creation efficiency, the movie was structured by multiple images like animation sending frames and data editing was easy.

3.2.4 Creating graphic, data creating The man-hours for the CAI courseware using typical image data, i.e., in creating the graphic data, almost agreed with the creation man-hours of the proposed method. We presumed the main factor as the agreement of the CAI system using the typical image data generated from the use of a depiction tool from an application program, almost the same man-hours as for the image complex function were needed with the proposed method.

3.2.5 Creating text data Because the man-hours for creating the CAI courseware using typical image data, i.e., in creating the text data, were necessary to superimpose the text data on the image display by LD, was taken time to rectify the display timing of the text data. On the other hand, in creating the text data with the proposed method, because the image complex function could be used to edit one frame in which the image data and text data were together, it was not necessary to worry about the above superimposing or display timing and because of this, the courseware creating function was separated to improve the efficiency.

3.2.6 Test In the test (edit and modification step) we presumed that the creation efficiency of the courseware improved because the proposed method was separated by the image complex function, the space design function, and the time scheduling function (like in creating the text data). Moreover, with this proposed method if we needed improved timing to add sound data to the courseware, the creation efficiency improved by the time scheduling function.

Consequently we compared the man-hours for creating the courseware in Table 2 and the most efficient creation step to create the text data. Moreover, it became clear that this contributed toward improving the efficiency of the editing and modification step in the test. In all cases of, we presumed the effect of the proposed method by separating the image complex function, the space design function, and the time scheduling function.

4. Conclusion

- By the proposed courseware creating method, the courseware creation efficiency for the teaching of PC maintenance work was improved about three times that of the conventional method.

- In the future, we plan to study a courseware creating method that supports the "Analysis of an object" (understanding of a PC manual).

5. References

[Fukuhara 91] Fukuhara, Y. (1991) Multimedia Authoring System for Practical Scene-oriented ITS (CAIRNEY): ICOMMET 91, pp. 215-218

[Fukuhara 93] Fukuhara, Y. (1993) CAI system (CAIRNEY) for tele-communication network operator: SIG-IES-9303-7, pp. 37-42

[Maruyama 95] Maruyama. (1995) Proposal of hyper link architecture in the distributed environment CALAT: AI symposium 95, JSAI

6. Biography

Y. Terahama is a Researcher of Systems Development Laboratory (S.D.L). He is engaged in the study of business performance and training support system.

H. Kojima is Senior Researcher of S.D.L. He is engaged in the study of business performance and training support. He holds a Ph.D. in Computer Application.

H. Yamamoto is a General Manager of Engineering Education Center. He is engaged in the study of CAI education support functions on self-study.

20. HOW A SMALL ENTERPRISE OBTAINED WWW EXPERIENCE AT A MINIMUM COST:- A CASE STUDY

J. B. Thompson and S. McCall
School of Computing and Information Systems
University of Sunderland,
Sunderland SR6 0DD, U.K.
Tel : (44) 191 5152769 Fax: (44) 191 5152781
e-mail: barrie.thompson@sunderland.ac.uk

ABSTRACT

A very successful occurrence of technology transfer between a University and a SME (small and medium size enterprise) is detailed. This involved the creation of a World Wide Web site for the organisation and the production of a detailed research report on Digital Commerce on the Internet. The work was undertaken by a postgraduate student following a Masters level "conversion" course in Computer Based Information Systems. Background information relevant to the project and the course is provided. Details of the research and development work are given. Finally an evaluation of what has been achieved is presented.

Keywords

Higher Education, case studies, networks, electronic commerce

1. Introduction

The explosive growth of the Internet during the 1980s and 90s coupled with the facilities offered by the World Wide Web (WWW) has provided many new opportunities for the commercial world. Together these two technologies have provided a simple and relatively inexpensive way for businesses to communicate with: other businesses, clients, and the public. They also present a means by which businesses can greatly enhance their sales and marketing efforts. The prime reasons for a business initially establishing a WWW site can be seen to be (McCall, 1997):

- to network and establish a presence,
- to make business information available to potential customers,
- to heighten public awareness,
- to serve existing customers.

Unfortunately, for small and medium sized enterprises (that is enterprises with less than 250 employees and known as SMEs in the UK) there can be major problems associated with the establishment of a WWW site. These are - a lack of experience and expertise in the area and the costs that would be involved in buying in outside expertise. Also such enterprises are often very wary of outside consultants when approaching new technological areas. This is because they are not sure of how impartial the consultant's recommendations may be and what resultant costs may be incurred. This paper documents an alternative approach involving a close link between an educational establishment and a SME which has resulted in very cost effective technology transfer.

At the University of Sunderland we operate a 'conversion' MSc in Computer Based Information Systems. The course takes only graduates from non-computing courses and after the equivalent of 12 months full-time study produces personnel who can operate very effectively in the computing sector. A significant part of the course is devoted to a practical project which is externally sponsored and represents a sizeable real world problem. One of the projects accepted by the University, during the 1996/97 academic year, as suitable for an MSc. Student involved the construction of a Web site for a SME which retailed pine furniture. The company "Principally Pine" was founded in 1990 and at the time of the project had four retail outlets in the North of England. The company primarily wished to explore the possibility of global advertising over the Internet but was also interested in the possibility of digital commerce in the future.

The following sections of this paper provides: some background information on our MSc course in Computer Based information systems, details of the project that was undertaken with Principally Pine, and finally an evaluation of what has been achieved.

2. MSc in Computer Based Information Systems

The MSc. in Computer-Based Information Systems at the University of Sunderland is a 'conversion' course intended for graduates who have little or no knowledge of computing and are interested in gaining a theoretical and practical understanding of the construction of computer-based information systems. The course is distinctive in that it is offered in five diverse delivery/learning modes (Thompson and Edwards, 1995):

1. Full Time over twelve months at the University,
2. Part Time Evening over 33 months at the University,
3. Part Time Day over 24 months at the University,
4. Block Mode over 36 months where formal attendance at the University is restricted to a maximum of four weeks per year,
5. Distance Learning Mode supported by in-house produced videos and related textual material. This mode is offered from approved centres both within the UK and internationally.

The course has a modular structure and operates within a Postgraduate Credit Accumulation and Transfer Scheme (CATS). The course consists of two main elements: a taught element (equivalent to seven months full time study, which has a value of 70 CATS credits at level M) and an externally sponsored project (equivalent to five months full time study, which has a value of 50 CATS credits at level M). Intermediate awards of Postgraduate Certificate and Postgraduate Diploma are available for students who wish to leave the course during or at the end of the taught part having gained 35 or 70 credits respectively. The detailed aims of the course are to:

1. promote a critical awareness of the natures, roles and limitations of computer based information systems,
2. develop the knowledge, skills and understanding needed to specify, design, implement, document and furnish continued support for an effective computer based information system, either alone or as part of a team.
3. allow the student to consolidate and display skills, knowledge and awareness in a selected application area for computer based information systems and gain experience of implementing such a system.

The project (which is externally sponsored) forms a major part of the course and each student is expected to devote at least 540 hours of work to it. The aim of the project is to extend and develop the student's ability to analyse, specify, design, implement and document an effective computer-based information system which satisfies an organisational need. The undertaking of the project should mean that students will be able to demonstrate their ability to:

- Plan, schedule, monitor and control the conduct of a substantial piece of research and development work
- Select and critically assess relevant material from original papers and articles, and to extend the lines of research therein
- Apply some of the methodologies developed during the course
- Plan and communicate, both orally and in writing, a programme of work in information system design and implementation.

Students undertake the course for a variety of reasons, for example: to convert to another discipline completely, to add value to an existing degree, to improve job prospects by being computer literate, to change career paths (often after redundancy or an intentional period out of the job market), to provide an entry into research or lecturing in further/higher education, and to gain additional skills relevant to a hybrid manager. The last is particularly true of mature students who undertake the part-time versions of the course (Thompson and Edwards, 1996). In all cases the project provides a major opportunity for the students to concentrate on an area of their choice (they select their project from those available) and gain knowledge, skills and abilities that should enhance their future careers.

3. The Web project with Principally Pine

The prime objectives for the project with Principally Pine were:

1. Research and investigate what makes an effective Web site for a company.
2. Investigate how to design a Web site.
3. Determine what Principally Pine want included on the Web site.
4. Create a Web site advertising Principally Pine.
5. Research the implications of digital commerce to a company.

The research undertaken concerning the factors that should be taken into account when designing an effective Web site encompassed both non-technical and technical aspects. The former included factors such as the purpose of the site, its audience and site organisation. The latter included factors that in general relate to page attributes and include length, links navigation, graphics, frames and forms. The prime sources used in the research were the papers and texts by: Bayne(1996), Chen(1997), Gallant(1997), Gantz(1996), Green(1996), Greenburg(1996), Handley and Crowcroft(1995), Oberndorf(1997), Raggett et al (1996), Sachs and Stair(1997), Scheler(1996), Selzer(1997), Tilton (1996), and Wilson(1996). Using these it was possible to compose a general check list (McCall, 1997) which could be used to determine the company's true requirements. Following this example site were developed to demonstrate both good and bad features so that the sponsor within the company could understand more clearly why particular choices had been made. Finally the "good" site was modified to incorporate enhancements which were identified during the sponsor's evaluation.

3.1 User Requirements and Design Outline

The check list us to determine the company's requirements for the site and the information obtained was as follows:

1. What is the purpose of your site?
The primary purpose of the site is to advertise the products and services of Principally Pine.
2. Are you presenting information?
Yes. The information should be in one place and in full detail.
3. Are you trying to sell a product?
Yes. The products should be easy to scan allowing quick recognition and evaluation.
4. Are you providing a form-based user interface?
No. Principally Pine currently does not have an established mailing list and therefore do not require forms on the Web Site.
5. Who is the expected audience?
A great proportion of the target audience will be home users on relatively low specification computers. The site should therefore be set up in order to cater for these readers. The use of highly technical features, such as 24-bit true colour images, are therefore inappropriate.
6. What sections should be included in your site?
Following requirement analysis with Principally Pine, the following sections were decided upon:

- About Principally Pine
- Opening Hours
- Reason for Success
- Shop Locations
- Furniture Suppliers
- Finance
- Special Offers
- Delivery

7. The first screen-full of information, on the first page of the site, should have no vital information beneath the bottom of the browser and should capture the reader's attention.
Agreed.
8. Can the content be separated into discrete sections?
Yes. Therefore multiple short pages should be used including a table of contents.
9. Each page should have a recognisable title.
Agreed.
10. The HTML title should accurately reflect the textual page title.
Agreed.
11. Are any of the pages of considerable length (Example: over four screenfuls of text)?
No. Therefore internal page links are not required.

12. Is there any special reason to use landscape page orientation?
No. Therefore use the standard portrait format.
13. All links, should if possible, match the title of the resulting page.
Agreed
14. A link should not be a whole sentence or a single word but should be placed within the text as if the link wasn't there at all. Try to avoid the use of "Click here".
Agreed.
15. The description of a link should be in absolute terms rather than using implied destinations, especially if frames are used. "Proceed to Chapter 3" is clearer in terms such as "Back", "Next" or "Return To".
Agreed.
16. Is your site a large, widely used closed system?
No. Therefore a palette of graphical navigation buttons is unnecessary.
17. Are graphics to be included in your site?
Yes. The low technological state of the expected audience dictates the use of 8-bit, 256 colour displays. Also the expected low-bandwidth connection of the audience suggests the use of one large graphic rather than several smaller graphics.
18. Are graphical bullets to be used in the site?
Yes. A small set of bullets should be used repeatedly rather than using a large number only once.
19. Does your site contain a list of similar topics each requiring its own page?
Yes. A frame-based site should be considered. This will give readers the option for any downloads, allows for better navigation and will aid site maintenance.
20. Are forms to be used in your site?
No. They are not appropriate to Principally Pine.
21. Readers should be given the opportunity to send their thoughts on the site.
Agreed. A link to an e-mail address will be supplied.
22. The date when the site was last revised should be included in an appropriate international standard.
Agreed.
23. The finished site should be proof read by the sponsor and if possible another person.
Agreed.

3.2 The Development of the Web Site

It was decided that two sites should be created. The first site, referred to as a 'dummy' site would not follow the design principles determined during the requirements phase and in some cases would actually go against these recommendations. There were two reasons for doing this:

1. It would demonstrate to the client what could happen if suitable design guidelines are not adhered to.
2. This site could be used to practice the necessary Web design techniques.

The second site would then be created incorporating the design guidelines determined during the requirements phase. This site would eventually form the working Principally Pine Web site. For both sites a exploratory prototyping approach was used whereby following a number iterations a fully working system was built up stage by stage .

The Dummy Site

Although this site neglected many of the design feature identified above, the single most disregarded figure was the blatant overuse of graphics. Indeed the site took on average 22 seconds to load, which is far higher than the recommended top limit of 10 seconds. Other design recommendations that were overlooked include the use of "Click here" and whole sentences as links. A copy of this version of the sit can be found at:
http://osiris.sunderland.ac.uk/~cs0jbt/pine/index.htm

The Actual Site

The evaluation prototype of the proposed Principally Pine site consisted of a title screen and two pages of the actual site. These were necessary to demonstrate the use of frames and the internal navigation of the site.

The title page contained a graphic of the company's name, a link to the main site, a link to the contact e-mail address, the date of the last update and details of where the site was created. The main site was frame-based and consisted of three separate pages. Two of the pages were fixed, one page holding the company logo while the second was purely for navigation and contained links to the contents of the site. The third page was the main viewing area of the site and was used to display the individual sections of the site. This is achieved by clicking on the links by in the navigational page. When a link is activated it remains highlighted as an indication to the reader that they have already travelled the link. The site took on average 3 seconds to load, which is well within the recommended top limit of 10 seconds. A copy of the site can be found at:
http://osiris.sunderland.ac.uk/~cs0jbt/index1.htm

3.3 Client Evaluation of Prototypes and Final development

To allow the client to view the two initial Web sites a presentation was arranged for Monday the 28th of July 1997. During this presentation the features, design and navigation of each site were demonstrated to the client. A simple form was used to gauge the client feedback. In addition to this further design and content features were discussed and noted. As expected the dummy site served its purpose by demonstrating to the client how the careful design of a site is essential. It was also important to discover that the client was satisfied by the design of the actual proposed site. This meant that further development of the basic design could be continued rather than having to start a new design from scratch.

Following the client evaluation, and appreciative response, further development on the actual site was carried out. The framework of the site was such that maintenance and development work was relatively straight forward. Some problems, however, were encountered in providing a "Furniture Suppliers" section. In this section pictures of suppliers' brochures were scanned in and used as an advertisement for their products. Several designs were prototyped but most were abandoned due to the slow speed of the download because of the graphics. It was therefore decided to add a further frame-set to this section. This proved to have a number of advantages over the other possible designs:

- The speed of the download would be vastly improved, as only one graphic
- would be displayed at a time.
- he size of the graphic could be increased due to the faster download speed,
- which would make it easier for readers to view the graphic.
- Readers would be given the option of whether or not to download the graphic.
- Maintenance would be made easier and faster.

The outcome of this decision was that a graphical bulleted list is used as a navigational page and it provides an index of the furniture suppliers. The bullets are all the same, in accordance with the design requirements, as they take a relatively short time to load (compared to that of multiple, different images). The brochure of the supplier is displayed in the adjacent screen, which also displays the name of the supplier. These developments can be viewed at:
http://osiris.sunderland.ac.uk/~cs0jbt/pine/index1.htm

4. Evaluation and Conclusions

In addition to creating the Web site for Principally Pine a Research report on Digital commerce on the Internet was produced. That the sponsor was extremely pleased with both is shown by the following extracts from formal written evaluations:

"I am very pleased with the standard quality of the site. it is simple and easy to use and looks good. All the requirements I originally suggested have been included. I think you have done an excellent job"

"The report provided was very interesting and informative. I cleared up many of the uncertainties I had regarding the subject. The report was easy to follow and understand. I was particularly interested in the sections that discussed encryption and 'Ecash'".McCall (1977)

There have clearly been three winners in this project. they are the sponsoring organisation (Principally Pine), the student and the University:

- Principally Pine have gained not only a trial Web site and the research report but by being closely involved with all stages of the project have gained useful experience and knowledge at minimum cost. There was no charge for the students time. The only expenses the sponsor is expected to meet are any additional costs such as postage, travelling and any necessary software for their own machines. They are also obviously expected to provide staff time for consultations and work with the student.

- The student has gained excellent practical experience and has also been able to develop effective research and reporting skills. Working with real clients improves communication skills and it develops the ability to address problems in a professional and efficient manner. The undertaking of such a project also provides a major element of practical experience to be included in a CV when looking for the employment following the course.
- The University has been able to forge a successful link with the business community and has been able to oversee a very effective occurrence of technology transfer. Since both the company and the student were learning together none of the tensions that can arise between consultant and client in a "I know best" situation occurred. Both have been able to develop their knowledge at a reasonable pace over a period of months and work in harmony. The technology transfer from University to the business has occurred almost transparently with the student acting as the catalyst.

In the case of our MSc in Computer Based Information Systems at the University of Sunderland we insist that every project must be "real world" with a sponsor. We do not allow the creation of "pretend" projects by academics as is the case at some other institutions. This forces us to look outside our institution, to make links with the outside world, and give our students real opportunities. This time and time again over the years has proved to be not only to the benefit of the students and the companies, we carry out the projects with, but also to the University itself. By progressing in this way barriers are broken down and the links for further research and constancy are built up. Also one hopes that this will result in the University being the first port of call for advice and help.

5. References

Bayne, K. M. (1996) *Is your Site a Success?* Marketing Tools, March/April.

Chen, P. (1997) *Hit-or Miss-Measurement. Counting Hits is Less Than Ideal.* Marketing Tools, March.

Gallant, J. (1997) *Focus your Site on the Customer.* Netmarketing, February 9.

Gantz, J. (1996) *Web Site Design: Is It Art or Design.* Computerworld, Vol. 30, issue 41, p37.

Green, T. (1996) Daiwa Securities: *Trade to the Internet.* Bank Systems and Technology, Vol. 35, Issue 10, Oct, p 12.

Greenburg, R. (1996) *Psst! Wanna Know How to get your Web Page Noticed.* Computerworld, Vol. 30, Issue 41, Oct 7, p100.

Handley, M. & Crowcroft, J. (1995) *The World wide Web - Beneath the Surf.* UCL Press. London.

McCall, S. (1997) *An Investigation into the use of the Internet as a Medium for Advertising and Trade in a Commercial Environment,* MSc. Thesis, School of Computing and Information Systems, University of Sunderland, England.

Oberndorf, S. (1997) *Making Web design a Piece of Cake.* Catalog Age, Vol. 14, issue 1, Jan, p51.

Raggett, D. Lam, J. & Alexander, I. (1996) *HTML 3 Electronic Publishing on the World Wide Web.* Addison Wesley Longman. England.

Sachs, D. and Stair, H. (1997) *The 7 Keys to Effective Web Sites,* Computerworld, Vol. 31, Issue 1, Jan 6, p64.

Scheler, R. L. (1996) *Baiting the Web.* Computerworld, Vol. 30, Issue 28, pp 76-77.

Seltzer, R. (1997) *How to Make Business Chat Work.* Internet-on-a-Disk, No. 19, February.

Thompson, J. B. and Edwards, H. M. (1995) *One Course, Four Delivery /Learning modes and World-Wide Availability: An Example of True Educational Flexibility and Efficiency,* Sixth IFIP World Conference Computers In Education, Birmingham.

Thompson, J. B. and Edwards H. M. (1997) *The Hybrid Manager: Achievement within a World-Wide Dimension,* IFIP WG3.4 International Working Conference, The Place of Information Technology in Management and Business Education, Melbourne Australia, July, 1996, subsequently published by Chapman Hall, Eds Barta B. et al ISBN 0-412-79960.

Tilton, E. (1996) *Web Weaving: Designing and Managing an Effective Web Site.* Database, Vol. 19, Issue 5, Oct/Nov, p 99.

Wilson, S. (1996) *World Wide Web Design Guide.* Database, Vol. 19, Issue 2, Apr/May, p 103.

6. Biography

J. Barrie Thompson is Professor in Applied Software Engineering at the University of Sunderland.

Stuart McCall gained a distinction in the MSc in Computer Based Information Systems at Sunderland University in September 1997, He now works in the computing industry.

21. EFFECTIVENESS OF VARIOUS CAI EDUCATION STYLES AND SUPPORT FUNCTIONS ON SELF-STUDY

H. Yamamoto, M. Nakayama, Y. Shimizu
Graduate School of Decision Science and Technology, Tokyo Institute of Technology
(*Hitachi Electronics Services Co.Ltd.,)
2-12-1, O-okayama, Meguro-ku,
Tokyo, 152 Japan.
Tel: +81 45 826 1260 Fax: +81 45 826 1262
e-mail: yamamoto@cradle.titech.ac.jp

ABSTRACT

This paper describes a comprehensive analysis of the effectiveness of four different education styles to study the enhancement of learning methods. The comparison result shows that collaborative teaching using CAI(I) is the most effective among them. Compared with face-to-face lectures there is a difference at 1% level of significance either in the group with lower scores, in the group with higher scores, or in all. The effect of "human-to-computer interactions" advocated by cognitive science was shown quantitatively. It was also found that self-study at local offices using CAI(II) was effective in reducing the time required for learning by 24%. Comparing the effectiveness of group learning and self-study, the authors focused on self-study and developed self-study support functions on the Web.

Keywords

CAI, training effect, collaborative learning, cognitive science, Web

1. Introduction

In these times of radical technical innovations, companies must educate their personnel on a variety of high-level subjects. A more effective education style is being called for in group learning. A different and more effective style of education employing conventional CAI would prove to be very useful. Especially, if the effectiveness of "human-to-computer interactions" is demonstrated quantitatively, it would also be particularly beneficial for furthering the study of cognitive science in the future.

With an expectation for extending educational opportunities in remote locations and for reducing the costs, the demand for distributed education has also be increased. If self-study is possible even in places unattended by instructors and the learning time can be reduced, it is expected that CAI will spread quickly. Therefore, in its implementation, an effective CAI method both in terms of scores and time is being demanded (Okamoto, 1995).

Although many studies have been performed on development and evaluation of CAI systems (Lee and Shirai, 1996), no study has evaluated the scores and learning time quantitatively with respect to the education style.

Setting up four education styles using CAI(I) which has been developed for group learning and CAI(II) which has been developed for distributed education, this study investigated the effectiveness of them on the test scores and learning time. Furthermore, it analyzed if there was a difference in the improvement in score between group learning and distributed education.

Finally, a method was studied to ameliorate the defects of distributed self-study and developed a system having new support functions for self-study.

2. Course Contents And Education Styles

2.1 Course contents

Materials for educating computer maintenance personnel are the basis upon which this study was conducted. The traditional style of classroom teaching was evaluated to compare four different educational styles in this study. This occupied approximately 20% (1 to 3 days) of the total time of the course. As with any computer system, similar topics are covered to gain the knowledge required to conduct preventive maintenance and troubleshooting.

2.2 Education styles

Four education styles were evaluated in this paper as shown in Table 1. Since the contents differ from one educational style to another, traditional lectures were conducted for comparison using the same contents. The characteristics of each educational style are also presented in Table 1.

Table 1 Characteristics of education styles

Education style			Learning time	Instructor	Use of images	Collaborative teaching	Self-study support
Group learning	(1)	CAI(I)-based schooling	Fixed	✓	✓	—	—
	(2)	Collaborative teaching using textbooks		✓	—	✓	—
	(3)	CAI(I)-based collaborative teaching		✓	✓	✓	—
Distributed education	(4)	CAI(II)-based self-study	Free	—	✓	—	✓
Face-to-face lectures for comparison			Fixed	✓	—	—	—

✓: Can be used to the fullest extent. —: Cannot be used fully.

Group learning is shown in Table 1, with education styles (1) to (3). As shown in style (4) for distributed education, self-study using CAI(II) was conducted. In group learning, the learning period was fixed in each educational style. In distributed education, each trainee was free to take any length of time for learning. That is, the learning time differed from one trainee to another only in style (4), self-study using CAI(II).

The instructor column is marked for the group learning in the table because there is always an instructor nearby. It is not marked for the distributed education because there is no instructor. As for images, both the CAI(I) system and CAI(II) system allowed retrieving and displaying on a screen. The "collaborative teaching" column is filled in from the viewpoint of whether or not trainees could learn mutually with one another by questions and answers and other means. The self-study support refers to such functions as an online glossary and hypertext which allow trainees to have access whenever they have their own questions.

The following details each education style.

(1) Schooling using CAI(I)

The CAI(I) system provides computer control of text, still images, video and audio. This system was developed to be used in group learning. It has a courseware creation function, learning function and other functions (Yamamoto, 1993).

Actually, one CAI(I) system was provided for each person in group learning. If a trainee did not understand the method of study or had a question, the trainee could ask the instructor a question at anytime.

(2) Collaborative teaching using printed materials

This education style used only textbooks and no CAI was used. The trainees were divided into teams of three to four persons each. Within this team, trainees taught each other to gain knowledge and deepen their understanding.

(3) Collaborative teaching using CAI(I)
In this education style, the trainees taught each other using CAI(I). As in the collaborative teaching using printed materials, the trainees were divided into teams of three to four persons each. Each team was provided with one CAI(I) system.

(4) Self-study at local offices using CAI(II)
CAI(II) was developed aiming at a Performance Support System (PSS) (Gery, 1991) allowing learning at anytime while working on the job (Yamamoto, Aizawa, Munemoto and Suganami, 1996).
In this educational style, the trainees studied on their own at their own locations using the same personal computers as they were employed in their daily work.

(5) Lectures for comparison of education styles
The trainees studied the computer maintenance as discussed in Section 2.1. However, in an actual course, the test problems differed from one system to another because of differences among the systems in terms of the scale of the systems from large to small. Therefore, the raw test scores could not be used for comparison of education styles. For comparison, traditional, face-to-face lectures were performed using the same contents to be learned by the trainees. The education styles were analyzed and evaluated with reference to the lectures.
In this traditional style of education, the trainees were gathered in a classroom and they were taught by an instructor using textbooks and blackboard.

3. Evaluation Methods

The total number of trainees was 1,516. Pre-tests and post-tests were given for all the trainees to calculate the achievement score by regression (Ikeda, 1982). This achievement score by regression allows an evaluation even if two education styles provide different scores in pre-tests. An achievement score by regression, Ar, is obtained by the following equation:

$Ar=S_{post}-(a \bullet S_{pre}+b)$

Where, S_{post} and S_{pre} are the scores in the pre-test and post-test. A regression line shows the score of the post-test which is predicted from the pre-test score that a trainee could achieve. Therefore, subtracting the predicted value from the actual post-test score leaves an achievement score by regression. An achievement score by regression works as an index of the education effect. Furthermore, by finding the difference in the achievement score by regression between the CAI(I)-based collaboration teaching and education based on lectures as a deviation score

(Nakayama and Shimizu, 1993), the effectiveness can be compared between different education styles.

4. Results Of Evaluation

4.1 Comparing the deviation score in each education style

A deviation score from traditional lectures for each educational style was found and from that was calculated how scores were improved in each education style. Figure 1 shows the results.

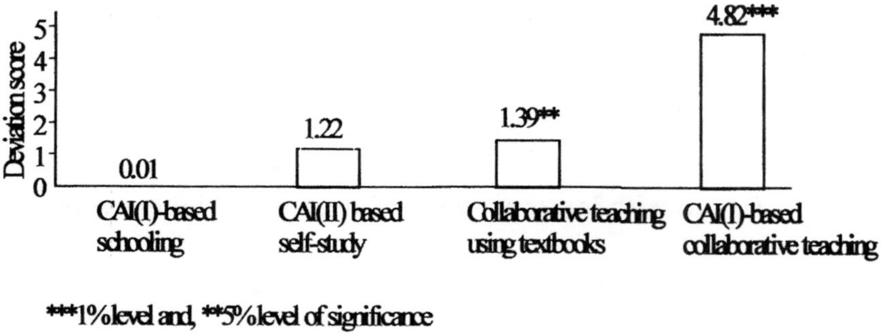

Figure 1 Deviation scores in reference to traditional lectures.

The deviation score of the CAI(I)-based collaborative teaching was 4.82, which showed a difference at the 1% level of significance. This shows the effectiveness of the collaborative teaching where, while one trainee was engaged in learning through CAI(I), the other trainee gave their comments and questions observing the same screen. In this approach, all the trainees reflect and learn more deeply through discussion among themselves. Still pictures and video might play an important role in making the discussion more concrete and active.

The educational effectiveness of the CAI(I)-based schooling is same as traditional lectures. Although the collaborative teaching using textbooks is effective even though effectiveness is not so significant by itself. However, it was found that the two educational styles combined together is significantly effective. The effectiveness of human-to-human interaction using a computer as the medium which has been advocated by cognitive science (Anzai, Ishizaki, Ohtsuda, Hatano and Mizoguchi, 1992) could be demonstrated quantitatively. Combining education styles improved the overall effectiveness which was of great interest.

4.2 Analyzing the group with higher scores and the group with lower scores

To further analyze the effectiveness of each education style, the trainees were divided into a group with higher scores and a group with lower scores according to the average of the pre-test.

The deviation score was calculated for the group with higher scores and the group with lower scores in each education style. Figure 2 shows the results.

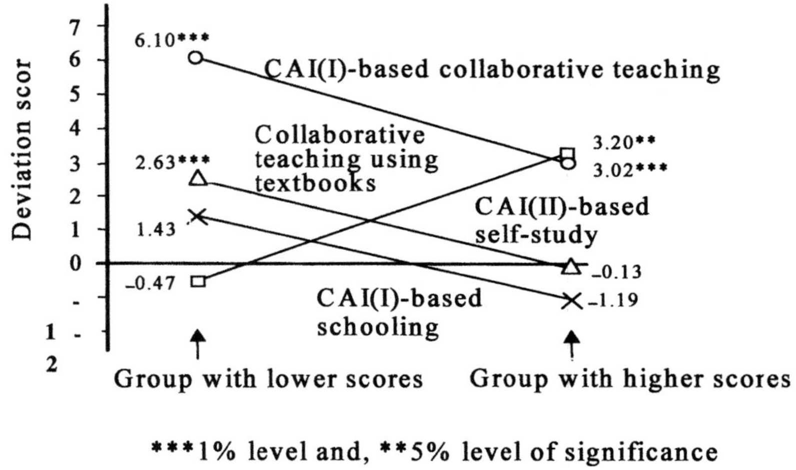

Figure 2 Deviation scores in reference to lectures (groups with higher and lower scores).

As shown in Figure 2, a higher deviation score is given by the group with lower pre-test scores than by the group with higher scores except for the CAI(II)-based self-study. Conversely, in the CAI(II)-based self-study, the group with higher pre-test scores shows a higher deviation score than the group with lower pre-test scores.

Studying this result from the viewpoint of education, it would lead to a conclusion that the presence of an instructor as in a school or a situation where the trainees can ask each other questions freely is effective for the group with lower pre-test scores. However, in the distributed education as in the CAI(II)-based self-study, the group with higher scores could learn and build up their knowledge efficiently by making full use of the hypertext and glossary functions. On the other hand, an instructor is needed by the group with lower scores to pose questions as they arise to the group to facilitate learning. This contributed to the reason why the educational effectiveness was not improved in the group with lower scores. It was also shown by questionnaires that the group with low pre-test scores requested a software function which allowed acceptance of questions at anytime.

4.3 Evaluation of learning time

In the CAI(I)-based schooling, collaborative teaching using textbooks and CAI(I)-based collaborative teaching, the learning time was the same as face-to-face lectures. However, in the CAI(II)-based self-study, the learning time differed from one person to another. Therefore, not only the test scores but also the learning times should be evaluated. The distribution of learning times are shown in Figure 3.

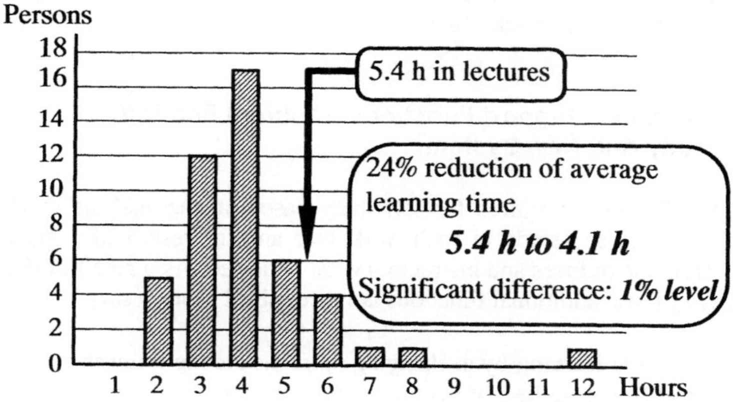

Figure 3 Distribution of learning time in CAI(II)-based self-study.

The same contents as CAI(II)-based self-study were taught in lectures lasting 5.4 hours. Compared with this time, the CAI(II)-based self-study required 4.1 hours on the average which is 24% less.

Next, the learning time was examined in the group with higher scores and in the group with lower scores.

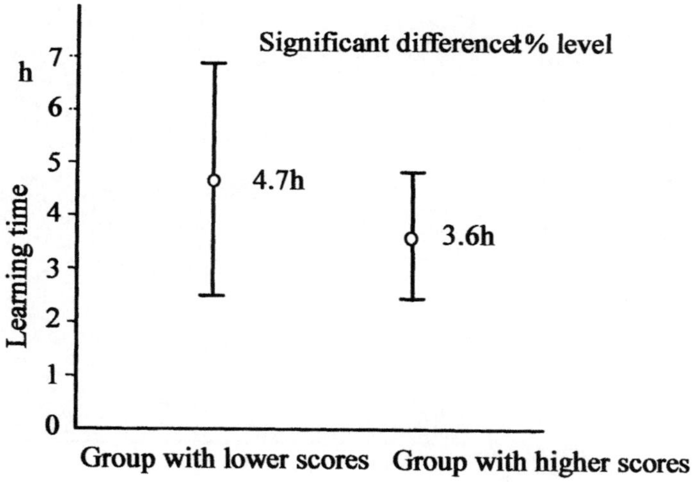

Figure 4 Learning time of the higher-scoring and lower-scoring groups.

The self-study using CAI(II) was effective in the group with higher scores in reducing the learning time as well as the achievement scores. An analysis of the scores and learning time revealed that the support function must be strengthened for the lower-scoring group in self-study.

5. Additional Support Functions Required For Self-Study And New System

The support functions required for self-study based on the analysis results of the scores obtained in self-study in each workplace and the results of a questionnaire collected from the trainees and instructors were reviewed. As a result of this review, the following seven additional functions are recognized as necessary:

(1) Collaborative learning by exchanging opinions among trainees
(2) Near real-time handling of questions and answers
(3) Schedule management for education
(4) Display of a list of educational materials and access to supplementary study
(5) References such as average score, highest score and lowest score
(6) Timely distribution of educational materials

For functions (1) to (6) listed above, a Web-based CAI system using the Internet/intranet and enriched functions was developed. Figure 5 is one of the screens of the newly developed Web-based CAI system.

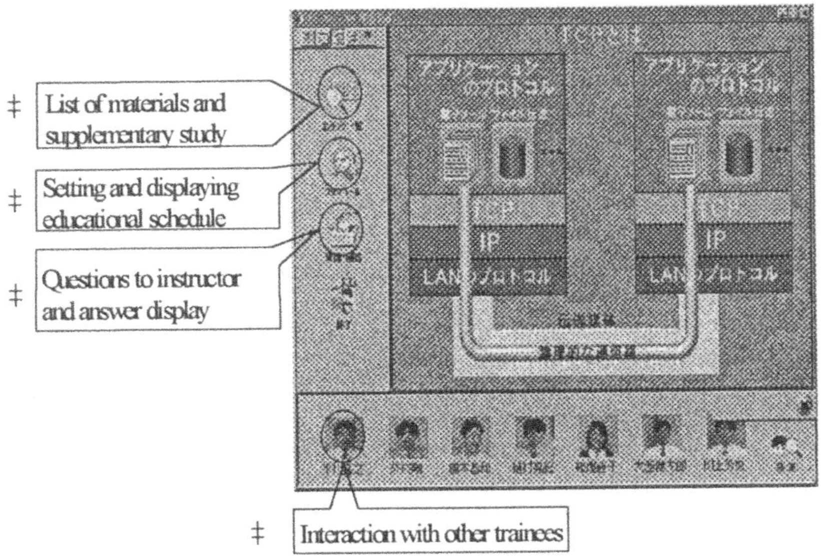

Figure 5 Web-based CAI screen.

The major new learning functions based on Figure 5 are described in the following.

(1) Collaborative learning by exchanging opinions with other trainees
This function facilitates the communication with other trainees and instructors. Not only textual information but also audio-visual communication is possible in real time. Through networking, this function is intended for providing the same environment as the collaborative teaching using CAI(I), which was effective in improving test scores. If a trainee has a question, he or she can feel free to ask it or seek an answer to it. In addition, the trainees can exchange information about their progress in the course.

(2) Questions to instructor and display of answers
This function provides a database of assumed questions, and past questions and answers and allows a user to find an appropriate answer from the database. The conventional question and answer method by e-mail required more than one day to receive an answer. This was a disincentive to trainees. In addition, time was wasted because a trainee could not proceed with the study because of lack of understanding. This function provides an answer immediately if such a question was answered in the past and stored. The user can retrieve a question just by entering a keyword; then all related items are displayed. If the question is not stored in the database, the user can request an answer by registering the question. The answers to the questions can then be given by the instructors in the education department or front-line specialists. Active learning is further enabled by an employment of this question and answer function.

(3) Setting and displaying the educational schedule
It is difficult to manage the progress of learning in self study. This function addresses this difficulty. This function can be used not only by trainees but also by instructors or managers at their workplace for reference or to give trainees advice as required.

(4) List of materials and supplementary study
This function displays a list of educational materials provided. It also allows the user to access pertinent sections in other materials or reference an easier material for reference.

(5) Other references such as average score, highest score and lowest score
In group learning, trainees tend to improve themselves through friendly rivalry over each other's scores. However, in self study, a trainee is hardly conscious of other colleagues, does not set goals well and does little to maintain or improve their aspirations. In addition to including exercise problems to solidify and confirm the trainees' knowledge, the system notifies the trainees of their test scores to improve the motivation for learning.

6. Conclusion

(1) In the three education styles of the CAI(I)-based schooling, collaborative teaching using textbooks and CAI(I)-based collaborative teaching, the group with lower scores showed higher results than the group with higher scores at 5% level of significance. In the CAI(II)-based self-study, the group with

higher scores improved more than the group with lower scores at 5% level of significance. The rate of improvement in test scores differed between the higher-scoring group and lower-scoring group depending on whether group learning or distributed education was used.

(2) For the learning time, the CAI(II)-based self-study cut the time required by 24% on the average, which showed a difference from traditional lectures at 1% level of significance.

Based on the analysis results above, a new Web-based CAI system was developed. Further study is needed for evaluation of this newly developed system.

7. References

Anzai, Y., Ishizaki, S., Ohtsu, N., Hatano, G. and Mizoguchi, F. (1992) Handbook of Cognitive Science, Kyoritsu-Shuppan

Gery, G. J. (1991) Electronic Performance Support Systems, Gery Performance Press

Ikeda, H. (1982) Tests and Measurements, in *Pedagogical Collection 25,* Dai-ich Hoki

Lee, K. and Shirai, K. (1996) Evaluation of the ICAI System for Assisting Speaker of Japanese to Learn Korean Writing, *IEICE Journal (D-II)*, **Vol. J79-D-II, No. 6**, 1146-57

Nakayama, M. and Shimizu, Y. (1993) Using Student Scores in the Evaluation of a Communication Satellite (PINE-NET) Lecture-Plus CAI-Based Distance Learning System, *Japan Journal of Educational Technology*, **Vol. 17, No. 2**

Okamoto, T. (1995) Education, Media and Artificial Intelligence, *Artificial Intelligence Journal*, 361-7

Yamamoto, H., Aizawa, T., Munemoto, T. and Suganami, K. (1996) Development and Evaluation of EPSS type CAI, *Shingaku-Giho*, **ET95-106**, 31-38

Yamamoto, H., Ohtani, A. and Kado, T. (1993) Development and evaluation of computer-mediated education system for customer engineers, *IFIP*, 205-14

8. Biography

H. Yamamoto received his B.Eng. in engineering from the Department of technology, Shinshu University in 1966. He then joined Hitachi Electronics Services Co., Ltd. He is now director and general manager of the Technical Education Division. Since 1998, he has been in the doctorate program of the Tokyo Institute of Technology.

Minoru Nakayama graduated with a B.S. in Science from the Faculty of Education of Tokyo Gakugei University in 1983 and completed the M.S. program in 1985. That year he became a Research Student in the Center for Research and Development of Educational Technology, Tokyo Institute of Technology. In 1990, he received a Doctorate of Engineering from the Tokyo Institute of Technology. He is currently associate professor at the Tokyo Institute of Technology. His research interest is educational technology.

Yasutaka Shimizu graduated from Tokyo Institute of Technology in 1964, and received Master and Doctor of Engineering in 1966 and 1971. Since 1969 he has been working with Tokyo Institute of Technology and is currently Professor and Dean of Graduate School of Decision Science and Technology. He was elected an IEEE Fellow "for contributions to research and development in the field of educational technology, electromagnetic compatibility, and surface acoustic waves" in 1994.

DISCUSSION REPORTS:

TELE-EDUCATION FOR NETWORK-CENTRIC ORGANISATIONS: AN ADULT EDUCATION VIEW

M.J. Ruohonen
University of Tampere
P.O. Box 607, FIN-33101 Tampere, Finland
e-mail: mr@cs.uta.fi

S.R. Kerridge
Centre for Electronic Commerce
Computing and Information Systems
University of Sunderland,
Sunderland, SR6 0DD, U.K.
e-mail: simon.kerridge@sunderland.ac.uk

T. Lainema
Turku School of Economics and
Business Administration
P.O. Box 110, FIN-20521 Turku, Finland
e-mail: timo.lainema@tukkk.fi

1. Introduction

The discussion group had a covering international representation both from developed and developing countries and from different levels of education ans service roles (See Table 1.)

Table 1. Discussion group participants

Mikko Ruohonen	(MR)	University of Tampere, Tampere, Finland
Simon Kerridge	(SK)	University of Sunderland, Sunderland, U.K.
Kouji Yosjida	(KY)	Mitsubishi Corporation, Tokyo, Japan
Jukka Viitanen	(JV)	Turku School of Economics and Business Administration, Turku, Finland
Wolfgang Weber	(WW)	Landesinstitut für Schule und Weiterbildung, Soest, Germany
Gilford Hapanyengwi	(GH)	University of Zimbabwe, Harare, Zimbabwe
Timo Lainema	(TL)	Turku School of Economics and Business Administration, Turku, Finland

Much of the discussion concerning tele-education is focused on technological issues. However, technological imperative is not enough when examining the potential of tele-education for network-centric organizations. Real networks are more than just cables and servers, they are also social networks and people-to-people connections. Educational contents can vary widely, from very structured, hard knowledge to a more fuzzy types in which end-results are different. In addition to that educational processes involve a number of stakeholders, it is not any more teacher-student interaction, it is growingly a teamwork of core learning contents providers and supporting organizations and people. Furthermore, this happens in an environment in which you need to work with multiple cultures, within a varying number of learning theories and redesigned educational processes (see more Ruohonen 1998). For example, Leidner and Jarvenpaa (1993) suggest that course contents, available technology and instructor factors influence the type of teaching method used. Student factors (experience, attitude, personality and learning style) and instructor factors mediate the impact of the teaching method on class interaction and in-class learning i.e. the type of material covered during class (factual, procedural, conceptual, or exploratory). In class-learning and class interaction affect learning and class performance. In this report the research model is extended to include also socio-cultural learning environment. Mediation is the keyword in this model. The tools (i.e. interactive technology) mediate learners (i.e. the active subjects), and object (mastering the knowledge). It has been noted that personality of a teacher affects the teaching practice. More research is needed in observing teacher practice in open, electronic learning environments. However, two other critical mediation forces are also present. The prevailing rules and approaches used before for teaching which can either promote or inhibit the modern IT-induced learning process. This is related to teacher training and introduction of service-oriented support personnel. Also the division of duties between, say network operators, software agents, information providers, teachers and learners affect and question the stability of the learning system. Open learning environments should be flexible to use available resources regardless of time or location.

2. The Big Picture

2.1 Research model

The following "triangle" (see Figure 1 below) describes the problem area in one dynamic picture. The relationships between different corners are important in interpreting contradictions of tele-education for network-centric organizations. In short the six main "corners" of the triangle are:

- Information Technology (the platform on which tele-education is based)
- Stakeholders (e.g. Teachers, Students and other involved parties)
- Subject Contents Area (the nature and how it is mastered)
- Pedagogical assumptions (what is the teaching model / theory behind tele-education)
- Social Learning Community (what is the interaction between students and other stakeholders)
- Process environment (the general learning environment and division of processes)

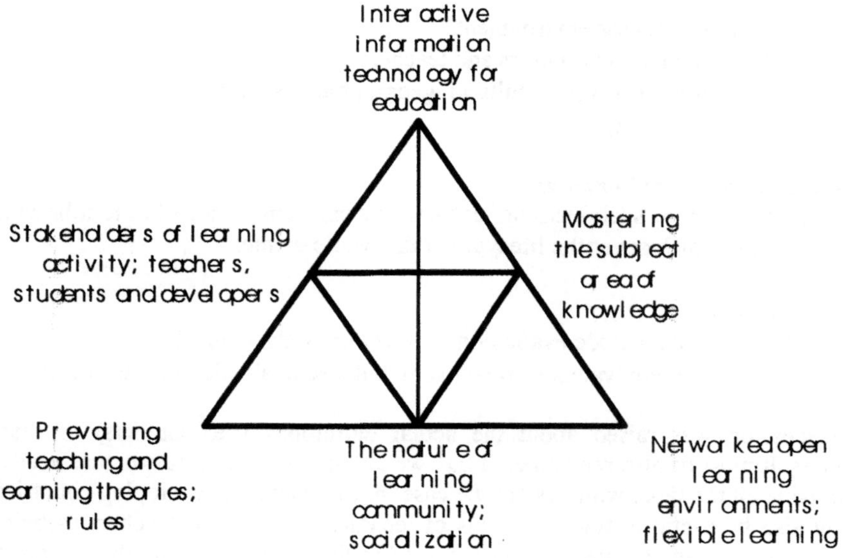

Figure 1. Research model for a deeper analysis of tele-education in the context of network-centric organizations (Ruohonen 1998).

2.2 *General issues from the big picture*

After first reflections based on the model the most urgent issues emerged to be, first, relationships between students, teachers, supervisors and other related groups, secondly, technology should be used just as a technical platform to transfer knowledge, not as an end itself and, thirdly, growingly learning communities are growing diverse and difficult to manage.

2.3 *Specific issues to be investigated*

The most interesting and least researched aspects of the six axes were: social learning community, satellite communication systems for education, motivating students to use the systems, co-ordination of stakeholders in the system, social community, human interactions in network environments, processes in network environments, the role of the learner, tailored learning, how to organise learning environments, using all possible learning materials and media, training teachers in the new pedagogies, stakeholders and learning activities, material development from multiple sources, ensuring the relevance of materials for technologies, real-time processes, business games for learning and networks for distributed training. Although this list is not comprehensive it gives a good indication of the bounds of the areas for future research and development.

In summary the following topics were seen as the most promising for future research:

- networked process environment
- collaboration between users and teachers
- community aspects (e.g. cultural, geographical, subject, etc),
- usable technology

Networked process environment
In general the flow of such learning/teaching systems can be seen in the following three headings, which cover the lifecycle of the whole theme:

- Planning
- Process (can include evaluation if done during the course)
- Evaluation (equivalent of final exam, but also evaluation of the teaching)

A discussion was raised about the actual definitions (i.e. contents) of these headings. It must be also remembered that we assume that the infrastructure needed is available all the time, which is not the case in, for example, developing countries. It may also be useful to think in terms of technical support for teachers as being perhaps a pre-planning phase. It was assumed in the discussions that the drivers of the system (teachers) know how to use it properly, which is not a trivial statement. However, this is questionable while the complexity of the tele-education systems is growing.

The experiences of the participants gave a good mix of inputs into the discussion. Experiences reported were such as using videos and video conferencing for modular teaching in Europe (EUROPACE), emails and a shared noticeboard for student communication (Open University), tailored distance learning packages for industry (University for Industry), using the lowest common denominator for discussion groups (i.e. email as not all had access to newsgroups), studies based on information from two Universities with homogenised results.

Teachers' and students' new roles

For taught versus research and the spectrum in between, a feedback is required into the teacher's knowledge. With the research side, new knowledge can be created. In new subject areas students may be more up to date that the teacher, the question was raised: "how does the teacher keep control / respect in this case?" New areas perhaps need new pedagogy, for example the entire group learns and the teacher is just a guide rather than a leader. There is the question of how many providers and how many students are optimal. It depends of course on the type of delivery and the cost effectiveness, for example, fewer students in a graduate class is needed than you would have in a general email group. It may also depend on how many active students you have, for example in the context of a newsgroup discussion list. Teachers will need aids to help them control the flow of information, for example generally known procedures should be adhered to (e.g. teacher will not solve administrative problems). Of course there are problems for the teacher if they cannot answer all questions – this will challenge their traditional role as a teacher.

Community Aspects

In general, aspects such as the human-human interface (as well as the human-group, and group-group interfaces) need addressing. The examples discussed involved the emotional content of communications; it is much easier to fire someone you have never met, rather than having to do it face to face; if someone is angry or upset it is difficult to convey that by (for example) email, and perhaps video-conferencing might be more appropriate for some types of communications. It is also important that a community can exist with shared spaces (of whatever type) and can synchronise in time.

Synchronization of technology use

Synchronisation must also be considered in a distributed learning environment. Email is useful, there are also concepts of notice boards and exhibition spaces which may be the equivalent if black boards and class room walls respectively. The most important thing is to balance the use of technology and competencies of learners and teachers. Otherwise overload or undercapacity will emerge.

3. Reflection on a case example; a distributed business game

Timo Lainema introduced the example – a business simulation to help executives and workers what the effect of their actions might be. It was agreed that different techniques would be required for different purposes, for example a system to teacher 100,000 garage mechanics how to tune an engine would be different from one which helped graduate research students understand quantum mechanics, where not all the possibilities are known. Learning if different from learning by experience / exploration / discovery. The triangle axes (see figure before) were useful for as a generic framework, but sets of solutions rather than a single one are. The business game, for example, has three phases i.e. setup, play and feedback.

All these should be moderated by an expert i.e. a facilitator, who will set up the system for the players, monitor the play and afterwards provide feedback. One problem is that the game might be too simple, and so it will be too similar each time, so it must be complex enough. However, it is probable that different types of users (e.g. groups from production, purchasing, sales, engineering, etc.) will use the system and this will provide and extra level of variation. Also contents of the game will affect results. A distributed system is required for a number of reasons, however it still sensible to allow a subset of the system to be a stand-alone system for smaller users, so rightsizing is important for effective game environments. Another main reason for having a distributed system is to allow added complexity by having multiple groups of users using the system at the same time and affecting each other. Groupings that use a computer moderator have been shown to be both quicker and more productive, balance between anonymity and identified contributions should be decided case by case. Another reason for having a distributed system is that you cannot actually get all the players physically together in one place or time (e.g. Sales Directors). You must also ensure that there are actual learning benefits for using the network rather than using it for its own sake and monitor the social aspects of communications (e.g. if a person is angry it should be taken into account by the sender / receiver). It may still be necessary to combine face-to-face meetings in order to have the full impact.

It is important to have some incentive and disincentive system for doing well / badly in the game in order that the players take it seriously enough. But not too much as they must learn by their mistakes and the teacher / facilitator may not know everything. It is also important to simulate things that cannot happen – or are extremely unlikely in order to simulate organisational change. The blackboard has to be flexible, so that anonymous as well as credited information can be entered, also it must have the ability to be open and closed to the outside world, as appropriate for different purposes in the simulation. The task of the teacher in the simulation is paramount. It should be decided are they as advisors , consultants or organisers or a hybrid version of all the roles? This will affect the design of the simulation, also it is important that it they are given the appropriate training in the use / control of the system.

4. Conclusive remarks

It was generally agreed that further work in the area was required, as although we could decide what we thought about various scenarios and teaching / learning methods, they should always be supported or otherwise by empirical studies.

REFERENCES

Ruohonen, M.J. (1998) Opportunities and Limitations of IT-Induced Learning and Education. In Multisilta, J. and Niemi, J-P. (eds) Proceedings of the LeTTeT '98 and MaTILDA '98 Joint conference. Publications of the Pori School of Technology and Economics A 18, Pori, pp. 23-35.

EDUCATING PROFESSIONALS FOR NETWORK CENTRIC ORGANISATIONS

Discussion Leaders: J. Barrie Thompson and Susan Kerridge
School of Computing and Information Systems
University of Sunderland, Sunderland SR6 0DD, UK
Tel : (44) 191 5152769 Fax: (44) 191 5152781
e-mail: barrie.thompson@sunderland.ac.uk
ws0suk@intdev.sunderland.ac.uk

1. Introduction

Two discussion group sessions were held during the conference followed by a formal reporting session to all the delegates during the last afternoon session of the conference. The first discussion session was primarily used to: explore the topic area, define boundaries, and identify the classes of professional and organisation that the group would consider. It also enabled the participants to express initial views and identify the types of organisation they were each concerned with.

The second session concentrated on identifying the forms of education relevant to Network Centric Organisations (NCOs) and then cross matching these with organisational and professional types. The first session had resulted in seven different organisational types and three distinct professional types being identified. This gave a matrix which was then populated in this second session with appropriate classes of education.

The remainder of this paper is organised as follows: Section 2 summarises the initial discussions, the setting of boundaries and the identification of types of professional and organisation. Section 3 covers the area of education. It reports one particular approach to technology transfer that was described to the group and documents the subsequent types of education that were identified by the group members as appropriate to NCOs. Section 4 presents the populated matrix along with recommendations regarding wider issues which group members felt should also be considered. Finally section 5 lists the group participants.

2. Professionals and Organisations

The first problem that the group addressed was the fact that the topic allocated "Educating Professionals for Network Centric Organisations" was also the title for the whole conference. Was this to mean that the group were supposed to consider all the areas already being addressed by the conference or even more? A rational decision was reached that the group should set clear boundaries that would enable the topic to be fairly addressed within the allocated time of two 90 minute sessions. The overall scope was set as that which was relevant to the area of Information Technology (IT) and then, working from the title, the group agreed to concentrate on discussions concerned with:

- Appropriate types of Education
- The Type of Professionals who need Education
- Different Types of Organisation

all within the context of NCOs which were assumed to be:

organisations who are or wish to use technologies based on networks in this definition "technologies" was taken to represent a whole range from e-mail and the use of the WWW to sophisticated forms of electronic commerce. It was decided to first concentrate on the different categories of professional and types of organisation. The reason for this was that it was felt that appropriate types of education could best be considered once parameters regarding professionals and organisations had been identified.

2.1 Professionals

The group decided to limit its discussions to three distinct types of professional within NCOs that could be aided by appropriate education. These were:

- New IT professionals entering the organisation (typically graduates with a degree in computing or IT)
- Existing IT professionals within the organisation
- Non-IT professionals in an organisation who nevertheless are concerned with IT or Information Systems and who can be regarded as significant stakeholders in the relevant area.

Such non-IT professionals could be involved in purchasing or specifying IT systems. Also they or their staff are likely to be the users of the systems. Depending on the type of organisation there could be a wide range of such professionals which could include:

- Managers in the areas of : Accounts/Finance, Marketing, and Production.
- Departmental/Division Heads and Administrative Heads
- Members of the Board of Directors
- Research Officers,
- Librarians
- Teachers/Lecturers

The group felt that the importance of non-IT professionals within a NCO must not be underestimated and that their needs for appropriate education must be fully considered.

2.2 Organisations

The group then spent time discussing a range of different organisational types which could make use of technologies based on networks. The types of organisation of which group members had experience ranged from very large multinationals (e.g. Hitachi) to small local organisations employing fewer than 10 people. Eventually seven organisational types were identified as being sufficient to represent the group's experiences. It was felt that with regard to organisations in the commercial, administrative and government sectors, these were best divided into five distinct groups according to size and whether or not there existed a distinct department or section which dealt with IT. The types identified were:

1. Very large organisations with distinct IT department(s); e.g. a large multinational manufacturer, or a sector of national government such as Social Security.
2. Large or medium sized organisations with a distinct IT department.. Included in this category, in addition to manufacturers, could be organisations within the fields of insurance and finance, health care, and regional, municipal or larger units of local government.
3. Medium sized organisations with no distinct IT department; examples of these could be smaller units of local government and sector specific manufacturers. IT would typically be supported by vendor supplied systems. Any IT specialist staff would simply be members of particular functional departments, such as accounts.
4. Small organisations with no distinct IT department or section.. Here, within any relevant department, IT functions could be supported by either vendor supplied software or off-the-self software which had been customised if necessary. Typically such an organisation could have between 30 and 150 employees some of whom may be regarded as IT specialists.
5. Very small organisations with no distinct IT department and no specific professional IT staff. Examples of these would be a small family business such as a retail outlet or a farming enterprise. Here IT functions will typically relate

to accounts and stock control and will be undertaken using a package which is acceptable to financial auditors.

To this list were added two other broad organisational types which it was felt would have very distinct needs. These types were:

6. IT Exclusive. This category was assumed to include a range of organisations from major international vendors of IT products, such as IBM and Oracle, to smaller organisations dealing with a particular market sector (for example, Sage in the field of small business accounts).
7. Educational. This category included: schools from junior and primary through to senior high, colleges and institutions of further education, and Universities and other institutions of higher education.

It should be noted that the categorisations given above reflect the particular views of the discussion group members and they should not be viewed as a definitive list. Other categorisations could be equally , if not more valid depending upon circumstances. However, for the purpose of producing a matrix to populate with appropriate types of education the group felt the above list was sufficient.

3. Appropriate Types of Education

The second discussion session commenced with a review of the decisions reached during the first session with regard to types of professional and categorisation of types of organisation. To start discussions in the area of education the group leaders circulated details of a case study example relating to Technology Transfer. Using this and analogous experiences the group then went on to identify eleven types of education that were appropriate to the professional and organisational types identified previously.

3.1 Example Case Study

The case study that was circulated related to an example of technology transfer to the type of organisation which in the UK are classed SMEs (Small and Medium sized Enterprises having fewer than 250 employees). It detailed a common problem such enterprises experience and outlined a solution detailing successful co-operation between the educational system and industry.

Problem

For SMEs there can be major difficulties in gaining even basic knowledge, skills and abilities in the areas of networks and the use of the internet and intranets. Their staff normally have a total lack of experience and expertise in these areas and they are concerned that significant costs will be involved in buying in outside expertise. In addition such enterprises are often very wary of outside consultants when approaching new technological areas. This is because they are not sure of how impartial the consultant's recommendations may be and what final costs may be incurred.

Solution and Benefits

To use undergraduate and postgraduate student projects to create links between an educational establishment and SMEs (such an approach was described in detail in a paper by Thompson and McCall within the main part of the conference). This type of solution can not only can result in very cost effective technology transfer to the SMEs it also produces great benefits for the students undertaking the projects and the University itself.

The students gain excellent practical experience and also are able to develop effective research and reporting skills. Working with real clients improves communication skills and it develops the ability to address problems in a professional and efficient manner. The undertaking of such a projects also provides a major element of practical experience to be included in a CV when looking for employment following the course.

The University is able to forge successful links with the business community. Technology transfer from University to the businesses can occur almost transparently with the students acting as catalysts. Also barriers are broken down and the links for further research and constancy are built up. This can also result in the University being the first port of call for advice and help in the future.

3.2 Types of Education

The group spent time considering the various types of education that would be appropriate to the organisations and professionals already identified. This included formal education courses from Universities, different types of training courses, general and professional education, government initiatives, and consultancy. With regard to consultancy the Japanese members of the discussion group were of the opinion that this was not used very often by small firms in Japan. More often they tended to rely on training and advice from vendor companies. The eleven types of "education" which the group finally identified were:

1. Technology transfer via student project work / year out / industrial attachment / internship.
2. Degree / Diploma in an IT related specialism. from University / College which if appropriate will have included an industrial attachment / internship.
3. Internal training courses.
4. External training courses (these could be from and educational institution, or an IT specific training organisation).
5. Consultancy
6. Staff development courses.
7. Vendor Training related to products from the Vendor.

8. General Training course from Vendor (e.g. Java).
9. Following new developments.
10. Government initiatives and government money to fund initial consultancy / advice.
11. Professional development (updating and courses) relating to IT professionals.

4. Populated Matrix and Recommendations

A matrix of Professional vs. Organisational types was drawn up. This was then populated with the educational types identified in section 3.2. The final populated matrix is shown in figure 1.

	New I.T. Professional	Existing I.T. Professional	Other Professional Staff involved in IS / IT
Commercial, Administration, Management, and Government Sectors			
Very Large (with IT dept)	2, 3, 4, 7, 8, 11	1, 3, 4, 5, 6, 8, 9, 10, 11	1, 3, 4, 5, 6, 7, 10
Large / Medium (with IT dept)	2, 3, 4, 7, 8, 11	1, 3, 4, 5, 6, 8, 9, 10, 11	1, 3, 4, 5, 6, 7, 10
Medium (no IT dept)	2, 4, 7, 8, 11	1, 4, 5, 7, 8, 9, 10, 11	1, 4, 5, 7, 10
Small (no IT dept)	2, 4, 7, 8, 11	1, 4, 5, 9, 10, 11	1, 4, 5, 7, 10
Very Small (no IT dept)	N/A	N/A	1, 4, 5, 7, 10
Exclusive Organisations e.g. IBM	2, 3, 4, 7, 8, 11	1, 3, 4, 5, 6, 8, 9, 10, 11	1, 3, 4, 5, 6, 7, 10
Educational: Universities, Schools & Colleges	2, 3, 4	6, 8, 9, 10, 11	1, 3, 4, 5, 6, 7, 10

Figure 1. Education applicable to professionals in different organisations.

In addition to producing the populated matrix the group also had some time to consider wider issues. The group's final recommendations with regard to the education of Professionals for Network Centric Organisations were that:

Education for NCOs should not only be in technical areas but should also include wider aspects such as:

- Ethical Issues
- Copyright
- Legal Aspects

5. Participants at One or More Of The DISCUSSION Sessions

Name	Affiliation
Mrs. Sue Kerridge	Centre for Electronic Commerce University of Sunderland
Prof. Barrie Thompson	University of Sunderland
Mr. Masayuki Yamauchi	Human Resource Development Centre Telecommunications Division, Hitachi Ltd
Dr. Hidekazu Tsuji	Mitsubishi Electric Corporation
Mr. Takeo Tatsumi	Media Network Centre, Waseda University
Mr. Shinobu Satoh	Hitachi Software Engineering Co. Ltd
Mr. Tsurayaki Kado	Hitachi Ltd. Information Systems Group
Dr. Rose Mazhindu-Shumba	Computer Science Department University of Zimbabwe
Mr Kazunori Sadachi	Hitachi Information Academy Co. Ltd
Prof. Joyce Little	Computer & Information Sciences Department Towson University

INDEX

GPSR Compliance

The European Union's (EU) General Product Safety Regulation (GPSR) is a set of rules that requires consumer products to be safe and our obligations to ensure this.

If you have any concerns about our products, you can contact us on ProductSafety@springernature.com

In case Publisher is established outside the EU, the EU authorized representative is:

Springer Nature Customer Service Center GmbH
Europaplatz 3
69115 Heidelberg, Germany

Batch number: 10755292

Printed by Printforce, the Netherlands